How to Succeed in Business
Before Graduating

How To Succeed In Business Before Graduating

307 TESTED MONEY-MAKING IDEAS FOR THE UNDERGRADUATE ENTREPRENEUR

Peter M. Sandman
and Daniel R. Goldenson

THE MACMILLAN COMPANY, NEW YORK

COLLIER-MACMILLAN LIMITED, LONDON

Library of Congress Catalog Card Number: 68-18874

First Printing

The Macmillan Company, New York
Collier-Macmillan Canada Ltd., Toronto, Ontario

Printed in the United States of America

Contents

Preface

Money-making is a topic of tremendous concern on the college campus today. As costs and enrollments continue to leapfrog merrily upward, the question of how a full-time student can earn enough money is beginning to bother not only students and their parents but even college administrators themselves.

Despite this increasing interest, *How to Succeed in Business Before Graduating* represents the first large-scale survey of successful money-making enterprises on campus. In the preparation of this book, questionnaire forms were sent to the financial-aid directors of more than 500 colleges and universities throughout the country. Additional forms were mailed to 200 college information officers, student newspapers, and student governments. To supplement the written data, scores of campus entrepreneurs were interviewed by telephone about the details of their operations.

One result of our research was the discovery that colleges vary widely in the extent to which student business opportunities are utilized. Dozens of ideas which earn big money at one or two colleges are unheard of anywhere else. A lack of information about what can be done is costing U.S. students an estimated $20 million a year in potential earnings. Twenty million dollars could pay well over 10,000 tuitions—compliments of student business. That is the aim of this book.

CHAPTER 1

Horatio Alger and All That

1. INTRODUCTION

Congratulations! You are a college student. That letter of acceptance your mother had framed is your ticket to four years of living off the fat of the land. You have earned the privilege of joining the ranks of America's unproductive citizens—a select but growing sector of the economy which includes, besides you, infants, some criminals, the aged, and the unemployable. Nobody is going to look down on *you* for not earning your keep.

The reason for your favored position is simple: You are in training. You are undergoing the rigors of a process society calls Higher Education, a process it admires so much it lets you go at it fulltime for four years. You are a student. You drink the eternal wine of wisdom—when you can't get beer. You grapple with the great minds of the ages—when you can't find the opposite sex. You prepare for a life of contemplation—when you're not preparing for Saturday's game.

Is there anything to college life besides alcohol and athletics, sex and study? More to the point: Should there be? The premise of this book is that the answer to both these questions is Yes. Specifically, we believe that participation in some sort of business enterprise while an undergraduate can add immeasurably to your college experience, not only by providing funds (for the alcohol, sex, athletics, and study), but also by developing skills and con-

1

fidence, friendships and a working knowledge of the real world beyond the campus.

The aim of this book is to help you figure out how to earn the money you want to earn in the fastest, most pleasant and most educational way possible. To this end, we have badgered administrators at more than five hundred colleges and universities to give us a picture of the employment and business opportunities for students on their campuses. Then we have contacted successful student businessmen at these colleges and asked each the secret of his success.

On one level *How to Succeed* is a list of proven money-making ideas for students. Such a list would be valuable—but not valuable enough. Ideas which earned thousands on one campus have been known to fail miserably on another. The difference was in the planning and imagination of the students involved. We can't help much with the imagination, but we can give you a detailed account of planning that *worked*.

Nearly every business possibility in this book is illustrated with a case history, each containing the information a successful student entrepreneur thought people ought to know if they were going into his business—information about manpower, advertising, prices, purchasing, and the thousand other details that spell the difference between just another good idea and cash in your wallet.

These "case studies" are supplemented by separate chapters on the two thorniest obstacles to student entrepreneurial success. Obstacle Number One, of course, is your dearly beloved administration, with its policies and peculiarities. Obstacle Number Two (this one you share with normal people) is the government, with its complex taxes and laws. If you can stay on the right side of the college and the government, you should have comparatively little trouble making it with your customers.

We want to make one thing clear at the outset. Despite the title of this book, it is not our purpose to enable you to retire at the ripe old age of twenty-five. Undergraduate Big Businessmen, with annual profits of $10,000 to $20,000, do exist, and they are sufficiently important and interesting to deserve the chapter we have given them. But for every mogul-in-the-making there are a good five hundred serious students who are working to earn their spending money and maybe part of their tuition. And they're doing it without cheating the pants off their dormmates and classmates. Most of the businesses we will describe net somewhere between $1,000 and $2,000 a year. For a full-time student, that's good money.

One final word to administrators: We hope your students will read this book, because many of them have to earn money to stay in school, and nearly all of them want to earn money to have fun in school. But we also hope you will take a look at it. Every dollar a needy student earns is a dollar less that you have to dig up for scholarships and loans. More than thirty financial aid directors at small colleges have written us that they "would like to develop job and business opportunities for more students, but just don't know how to go about it." Much of this book is aimed at answering these queries.

If this were a book on sexual technique, Chapter One would open with a discussion of the beauty, magnificence, and humanistic grandeur of sex. Since money-making has often been condemned as every bit as earthy and suspect as love-making, we feel the need for the same sort of apologia. So if you already *know* your philosophy of collegiate business, and all you want to do is learn how to make your wad, skip to Chapter Two. Otherwise, prepare to ramble through the pros and cons and reasons and histories of student money-making.

2. CHANGING TIMES

Once upon a time, so we are told, the only people who went to college were the scions of wealthy landowners and preachers. Henry Adams and his contemporaries were as unlikely to work to earn money as they were to work to earn top grades. Neither was appropriate behavior for gentlemen. There were exceptions, of course: Zachariah Bridges, Harvard Class of 1657, worked to meet his expenses by "ringinge the bell and waytinge" and was accredited "by his wages fifty shillings and a scholarship three pounds, fifteen shillings." His classmates no doubt thought his behavior a bit odd.

Zachariah's sterling example was forgotten, and the next recorded instance of student employment appeared in the middle of the nineteenth century, when an impoverished Denison University undergraduate decided to earn his keep as a janitor. A few years later, three students at Dickenson College managed to support themselves completely for an entire academic year, two by pressing suits in their room, one by opening a shoe-repair shop in his.

By 1880, dozens of cases of working students had been reported—but each case was still an untraditional exception. Then, suddenly, the spirit of Horatio Alger descended upon the land. Any boy with gumption and guts, it was said, could make it up from the slums or the farm to fame and fortune. Thousands tried the college route up, and every one of them worked his own way through. In the 1930's, more than 20,000 working students were enrolled in colleges and universities across the country. By 1935, the figure had increased to 200,000.

Two kinds of students went to college in the thirties: those who could afford it and those who had to work their way through. The latter may have been a tribute to the indomitable American spirit, but the former were damn glad not to have the problem. About 1,000,000 men and women a year were enrolled in college, so only about one-fifth of them were members of the student working class.

Between 1935 and 1938, increases in the number of students attending college, the cost of college, and the average annual family income kept pace with one another. This meant that, while the percentage of poor students may have gone up, and the number of poor students certainly did, the distinction between the needy (who had to work) and the well off (who did not) remained firm. Since 1958, however, private school costs have outrun incomes, while the price of state-supported schools has quickly risen to the point where they, too, are now beyond the budget of the average American family. Meanwhile, "college consciousness" has increased tremendously: From a figure of 3,226,000 in 1958, college enrollment soared to over 5,000,000 in 1965. Experts predict that more than 8,580,000 students will be attending colleges and universities in the year 1975.

The upshot of all this is that just about nobody today can afford to send his children to college, and just about everybody is planning to. Scholarship and loan plans have multiplied fantastically to meet the need—more so has student money-making. More than 3,500,000 students today earn some part of their college expenses. This is more than three-quarters of all undergraduates, and at some schools, including the prestigious and once-patrician Harvard, the figure is up near 90 percent. Colleges themselves pay out at least $100,000,000 a year to students in exchange for term-time work. Off-campus employment and business ventures contribute an equal amount, bringing the average term-time earnings of workers to about $600. Most of the undergraduates who contribute to this statistic work somewhere between 12 and 15 hours a week, and most hold unskilled, low-paying jobs. Those who work longer hours, or work for themselves, or find skilled jobs, earn a good deal more.

Even among the minority of today's college students who do not require scholarships, work, or loans to pay their college expenses, most work anyway to earn extra spending money. Daddy may be paying your tuition, but he probably is not paying to keep your bar stocked and your car's gas tank filled. With even well-heeled students out earning money, the distinction between poor undergraduates who have to work and wealthy ones who do not is very nearly a thing of the past. Student money-making may not be very prestigious anymore, Horatio Alger being more or less forgotten, but it is nearly universal.

3. OTHER WAYS OUT

It is possible to go to college without having to earn money. The easiest way to achieve this is to have wealthy parents. If you fail at that, the second method is to apply for financial aid.

Financial aid is the term educators use to describe any means of paying college expenses which is not dependent on the resources of the student or his family. Strangely enough, student employment and business activities are often considered a variety of financial aid, and the ugly word "workship" has been coined to refer to such arrangements. Besides workships, the two principal forms of financial aid are scholarships and loans (which are not yet referred to as "loanships," even by educators).

We have already said that student employment or business is rarely enough to pay all your college expenses. The same point must be made for scholarships and loans. Colleges offer very few scholarships, and almost no full loans. Commercial institutions are likewise reluctant to lend you enough money to cover all your college expenses, and those that will do it leave you with a $10,000 debt on Commencement Day—something you can do nicely without.

The usual form of financial aid is a neat package with several strings attached, a confusing concoction of scholarships, loans, and jobs. Even if their particular aid package doesn't require it, most students on financial aid today want to work. They want to earn extra spending money and, if possible, to reduce the size of their loan. Moreover, the working student is eligible for better scholarships and loans. In 1958, Dean William F. Griffith of Colgate University stated categorically that "we wouldn't make a grant to a boy who wasn't interested enough to take some financial responsibility for himself." Most administrators are less frank, but the statement of one Midwestern dean is typical: "We are more apt to give a scholarship to a student who has already earned a good part of his tuition costs than to anybody else. He has already demonstrated how much a college education means to him."

The same is true for loans, whether they are commercial, government or college-sponsored. A job or a business activity makes a student a better financial risk. Students with part-time jobs in industry occasionally qualify for company tuition benefits, and find themselves with their college expenses paid for by their employer. Finally, even parents are likely to contribute a more sizable chunk if they know that junior is doing his part by earning money part-time.

4. "THE PROPER BUSINESS OF STUDENTS IS STUDY"

Despite the interdependence of loans, scholarships, and work, a good number of college administrators deplore the tendency of their students to want to earn money. From Avila College in Kansas City comes the following comment on undergraduate businesses: "Our campus is striving to create an atmosphere of learning and living, physical, cultural, academic, and social. We've no time to prowl and hawk!" Says the dean of St. Benedict's College, Atchison, Kansas: "We want our students to get their degrees in four years and then go on to make a living. The two don't mix—at least not at our college." "A student's main purpose should be to learn," an administrator at Upsala College in East Orange, New Jersey, wrote "particularly in an academic, non-vocational sense."

In place of student money-making, critics suggest greater reliance on scholarships and loans. Wagner College in Staten Island, New York, boasts a financial aid program which "makes it unnecessary for any student to *have* to run businesses to make money to get through college." Wagner's financial aid director commented on our questionnaire as follows: "I should like to say that somehow I get the impression that a 'forward-looking college' ought to be classified that way because it encourages student businesses. We want to be considered 'forward-looking' because we have a college policy of aid which goes beyond this need."

When scholarships and loans prove insufficient to meet college costs, opponents of student business reluctantly unbend to the extent of approving part-time employment ("workships"), which they seem to consider less unscholarly than student entrepreneurial adventures. The financial aid director at St. Edward's University in Austin, Texas, was representative of this view: "The primary purpose of a higher education institution should be to provide an atmosphere conducive to learning and not private enterprise. Part-time jobs on and off the campus seem to fill the financial aid gap at least at this institution anyway. . . . Furthermore, using the dorms for a marketplace seems inconsistent with the purpose they were constructed for."

A large part of the dispute seems to center on the effect of student business on academic performance. Educational psychologists have been studying this question since the thirties, and have reached one irrefutable conclusion: Sometimes a student's grades go down when he starts earning money, sometimes they

stay the same, and sometimes they go up. Clemson University in
Clemson, South Carolina, compared the academic records of
working and non-working undergraduates, and discovered that the
former had a mean grade point average of o.8 less than the latter.
"As a result," noted their financial aid director, "we are becoming
somewhat disenchanted with the Horatio Alger concept and prefer,
instead, to guide our needier students into scholarship-grant-loan
packages." At the other end of the statistical spectrum is Arizona
State College at Tempe. Arizona's President Grady Gammage has
commented that "year in, year out, more top grades are captured
by the worker than the nonworker."

Researchers at the University of Washington placement office
compared the grades of both working and non-working students
with their predicted grades at matriculation. Their finding: Working students did better, relative to prediction, than students who
did not work. Two newer studies using a similar method on other
campuses found no significant differences in academic performance
between workers and nonworkers.

Though these research findings would hardly justify a recommendation that students take outside jobs or start businesses in
order to improve their grades, they give just as little support to
the fears of the administrators we quoted earlier. There is no
doubt that holding a job or running a business can teach a student
some lessons about organization and concentration which, if applied to his classwork, will help him in his studies. There is also
no doubt that money-making takes time, and some of that time
could have been spent studying. Which of these factors will have
the greater influence depends wholly on the motivation of the
individual student.

Moreover, the student businessman who really lets his work
slide does so because there is something so enticing, so exciting,
so involving about what he is doing that it makes classes and
assignments seem trivial and irrelevant. This is a danger to which
editors of student newspapers and presidents of student governments are at least as vulnerable—yet no responsible college administrator today denies the importance and value of extra-curricular activities. Undergraduate money-making at its best—which
is what this book is trying to promulgate—has all the values of

extra-curricular activities, with the additional advantage of helping to pay college expenses. If large numbers of students at any college are neglecting their scholastic activities for their business activities, then the students must be doing something very right, or the college something very wrong.

5. COCOON TYCOONS

Before leaving the opposition case and going on to talk about the positive values of student money-making, we want to refer briefly to a more fundamental criticism of student business involvement. Social critics frequently accuse our country of supporting the most "crass," "valueless," and "materialistic" society known to man. U.S. policy and culture, so the argument runs, are controlled by U.S. businessmen, who in turn are controlled by the business ethic: Do others before they can do you. Our colleges and universities are indicted for having failed to teach young men and women that morality and culture are more to be treasured than gold. Today's college graduates, it is said, leave school with a strong sense of rapacity and a weak sense of ethics. Anything which encourages students to engage in business while they are still undergraduates accentuates this trend and is therefore evil.

We cannot help feeling a little sympathy for this argument. The nineteenth century's Captains of Industry did have much in common with the sixteenth century's captains of pirate ships, and a little of that tradition lingers on. But not much of it. American businessmen today recognize, however regretfully, that their profits and perhaps their very existence depend upon their acting with social awareness as well as business acumen. And to whatever extent the business world is still a jungle, it is today's college student who will have to do the clearing—which is impossible unless he enters it.

In any case, the vast majority of working students are not trying to become Big Businessmen on Campus, and we are not trying to encourage them to do so. Students want jobs or businesses which are relevant to their career goals, which involve skills they want to learn or practice, which can provide needed services for their school or community and satisfaction for themselves. There may be a kind of satisfaction in producing a better napalm bomb or bilking a naive freshman, but most students would rather program their college admission procedure for a computer, or see to it that their classmates have snacks available after hours, or provide music for a prom. These are the sorts of businesses students now want, and they are the sorts this book is about.

6. BENEFITS OF STUDENT BUSINESS

Almost without exception, the principal reason students give for taking a job or starting a business is money. But when asked to evaluate their money-making experience, or when deciding among a number of equally remunerative possibilities, these same students take into account a number of non-financial factors.

The most frequently mentioned consideration is the development of skills. For better or for worse, most people spend most of their adult lives earning money, or at least trying to. For a young man planning a career in management few experiences could be more edifying than running his own business. But paradoxically enough, business skills are not the only skills developed by business. In the case of many students, they are not even the principal ones. We know of music majors who play in professional orchestras, math majors who program computers, biology majors who care for department greenhouses, art majors who make knickknacks, pre-med majors who work as orderlies in hospitals, journalism majors who edit and sell their own newspapers, history majors who do library research, agriculture majors who test soil samples, and so on, *ad infinitum.* For almost any career choice there is at least one job or business available to undergraduates which will provide worthwhile vocational training and experience.

Much of what can be learned through running a business or holding down a job has less to do with specific vocational training than with general abilities such as organization. In a survey conducted at the University of Minnesota in the 1930's, more than 20 percent of working students listed "acquired basic mental concepts essential to success" and "learning the value of time and money" as important benefits derived from their work. The same values are inherent in student work today.

The best evidence of the lessons learned from undergraduate money-making is the experience of each year's graduates when they start applying for jobs. Time after time they are asked: What percentage of your college expenses did you earn? What sorts of jobs have you held? What did you do at school besides study? The president of one major company has frankly stated: "I'll employ the worker with lower grades over the 'A' student who has no work experience." Most corporation personnel directors today agree with him. They have learned through experience that the graduate who worked somewhere as a student is likely to try harder, stay with the company longer, and perform better.

"Meeting people" is another frequently mentioned advantage of a business or a job. The crass word for this is "contacts," and a number of our informants were justifiably proud of having met and come to know important people in various walks of life, people who might be of assistance to them after graduation. But just as on-campus business activities are more common than off-campus ones, so too the more frequent comments concerned the pleasures derived from meeting and forming close friendships with other students.

Many student businesses have an advantage not too often found in the adult business world: fun. Students across the country are searching for jobs in which they can say, as one Harvard research assistant recently said, "I'm doing something I love, and they're paying me for it."

In the 1932 University of Minnesota study we mentioned earlier, nearly 20 percent of all working students cited "freedom and independence" as one of the most important benefits of the experience. Many things have changed since then, but the irresistible urge of young people to get free of parents and stand on their own has not. The Student Agencies director of Rutgers University in New Brunswick, New Jersey, puts it this way: "My own experience has adequately demonstrated that student interest in 'entrepreneurship' is widespread and strong. The appeal of being 'one's own boss' has traditional roots in the American way of life that have been inherited by an adequate number of today's youth." A coed at Agnes Scott College, Decatur, Georgia, said the same thing more simply: "We want to avoid the allowance bit. We want to be able to say 'I'm independent. I don't have to write home for money every month.' "

Closely related to the urge for independence is the desire for achievement. Part of this is simply the wish to stand out, to excel—something which gets increasingly difficult on campus as crowds of active students make the BMOC nearly a thing of the past. Part of it is the satisfaction that comes from doing a job well.

In stressing the various benefits that students derive from business activities, we have so far ignored the other side of the coin. The college and the surrounding community are equally the beneficiaries of these enterprises. It seems almost unnecessary to mention that an early-morning doughnut shop and a late-night snack bar become centers of student conversation, that every baby-sitter and every hedge-trimmer is an ambassador to the surrounding community, that laundry and typing agencies provide essential services to students, that beer mugs and wall banners are treasured mementoes of undergraduate years—that all of these add color and richness to the college experience. "One aspect of student-run businesses often overlooked," noted a Rutgers University administrator. "is the 'self-contained service' aspect. That is, many services and conveniences required by a university community can be provided by student businesses. At Rutgers College most convenience-type services can be found within Rutgers Student Agencies at the present time, making student-run businesses an integral part of the environment on campus."

Our correspondent at Dean Junior College in Franklin, Massachusetts, said it more tersely. Describing his college, he wrote: "No business; ergo no color."

7. THE REAL WORLD

There is one further advantage to student money-making. We have saved it for last, partly because it is somewhat difficult to describe, and partly because we believe it to be extremely important and yet generally overlooked. We are referring to the contact with "the real world" that student business affords.

Psychologists and sociologists say that adolescence is a comparatively new phenomenon, an artificial transition period which modern society has inserted between childhood and adulthood. Through four long years of high school, a biologically mature adult dutifully plays his appointed role as a child, wholly dependent upon and almost wholly subservient to his parents. Then, for many, comes college, and more of the same; and looming ahead for a good number, is graduate school. During all this time, the student is *preparing himself* for adulthood. He serves no useful function in society. He is expected to serve none. His job is to study, to better himself, to get ready.

We are not trying to buck this trend. To do so would be foolish, for today's society depends for its very existence on ever-increasing numbers of educated, trained specialists—and that sort of training takes time. But prolonged adolescence leaves its inevitable mark on the student: It frustrates him. A large measure of an adult's self-worth is derived from his ability to support himself, his loved ones and to some extent his country by doing something that is useful for others. The activities of a college student will make him more useful to others in the future, but in the present they are useful only to himself—and meanwhile it is his country and his loved ones that are supporting him. Little wonder that today's undergraduate occasionally feels a distressing sense of rootlessness and aimlessness, of preparing and preparing and preparing for that distant day when he'll actually do something.

Student money-making is one way out of this dilemma. An undergraduate who runs a business or takes a job is doing something which is of value to others right now. And he knows it, because he has his profit or his paycheck to prove it.

There are other solutions, of course. One very successful alternative is student activism; the way the world looks today, nobody could do it any bigger favor than to change it a bit. But for those of us who are not revolutionaries at heart, activism is not a viable answer. Furthermore, the kind of frustration we have described often makes a student activist overanxious to see the results of his handiwork. That is when activism begins to look like hooliganism—which is itself a favored method for college men and women to blow off steam. Where the desire to *do something* is stronger than the conviction of what ought to be done, the results are rarely desirable and always unpredictable. Student business seems a less risky and much more constructive safety valve.

It is the impulse to concrete achievement now, we feel, that has turned the college student into a "professionalist." The word "hobby" today has a negative connotation to students, implying the leisure activity of a kindergartner or a suburban housewife. A generation ago, perhaps, undergraduates with musical inclinations formed combos for their own entertainment; today they advertise for that missing bass player, agonize for hours over a suitable name, schedule regular rehearsals, and seek bookings all over the state. A generation ago, perhaps an amateur mathematician played with his equations in satisfied solitude; today he fights hard to get his work published in the "right" mathematical journal.

Academic work cannot fill this void. There is tremendous satisfaction to running a chemical analysis or writing a research paper, but that satisfaction is always tempered by the knowledge that the analysis will be checked and the paper read only by a professor who wants to find out how much you have learned. Rarely does anyone go over your academic work in order to learn something himself. Extra-curricular activities can fill the void (nobody reads a yearbook or a newspaper to find out if the editors did a good job) but they fill it on a small, campus-confined scale, usually with the supervision and financial support of a paternalistic administration, and generally without pay.

Buell Gallagher, president of the City College of New York, recently said of today's college students: "This generation has no Utopia. Its idea is the Happening. Let it be concrete, let it be vivid, let it be personal. Let it be *now!*"

That may not sound like a description of why undergraduates work to earn money, but for thousands of students across the country that's just what it is.

8. DECISIONS, DECISIONS

The number of job and business opportunities open to college students approaches, as the mathematicians like to say, infinity. In fact, it damn near passes it.

So once you have resolved to dive in, the first crucial step is to decide how you like your water. Does the treacherous but exhilarating ocean of a full-scale business enterprise appeal to you, or would you prefer a safer dip in the pond of a small campus concession? Do you dare to stand upright in the quick-running rapids of your own business, or would the placid pool of a part-time job suit you better? Would you like to swim alone, and against the tide, carrying forward a new idea, or would you rather paddle with others in an established, successful venture?

Forgoing florid metaphor for a while (hopefully for a good long while), there are in fact a number of variables which you should consider in choosing the sort of money-making effort which is right for you. To wit:

Time: There are only twenty-four hours in a day, seven days in a week. This is a fact of life which every prospective student worker must face up to. Every hour you spend working you will be unable to spend doing something else. Something else includes studying; it also includes running for president of your class, shooting the bull with your roommates, doing your nails, going to football games, going to frat parties, going to concerts, and going to bed.

Most college administrators recognize this fact of life, and try to steer students away from packing full-time study, full-time work and part-time collegiate fun into each exhausting week. Homer D. Babbidge Jr. of the American College Personnel Association advises that the number of hours spent in the classroom plus those spent earning money should not total more than 35. Figuring an average of 15 hours a week in class, that leaves you 20 more in which to work, without seriously impairing your studies or your college life.

Recommended maximums for work vary greatly from school to school. A 1960 survey conducted by *Changing Times* found that Kent State University and Wellesley College set the limit at ten hours, Grinnell, Oregon, and Montana State let it go at 20, while the University of California at Pasadena thought students could safely work up to 30 hours a week. At many schools these recommendations become compulsory for on-campus jobs, so if you're planning on one of those, check it out.

Freshmen are a special case, at least in the view of most administrators. Many college authorities would prefer that freshmen did not work at all, particularly during their first semester. Some schools see to it that they don't, on campus anyway, and a good number restrict freshman working hours more stringently than those of upperclassmen. The argument, of course, is that the freshmen need time to adjust to the college environment and to discover how onerous the work load is for them. Princeton's director of student aid, W. Bradford Craig, disagrees. "Actually," he writes, "this fear of facing up to the necessity of engaging in term-time employment right from the start is exaggerated. The entering student must, of course, adjust to the college academic schedule . . . but it is possible for him to do this and still maintain a program which calls for ten to twelve hours of employment a week. Having a job may even assist in the adjustment to college life."

An estimated one-quarter of all working students put in more than 20 hours a week. For some, this requires a decrease in course load; for many, it means juggling courses to fit job schedules, or passing up an occasional rough subject because it would require too much time. But long working hours inevitably take their greatest toll on participation in extra-curricular activities and informal campus events.

It is occasionally possible to beat the system. Some students find work that requires little more than their mere presence, and can spend the bulk of their job time studying. The best bet in this line for men is a position as a watchman or caretaker at the school library or chapel, an academic or administration building, a business or even a private home. For women, work as a baby-sitter or "mother's helper" can have the same advantage.

Another way to save time is to find a position that fills two needs at once. We have already pointed out that student business at its best shares many values with non-paying college extra-curricular activities. If you are willing to sacrifice contact with the outside world for contact with your fellow students, a business can be arranged that has all the characteristics of a campus club—plus pay. The most frequent examples are profit-making student publications and bands, but even a food concession can be made to provide all the cameraderie, enjoyment, satisfaction and campus recognition of a successful extra-curricular organization.

A third time-saving possibility is to organize a business that can be run during "dead time"—periods of the day when you would be doing nothing worthwhile anyway. Even better, find a money-maker which, once it is set up, takes no time at all. Campus businesses which nearly run themselves are not unusual, and many such enterprises will be described later in this book.

Profit: Time is money, so they say, but if you want to spend much time spending money, you have to make some money, whereas making time is usually free.

The question of profit is double-barreled. How much money you want to make is half of it, but it is also a good idea to ask yourself how *certain* you must be of making the money you want to make. If your earnings are needed for your tuition or part of it, and it's a matter of $25 a week or a trip to Viet Nam, you're probably best off taking an on-campus job. On the other end of the scale, if you're already financially comfortable and you're looking for kicks and a chance at The Big Money, then you might as well live a little and start your own industrial empire.

If we ignore the need for a secure, certain income, there is no doubt that successful campus concessions pay better than jobs, while off-campus or multi-campus operations have still greater profit potential. The key words here, though, are "successful" and "potential." You can lose a job, but you can't lose money on it; hundreds of students across the country have learned that you *can* lose money running your own business.

You can also make it big. Averages are hard to come by, but if the student businessmen we have talked to are representative, then you can expect to earn at least $1,000 during the school year in a moderately successful venture. If you hit on a good thing and play it right, an income of $10,000 or more is not impossible. Less time-consuming enterprises net less cash, but more than a few undergraduates have turned a quick $200 or $300 peddling fad items (such as kooky buttons or op art posters) for a few weeks.

Job incomes vary also—from low to lower. On-campus jobs are the worst from a financial viewpoint, though they are often the most convenient and always the most secure. If you can get $1.50 an hour out of your school for doing anything, you're doing well. Bus boys, counter girls, library assistants and file clerks command around $1.00 an hour; cashiers, paper graders, research assistants and typists go for about $1.15; artists, lab assistants, and researchers sometimes get as high as $1.30. These are not averages. They are reports from major colleges and universities, which pay considerably more than the average. Most student jobs at most colleges pay under $1.00 an hour, and some pay as little as 45 cents an hour for coolie labor.

If you can land a job off campus, the pay scale is bound to be higher. Typically, if you're getting $1.10 an hour as a typist for the biology department, you can earn $1.35 or more doing the same work for Sticky Wickets, Inc. Yardwork, retail selling, janitorial work, housecleaning and the like all pay about $1.50 an hour. Employees with experience or special skills naturally do better.

Not only are campus jobs less remunerative than off-campus ones, they are also scarce—and getting scarcer. As colleges become larger and more bureaucratic, they tend to hire more and more full-time staff to take over the positions students once filled. Even part-time jobs are often handed to "townies" as a gesture of town-gown amity and part of the school's private War on Poverty. The result is that campus jobs are often hard to get. At Louisiana State University, for example, you need a 'C' average to qualify for a campus "workship." Financial aid directors struggle hard to convince administrators to use more student help, but an ever-increasing part of their job today is finding off-campus positions for needy undergraduates.

Sex: At college, like most everywhere else, women have a harder time than men finding work, and are paid less for it. Baby-sitting and housework are the coed's staples, and they don't pay very well. Most retailing and secretarial jobs off-campus are filled by full-time employees, while part-time waitresses are notoriously overworked and underpaid. As a result, many colleges reserve a disproportionate number of campus jobs for women. So far there has been no ruling on whether or not this violates the federal civil rights laws, but it would be most unchivalrous to complain.

Location: Where you are will determine to a large extent what you can do, and how much you will be paid to do it. New York City requires few farmhands, nor is the demand for part-time taxi drivers very great in the Kentucky hills.

Generally speaking, you can expect the lowest pay in the South and Southeast. New England and the Midwest are somewhat better, and the top wages and profits are to be had in the Middle Atlantic and Far West regions.

In terms of job and business potential, the best place to be is a large, residential college in an urban area. At such schools (Harvard, Wisconsin, Stanford, etc.) there are a maximum number of work opportunities available, both on and off campus. Next best is a commuter school or a small college in a big city. On-campus jobs and businesses are rare at these places, but off-campus positions and even business opportunities are plentiful. If for one reason or another urban areas are out, a large university in a university town is the thing to look for. Many of the Midwestern state universities fall into this category. On-campus jobs are numerous, and the chance to sell goods or services to your 50,000 fellow students is golden.

The final alternative is one to avoid. This country is peppered with thousands of tiny colleges in tinier towns, places where the president's young son holds the only three part-time jobs around. We have received letters from hundreds of such institutions, succinctly informing us that "there are no student money-making activities here." They're telling the truth. If you wind up at such a school, and you have to earn money, try a mail-order business; it's your only chance.

Security: We have already mentioned that the desire for a high income must often yield to the need for an assured income. A business, like a woman, is a sometime thing, and if you can't afford to flounder for a while, you shouldn't be in one. Jobs are much safer, and on-campus jobs are safest.

With increasing college costs and academic work loads, there seems to be a strong trend today among college students to opt for the safe way. At Utica College in Utica, New York, for example, "trends toward campus-run businesses are undiscernible. But more than 50 percent of our student body works full or part-time, on or off campus." Flint College of the University of Michigan reports that "our students do not seem to be entrepreneurs. They are most interested in a definite job for so many hours per week at a definite salary. No projects involving risk of capital or loss of time." Loyola University in New Orleans notes that "most of our students do want to have part-time jobs while in school, but few of these students want to initiate their own businesses." The girls at Pembroke College in Providence, Rhode Island, are even more picky. According to the placement office, Pembroke students "seem to prefer a campus job (library or office) which makes no demands on them other than the ten hours a week and *does* guarantee them a salary of so much per hour. The security of such a job seems very important to them. . . . Pembroke students are not interested in sales jobs or jobs on commission; they prefer a steady, salaried job with defined hours."

Interests: What can you do well? What do you want to learn to do better? These are essential questions to ask in choosing the job or business that will be most rewarding for you.

Skills mean better-paying jobs, higher-profit businesses. Typing, bookkeeping, fixing a flat tire, vacuuming a rug, and mixing a malted are skills. So are library cataloging, sewing, playing a musical instrument, cutting hair, and coaching a tennis team. There are at least a dozen things that you can do better than most people, and half of them probably need doing at your college or in your community. Each is a made-to-order job or business.

Think not only about what you can do, but also about what you like to do. Do you like to work with people? With animals? With machinery? With paper and pencil? Find a way to make money doing it. Do you feel you need more physical exercise? More mental challenge? More relaxation? Find a way to make money getting it. Do you want to meet faculty members? Classmates? Important business people? Find a way to make money meeting them. Are you thinking of a career in teaching? In finance? In engineering? In medicine? Find a way to make money trying it.

Balance your interests and your skills, your sex and your location, your need for cash and your need for security, your personality and your available time—and find a way to make yourself some money. Thousands of students have solved the problem before you. Some of the best solutions are reported in this book.

9. AND NOW, THE FEATURE ATTRACTION

We have now generalized, philosophized, counseled and commented as much as we're going to. The next chapter begins our catalog of successful student business ventures, garnered from college administrators and students themselves across the country.

Chapter Two will be devoted to the wondrous assortment of objects which students have managed to sell to other students. These range from tweed jackets to embroidered panties, from beer mugs to powder puffs, from hotdogs to refrigerators. In Chapter Three we will examine the similar list of on-campus services which have proved profitable, from motorbike rentals to charter flights, paper typing to paper copying, linen supply to book supply. Chapter Four will leave the dormitories and deal with student businesses and jobs that serve, or at least live off, the community.

Special skills, from computers to coaching, will be the subject of Chapter Five. In Chapter Six, we will discuss the student tycoons, the men and women who succeed far beyond their campuses and their expectations. The seventh and eighth chapters will attempt to illuminate two of the most painful problems confronting a student entrepreneur—college policy and the law. Finally, in Chapter Nine, we will try to summarize our observations.

CHAPTER 2

Knapsack on
Your Back

1. DOOR-TO-DOOR FOOD

Students buy a fantastic assortment of objects, but the thing they buy most readily is undoubtedly food. And there is always a fellow student around who is willing to capitalize on the appetites of his classmates. The result is that refreshment agencies of various sorts are ubiquitous money-makers on more than half the campuses in the country.

Many colleges forbid door-to-door hawking of snacks on the grounds that it "would make the school look like a carnival" or "would distract our students from their studies." It is a rare undergraduate, however, who complains about the opportunity to interrupt his evening's work for a hamburger, a submarine sandwich, a Coke, a doughnut, or a cup of coffee. At colleges where it is permitted, organization of an agency to dispense such items is a sure way to pick up needed cash.

Practically any eatable will do. A University of Illinois undergraduate earns $900 a year peddling sandwiches; milk and doughnuts net a Middlebury College entrepreneur $65 a week; a student at Ursinus College pockets an easy $240 a year on sticky buns; an enterprising Ohio University senior pays his tuition and expenses and banks a surplus $800 a year selling potato chips, soda pop, and sandwiches. Grinders, milk, fruit juice and six varieties of sandwiches compete for the attention of hungry Dartmouth students. Ice cream, doughnuts, brownies and even potato pancakes turn a profit at Luther College in Decorah, Iowa. At Swarthmore it's hoagies; at the University of Pennsylvania it's sandwiches and soft drinks; at Princeton it's doughnuts, milk, soft drinks, grinders, and pizzas; and at Rutgers University it's simply "a wide variety of refreshments."

This simple do-it-yourself gold mine has only two problems worthy of the name. The first is convincing your college administration to let you loose on its wards. Remind them that doctors say we sleep better if we eat something before retiring. Tell them your business will keep students from venturing into the Big Bad City for evening refreshment. Remark that psychologists have found that an occasional study break makes for more efficient learning as well as better social adjustment. If all else fails, try to get a student referendum; the votes are certain to go your way.

The second problem is purchasing. For a small operation, the local supermarket should do; your profit will come from putting the materials together and delivering them to your customers' doorsteps. But as soon as your nightly sales pass the hundred mark (sandwiches or grinders or ice cream bars or bottles of pop or whatever), you should consider buying wholesale. Contact as many suppliers as you can. A number will be unwilling to sell to you, some because you are a student and too small-time, some because they already do business with your "competitors" in town. If you can afford to pay cash or pick up the goods yourself, be sure to say so; it will be a big plus in your favor.

Most state and local governments require food peddlers to obtain special licenses. If you are selling on the campus or a private college or university, you are probably exempt, and even at a state school the permits already held by your school will most likely cover you—but check. Especially if your route will take you off campus to the fraternities, sororities or student rooming houses, make sure you know the law. Several student peddlers recommend that you look into the legal aspect of your plans by asking someone connected with the college. "If you go directly to the police station for information," notes a Midwestern sandwichman, "you're likely to find that a lot of obsolete regulations nobody ever heard of suddenly apply to you."

Your prices should be roughly comparable to what the res-' taurants in town are getting. The convenience of door-to-door service is such that you will do well even if you charge somewhat more, but the experience of dozens of students has shown that lower prices mean more sales, which in turn mean purchasing in greater quantities at a lower cost—and that means larger profits. A Middlebury College student buys 35 quarts of milk and orange drink and the materials for 150 sandwiches daily. His food costs are $35 a week. He sells his sandwiches at roughly three times that amount, leaving him between $65 and $70 weekly profit. An entrepreneur at the University of Illinois buys the materials for 300 sandwiches daily. His cost per sandwich is 11 cents. His selling price 60 cents.

Make use of college facilities wherever possible. Several students have managed to work out an arrangement with their school's dining hall or student union to sell leftover snack material each evening. The student union may also help out with refrigeration and heating problems, though a fraternity kitchen is a more usual solution, and one Illinois peddler wraps bread in his electric blanket to keep it warm. Fraternity, dorm, or student union leftovers are also a good source of inexpensive menu variation. If your frat has chili for lunch one day, you should be offering chiliburgers as well as hamburgers that night.

Getting your goods to your market presents no major problem. A wire basket which can be suspended from the neck is fine for sandwiches, doughnuts, or anything else that is sold at room temperature. A metal cart or a large basket on a bicycle makes for easier traveling and fewer profitless trips back to home base for more provisions. Your school's grounds department may be able to lend or sell you something suitable. A large thermos is perfect for keeping coffee hot or soda cold. A tight-fitting metal-lined box will do the same for hot sandwiches or pop bottles; with the addition of a small piece of dry ice, it will keep ice cream solid all evening.

Prime selling hours start about two hours after the end of dinner (say 8:30 or 9:00 P.M.) and run till students start going to bed (generally 11:30 or midnight). Since you will be peddling your wares door-to-door, posters or other advertising is unnecessary. A news article in the student newspaper wouldn't hurt, though, and it's free; simply drop in at the paper's office and tell them what you'll be selling, your route and your prices. For the first week or two, hawk your goods aggressively, announcing what you have for sale and how much you charge. Once everybody has learned of your existence, work out a set pattern, and stick to it every night. It will become your trademark. A little originality in your pitch can boost sales enormously. A pastry peddler at Princeton found his cherry tarts moving more slowly than he had expected. One evening he decided to hawk them as "virgin cherry tarts." He quickly sold out, and virgin cherry tarts are today one of his biggest items.

Occasionally it is desirable to take orders for your food by telephone. This hardly pays for sandwiches, soda pop or the like, but for more expensive and less durable items such as pizzas it is the only way. Student pizza agencies usually use the college kitchens, cook the pies to order, and deliver them by bicycle. This is practical only if students have easy access to a phone. If they're going to have to walk some distance to telephone you, they may as well walk into town for their pizza. Your phone number must be immediately available. Advertise it in the school paper, the school telephone directory (if there is one), and any other medium that will wind up in a student's room. Distribute handouts several times a year telling students what you have to offer, and advising them to save the sheet so that your telephone number will be handy when they feel like a pizza.

A little promotion never hurt any business. Offer an occasional sale on a new item or one which is not moving very well. Try reducing prices on all items for one dorm or frat house each day. As student interest in your comings and goings rises, business will increase, not only at the particular house chosen, but at others as well.

At a school with more than 500 resident students, the time will quickly come when you cannot handle everything yourself. If you feel like cutting your responsibility and your time (and your profits) in half, take in a partner. The most common partnership arrangement is for one student to make the sandwiches or whatever, the other to sell them. A more efficient method, it seems to us, is for each partner to run the business alternately for an equal number of days. The period between dinner and 9:00 P.M. is dead time anyway, since nobody's hungry, and it's perfect for preparing the food. Alternating days thus leaves you with half your evenings (and your afternoons, if you pick up materials yourself) completely free.

If you like responsibility and money, don't look for a partner at all. Instead, hire other students to work for you. Standard pay for selling door-to-door is $1.00 an hour plus a penny commission on each item sold. For making the snacks, $2 an hour or more is appropriate. Your college financial aid office will be able to provide as many employees as you need. For a really big operation like Dartmouth's sandwich agency, you can hire men to pick up the food, men to prepare it, and men to sell it—leaving you free to keep an eye on things and count your profits.

Selling snacks in the evening cannot fail on a residential campus. Gear your product, your volume, and your pitch to the size and character of your school. Girls will buy less than men, and will demand low-calorie foods; diet soda and fruit go over well on women's or coed campuses. For men, big heavy sandwiches or grinders will be most popular. If there are food machines in or near the dorms or frats, they are bound to cut into your sales; try to offer something the machines don't, such as hot sandwiches. If other students are already selling food items in the evening, test the market carefully before trying to compete— there may not be enough hunger to go around. If you are the first on your campus, ask the administration if they will guarantee you a monopoly. Many schools permit only one student business of each kind, and yours could be the one. Start small, but think big.

The advantages of this enterprise are high profits and reasonable security. You can't lose very much money, and your chances of earning a great deal are better than for most student businesses. In addition, some students find door-to-door selling fun. "You'd be surprised," a Midwestern food concessionnaire told us, "how many people you can get to know by selling sandwiches in the dorms. I'll bet I've made more friends that way than through my classes." "It's enjoyable work," echoed a Middlebury College student. "You get a chance to throw the bull with other students in the halls."

The fun soon wears off, however. The main drawbacks of this business are the time it consumes and the boredom it engenders. Two hours of preparation and three hours of selling per night are par, and to become a campus institution you have to be at it every weeknight, every week, all year. Even the most enthusiastic salesmen admit that it gets to be a drag after a month or so. Once the business gets big, of course, you can hire other students and cut down on both the time outlay and the boredom.

In any case, the money can't be beat. At Elizabethtown College in Elizabethtown, Pennsylvania, we are told, "enterprising outsiders earn $50 a night selling hoagies on campus." Some student at Elizabethtown College—and perhaps at your school—should get hopping.

2. VARIATIONS ON THE THEME

Lugging food door-to-door requires for success lots of muscles and lots of doors. If your dormitories are not laid out in an entryway system, it may be nearly impossible to stand outside each student's window and hawk your wares. Your college may be justifiably reluctant to have you shouting through the halls of its buildings, and you may be justifiably reluctant to carry your basket or your cart up six flights of stairs. Faced with both these problems, the enterprising doughnut girls at Wellesley College have found a solution: They deliver boxes of doughnuts to the lobby of each dorm. Hungry students walk downstairs, drop their dime in a box, and grab a doughnut. Wellesley does it on the honor system, but you may wish to enlist dorm residents to sit by the doughnuts to prevent grabbing without dropping.

A student at Ohio University solved a similar set of problems, and avoided administration disapproval as well, by locating himself just off campus. He dispenses his food from a six-foot openfront trailer parked on a grassy spot near the dorms. A lantern lights the way and notifies customers that he is open for business. Known as The Sandy Wagon, his stand is still more convenient than any of the restaurants in town, and students come as much to chat with their classmates as to buy his food. He works only three hours a night, and earns more than $1,500 a year, so he must be doing something right.

3. RESTAURANTS AND SNACK BARS

From The Sandy Wagon it is just a short step to more ornate food dispensaries—restaurants, snack bars, tearooms, coffeehouses, nightclubs, and the like. Just about every college has its school-run student union with snack bars and so forth, so your job is to offer something a bit different. It can be done. A University of Delaware coed has been very successful running a "spaghetti diner" for students. Waldorf College in Forest City, Iowa, has "The Unique," a coffeehouse open to both students and faculty. A student at Carnegie Institute of Technology in Pittsburgh runs a nightclub of sorts every Friday evening during the school year.

Some sort of gimmick is necessary to attract students, especially at schools where there are plenty of eateries in town. Carnegie Tech's enterprise uses student help and student entertainment. A four-piece combo specializing in jazz and a congenial atmosphere have produced a nightspot designed, according to its manager, "for people who want to get together and groove a little." Upwards of 600 customers spend some part of each Friday night grooving. Waldorf's "Unique" has an additional come-on: it supplements student entertainment groups with faculty volunteers. To wean students away from town restaurants to Delaware's spaghetti diner, its manager supplies a service through which girls can sell or exchange outgrown clothing.

Running a restaurant of any sort is a complex business; everything from dishwashing equipment to fire insurance must be looked into. With rare exceptions, the profits are not worth the work unless you can win the support of your school administration. If you can get the college to run the food side of the business, leaving you free to concentrate on entertainment and promotion, then it may pay to give it a try. On campuses where existing centers for student eating and entertainment are inadequate, the administration may cooperate, and the student body is bound to be enthusiastic. But make sure there is a real need before you start; a empty restaurant or coffeehouse means a lot of wasted time and money.

4. FOOD STANDS

Students may eat most heartily during the evening, but they don't fast through the daylight hours either. Strangely enough, we have found very few student entrepreneurs selling food in the daytime. One successful venture at the University of Florida at Gainesville is known as "Honor System Apples." This consists of a dozen or so small wooden fruit stands, painted white to attract attention and strategically located at convenient spots on campus. Each morning before classes begin, the stands are filled with apples and bananas, purchased from local merchants. Built onto each stand is a money box. Students are on their honor to deposit a dime for an apple or 15 cents for a banana.

It is not necessary to rely on the honor system. The dorms may not be sufficiently populated in the afternoons to justify door-to-door peddling, but a small refreshment stand near the library, the gym, or the classrooms is bound to pay well, particularly if these buildings are located a healthy distance from any other source of nutriment.

The time and effort required to set up and run a stand of this sort is negligible. It won't get you into *Fortune Magazine,* but it will go a long way toward paying your college expenses—and it's easy and almost foolproof.

5. BREAKFAST

A standard money-maker for organizations and class treasuries is a "breakfast in bed" day. It works best at women's colleges, and even there only once in a while, when the entire school can be whipped into a breakfast-in-bed spirit.

But breakfast should not be abandoned as a possible daily business. A large percentage of students, forced to choose between the regular college breakfast and an extra hour of sleep before classes, select the latter. They get up at 9:30 yearning for a cup of coffee and a bun. The undergraduate who sells them will earn the life-long gratitude and a good part of the loose change of his fellow students.

The problem with hawking breakfast door-to-door, of course, is that you will wake up your potential customers—which is a move not calculated to put them in a buying mood. Several possible solutions suggest themselves. One is to lay out a tight schedule for yourself, notify students when you will be around to their dorm, and then stick to it. A second is to leave your wares in dorm lobbies, to be paid for under the honor system. A third is to take advance orders; let students pay you by the week or month to deliver a small breakfast to their rooms at a specified hour each weekday.

A further possibility is to set up a breakfast stand somewhere on the route from the dorms or frats to the classrooms. Students struggling bleary-eyed to their first class of the day will pay anything for a cup of coffee. Why shouldn't they pay you?

To the best of our knowledge no one has yet capitalized on the college student's need for a late, convenient, inexpensive breakfast. You just could be the first.

6. FOOD AND DRINK DELIVERY

At colleges where students are allowed to have refrigerators in their rooms, it is a daily struggle to keep the things filled. Food delivery agencies meet this need.

Ivy League schools and large state universities have had such services for many years. At schools where students entertain guests in their rooms on weekends (or during the week), the most popular goods are soft drinks, mixers, pretzels, potato chips, and alcoholic beverages, where permitted. Other foodstuffs—bread, crackers, peanut butter and jelly, etc.—are occasionally added to the list.

Food supply agencies generally hand out mimeographed sheets describing their products and prices, then take orders by telephone. A student can order a six-pack or case of soda for a particular weekend, or he can put in a standing order for so much per week. Empty bottles are picked up at the next delivery; payment may be on delivery or by the month. Not every college needs a food delivery service, but at those that do the agency is easy to set up, easy to run, and very profitable. If you buy your food and drink wholesale, you may figure at least a quarter profit on each six-pack of soda, a dime on each bag of chips. A hundred six-packs and a hundred bags a weekend represents a clear $35 profit for a few hours' work.

Liquor and beer delivery agencies are forbidden on most campuses, and are of questionable legality in most states to boot. Where they are permitted, however, they invariably earn a small fortune. Contact the manager of a local liquor store and offer him your exclusive patronage in return for a discount; if your volume is fairly large, he can afford to give you 10 percent off and still do nicely. You can then sell on campus at liquor store prices plus a moderate delivery charge, and do very nicely yourself.

7. ATHLETIC REFRESHMENTS

Everyone associates athletic contests with hot dogs, soda pop, beer, and the like. When the athletic contestants are students, the vendors of these goodies should be students also.

Just about every school that has intercollegiate athletics has a student refreshment agency working the popular home games. Such concessions are frequently awarded to honorary fraternities, lettermen's clubs, and so forth. They are nearly always monopolies granted by the college administration. If your college has sports events and its sports fans are going hungry, contact the student aid office or athletic office and offer to do something about it.

A typical concession of this sort is run by a senior at Williams College for the four home football games in the fall. His food is supplied by the college, as are the twenty salesmen he employs for each game. He sells hot dogs (35 cents), Coca-Cola (15 cents), coffee (15 cents) and candy (10 cents to 15 cents), and his gross receipts for each game are roughly $400. The college buys the food wholesale and in quantity, so nearly half the gross is profit, even after paying the salesmen. The school athletic department drains off most of the profits in return for the monopoly, but still leaves our enterprising student with $300 for his dozen hours' work.

If you're willing to handle the whole thing on your own, and the school doesn't mind, you can double your profits along with your time investment. Order your food wholesale well in advance, and pick it up the morning of the game. A propane gas stove is perfect for your cooking; if the college can't lend you one, you can rent it from any catering service. Plan on spending at least eight hours per game (including game time) if you run your own show. Your profits will of course depend upon the size of the crowd, but they should be roughly 40 percent of the gross.

Students in this business advise a wage of about $1.50 per hour for student hawkers, plus free entry to the game. They caution that food permits must usually be obtained from your local health department well before you start. If you plan on using a gas stove, a gas permit may also be required.

8. FOOD FOR SPECIAL EVENTS

Judging from the abundance of refreshment concessions at sports contests and their scarcity anywhere else, one would think that athletics are the only campus activities that draw student crowds. Thousands of movies, plays, concerts, speeches, and debates take place each year on college campuses—with no refreshments.

Such a scandalous state of affairs should not be permitted to exist unchecked. Anything which attracts an audience of more than 100 should attract an ambitious student entrepreneur as well. The principles are the same as for the other varieties of food sale: Choose an attractive item; buy in quantity, wholesale if possible; sell at a mark-up of at least 100 percent. The mark-up on soft drinks can range up to 200 percent. On coffee, which costs practically nothing if you make it yourself, a profit of 1,000 percent is not unreasonable.

Contact the person in charge of each event well in advance. Even if he was already planning some sort of refreshment stand, he should be easily convinced that you can do the job better than his already beleaguered ticket manager. Offer him a small percentage of your profits to clinch the deal. You are bound to get more acceptances than rejections.

On a large campus, an enterprising student might easily earn his full expenses by "catering" intermissions at a variety of non-athletic events.

9. CRAM KITS

At Dartmouth College they're known as "survival kits." The College of Idaho calls them "finals food packets." Luther College knows them as "care packages." The University of New Hampshire refers to them as "exam packs." On most other campuses, they're labeled "cram kits."

If you're a college student and you have to ask what we're talking about, then your college is a bit behind the times and you have just found yourself a ready-made source of income. Cram kits are cartons of food designed for snacking while studying for exams. They can be sold directly to students, but a more profitable and more usual arrangement is to take orders for them from parents.

About six weeks before exams each semester, send a letter to the family of each student, telling them of the ordeal ahead and of their son or daughter's urgent need for convenient nourishment during the crucial examination period. Offer two or three different kits, varying in size, composition, and of course price. Enclose an order blank and a business reply envelope, and set a firm deadline for orders at least two weeks before exams. This will give you plenty of time to buy your food and make up the kits after all orders have been received, thus making advance outlay of capital unnecessary.

A typical cram kit would offer hearty portions of peanut butter, crackers, cheese, fruit juice, raisins, cookies and candy for about $4. An $8 kit would include larger quantities of the same, plus fresh fruit, pretzels, canned goods and a can opener. Plan your kits so that the materials for each cost about a third of your sales price. You may count on roughly a 30 percent response from the parents.

Lists of home addresses are usually available in the form of "freshman handbooks," student directories, or yearbooks. If they are not, try to get a list from your school administration. A printed or multilithed letter would look official and gain a few extra sales, but a mimeographed one will do nicely. Be sure to include a postal reply envelope one size smaller than your outside envelope. Any printing company will whip off a few thousand of these for you; the savings from not having to put postage stamps on unreturned envelopes will more than cover the printing costs. When the orders are in, buy your food, pack it in cake boxes or similar cartons, and deliver the completed kits to students' rooms. Include a mimeographed note explaining whom the kit is for and who paid for it.

When things get too big for you, hire a few student envelope-stuffers, letter-answerers, carton-fillers and kit-deliverers. Handle this two-month, part-time business right, and you can expect a profit after all expenses are paid equal to three-fifths the number of students enrolled in your school. With a student body of 1,000 for example, you should make roughly $600 each semester.

10. BIRTHDAY CAKES

Another much-used method for profiting from the parents of your classmates is the birthday cake agency. The idea seems to be most popular in the East, where it originated, but it has been tried successfully as far west as the University of Texas at Austin, and there is no reason why it shouldn't work everywhere.

The procedure is simple. First obtain the names, home addresses, and birth dates of all students. (After the first year, it will be necessary to do this only for incoming freshmen.) Contact a local bakery and work out prices for two or three different sizes and flavors. You may expect as much as a 20 percent discount from the bakery if you can guarantee them a few hundred orders. This discount, plus a "service charge" of $1.00 or more above the regular retail price, will be your profit on each cake.

Arrange your list of students in chronological order by birthdays, and discard those whose birthdays come when school is not in session. Address envelopes to the parents of each student. Fill them with a printed or mimeographed letter explaining your service, and order blank, and a printed business reply envelope. Seal and stamp the envelopes, and you're ready to roll.

Several weeks before each student's birthday, drop your letter to his parents into a mailbox. As orders come in, phone, mail, or bring them to the bakery to be filled. On the morning of the student's birthday, deliver the cake to his room.

A number of variations in procedure have been tried. At several schools, the bakery handles delivery of the cake. This frees the student from running around campus making deliveries, but it also cuts down on his profit. On the other end of the ambition spectrum, Vassar College's cake girl buys a plain iced layercake from the bakery, adds the frills and inscriptions herself in her dormitory kitchen. The extra work comes to about 20 minutes a cake, which is more than justified by the savings in bakery prices.

At Bowdoin College in Brunswick, Maine, letters to parents are mailed out during the summer. Those who are interested send in the birth date of their son or daughter along with their order. This procedure undoubtedly loses a few sales because of the time span between the letter and the birthday, but it saves an immense amount of time, and it does not require you to know the birth dates of your fellow students. A hidden cost of this method is that letters must be sent to the parents of all students; if you know the birth dates, you can eliminate those coming in the summer or over vacations, and save one-quarter of your printing and postage expenses.

Obtaining your list of names, addresses and birthdays may be easy at some schools, nearly impossible at others. Our correspondent at Middlebury College, for example, simply stopped in at the Dean's Office and copied out his list; at Trinity College in Hartford, Connecticut, by contrast, the cake concessionnaire had to painfully piece together his list from information in the college newspaper office and at the infirmary.

Your letter to the parents should be short and to the point—but pleasant. Last year's letter from Middlebury College is an excellent sample:

Dear Parents,

In a short time your son or daughter will have a birthday. We hope that you will be able to join in the traditional birthday song, but if you are unable to, we know that you would want this to be a most happy one.

The Middlebury College Financial Aid Committee has granted us this activity as a campus concession.

You can order a cake, freshly baked in a local shop, packaged, and delivered personally to your son or daughter.

The letter goes on to list sizes, flavors, and prices, with a convenient order blank at the bottom of the page. The blank includes spaces for the name and birth date of the student, and the size and flavor of cake desired. It also includes the name and address of the concessionnaire.

Cake agencies typically offer three sizes—eight-inch, ten-inch and twelve-inch—for approximately $4, $5 and $6 respectively. At least two flavor alternatives (vanilla and chocolate) should be given for both the frosting and the cake itself.

The volume of responses from parents varies from college to college. It rarely goes below 20 percent, however, or above 65 percent. In any case, your profit should be between $1.50 and $2.50 on each cake. Out of that must come printing and postage, your only expenses. These should amount to about $100 for the first 1,000 letters, $60 for each additional thousand. All told, you stand to make a total profit of at least $500 and probably over $1,000.

The big advantage of a birthday cake agency is the very small amount of time needed to run it. Once your letters are printed, stuffed, and ready to go, a couple of hours a week is all the time you'll need.

11. VARIATIONS ON THE THEME

Once your agreement with the bakery has been worked out, there is no reason to confine your customers to parents. At Vassar College in Poughkeepsie, New York, the cake agency nearly doubles its income by taking orders from students as well. Girls order cakes for other girls' birthdays, and also for parties of various sorts—end of exams, completion of a term paper, Halloween, pinning, engagement, etc. All you need do to expand in this direction is to have a telephone. Distribute handouts with your phone number, your products, and your prices, and some suggestions about cake-worthy events. A few posters in strategic locations would also help.

Another way of putting your preparation to double use is to send out mailings to parents for occasions other than birthdays. Dartmouth College, for example, combines its birthday cake and cram kit agencies, since both use the same list of customers. At a few schools, parents are offered baskets of fresh fruit for their sons and daughters several times a year. The only limits to this sort of promotion are your own imagination and your classmates' parents' pocketbooks.

12. OTHER FOOD IDEAS

Special foods for special days, events, and interests are an ever-present possible money-maker. The most popular business of this sort is the sale of foreign foods by language clubs in connection with their other activities. But you should also be aware of the opportunity to peddle Halloween candy in October, turkeys in November, etc. At colleges with a substantial Jewish population, matzoth and Hamentaschen are good seasonal sellers. Look around for special food demands on your campus.

Two other food ideas are top money-makers at many schools. They are installation and management of food vending machines in dorms, frats, sororities, etc.; and catering of organizational or fraternity parties. Since both of these are closer to services than to direct sale of goods, they will be discussed in Chapter Three.

Students are suckers for any food product, any time, anywhere, at any price. At the College of St. Catherine in St. Paul, Minnesota, a girl earns pocket money peddling commercially made chocolates in the dormitories. She has to compete with the perennial home-baked cake and cookie sales that are ubiquitous on every college campus with at least one girl and one kitchen—but she still does well. After all, she's selling something edible. College students will buy anything edible.

We now move from food to the multitude of other items that students have successfully peddled to students.

13. BEER MUGS

It is a tribute to the chauvinism of the American college student that ceramic and metal beer mugs, embossed with the seal of the college, are a perennial sales favorite even on campuses where consumption of beer is forbidden. True, the mugs have some decorative value, and many find use as shaving mugs, pencil holders, and miniature garbage cans—but their main appeal, we are convinced, lies in the pure rah-rah appeal of possessing a genuine Yahoo State beer mug.

Whatever the reasons for their popularity, college beer mugs are guaranteed to net you a fast couple of C-notes. Profits vary with the size and wealth of the school, ranging from $120 at tiny Ursinus College in Collegeville, Pennsylvania, through $450 at Hartford, Connecticut's Trinity College, to a not-yet-counted fortune at giant Michigan State University.

The major problem with selling beer mugs is that somebody probably thought of it 20 years ago. If your college has a school store or a college co-op, the odds are ten to one that it already carries an impressive collection. But if not, simply contact the dozen or so companies that manufacture the things, and do a little comparison shopping. What you want is an attractive assortment of mugs, varying in size, color, material, and decoration. Your stock should range from an inexpensive ceramic mug with the college seal stenciled on to an ornate metal job with embossed lettering. Your school colors will be popular for the enameled mugs, but some students just don't like pink-and-purple, so be sure to include a variety. The opportunity to have the customer's nickname painted on his mug is an added sales attraction, so arrange for it.

Once you have found the least expensive company that does good work, have a set of sample mugs sent to you. Your job is to take orders, and deliver the mugs when they arrive.

You should price your mugs so as to leave you a forty to fifty percent profit. A mug that costs you $2.75, for example, should sell for around $5. The first year you can expect to sell somewhere between one-third and one-half of the student body; in succeeding years, count yourself lucky if you can talk 20 percent of your classmates into buying. Still, at a school of 1,000, 200 mugs are good for a quick profit of over $400.

Door-to-door canvassing is your best sales method, but a little judicious advertising in the college paper and a barrage of posters and bulletin board notices should do nearly as well. A student at Trinity College sold 200 mugs in under 20 hours, simply by bringing his samples to the frosh dining hall and taking down names.

14. HOME-MADE MUGS

A variation on the beer mug game was attempted last year at Michigan State University, when an Education School course in "Advanced Woods" decided to manufacture and market wooden mugs as a class project. The group quickly incorporated as "Moo U Mugs, Inc." and set about work. The finished mugs were hexagonal in shape, and stained a dark oak color. A rope handle and copper bands contributed to the rustic look, while fiberglass inner coating prevented leakage. MUMI sold 500 mugs for $2 apiece, leaving a total profit of $500 after all materials were paid for.

We wouldn't advise anyone else to try it—unless you've already taken Advanced Woods.

15. VARIATIONS ON THE THEME

The popularity of beer mugs is unsurpassed, but anything with the college seal on it is bound to sell well; if your classmates don't want your items for themselves, they'll buy a few to send home as gifts.

The list is nearly endless. Embossed ashtrays and cigarette lighters are popular on many campuses. Commonplace tumblers, highball glasses, wine glasses, and shot glasses become glamorous sales items with the simple addition of a decaled college emblem. Tablecloths, napkins, stuffed animals, matchbooks, pennants, banners, and practically anything else you can think of will earn you money if you can find a company that will produce it with your school seal on it. As in the case of beer mugs, the procedure is simple. Once you have found a supplier, simply carry your samples door-to-door, or bring them to a central location where students congregate. Take orders, and when the goods arrive, deliver them.

16. COLLEGE CLOTHING

Another type of merchandise which sells well when imprinted with the college seal (or its name, or a picture of its mascot) is clothing. The staple item is of course sweatshirts, with tee-shirts, scarves, and night shirts coming in second, third, and fourth. Here again, the college co-op is probably way ahead of you, but if it isn't, find yourself a manufacturer and start raking in the cash.

Clothing has all the variations in color, material, and decoration that we mentioned for beer mugs, plus an additional one—size. As in the case of beer mugs, you're sunk if you try to keep up a stock. Take orders, and be satisfied for your profit with the difference between the wholesale and the retail price. You should make about $1.50 per shirt.

More unusual clothing items also fare well in the collegiate market, if they have that magic seal. We will give only one example. The stalwart men of Princeton pay two ingenious undergraduates hundreds of dollars a year for "Princeton garters" and sheer "Princeton nighties" for their girl friends and—just conceivably—their mothers.

17. COLLEGE JEWELRY

School rings, pins, charms, lavalieres, brooches, and whatevers are another sales possibility capitalizing on the college emblem. Here again, the co-op and local jewelry stores probably carry a complete line already. If not, find a manufacturer and you're in business.

Even if the school jewelry market is already being served by a local store, you may be able to get your hand in by offering to solicit orders door-to-door. A surprisingly large number of students, it has been found, will spend four years at college without ever quite remembering to drop around the jewelry store to buy a school ring. If someone knocks at their door, however, they may well succumb to the combination of temptation and convenience.

If nobody at your school is now selling college rings, that is definitely the line to carry; commissions often run as high as $10 on each ring. As you probably remember from high school, the Balfour Company is the country's largest manufacturer of school rings. They will provide you with a set of sizers and order blanks, as well as a list of available styles. The rest is up to you.

18. COLLEGE STATIONERY

Stationery is another everyday item that becomes suddenly irresistible when embossed with the school seal. It is a big moneymaker at LaGrange College in LaGrange, Georgia (pop. 600), the University of Pennsylvania in Philadelphia (pop. 13,000), and just about everywhere in between.

Any of the major stationery companies will supply a complete selection of papers, type styles, emblems, sizes, and so forth. It is also possible to arrange for the customer's name and campus address to be engraved or printed on his letter paper and envelopes. Your commission for taking the order and making the delivery comes to about 15 percent of the selling price.

19. COLLEGE SOUVENIRS

Major football and basketball games, alumni homecomings, victory rallies, and similar raucous displays of spirit owe no small part of their excitement to the multitude of friendly souvenir vendors. If your college has some of the former but none of the latter, you should consider going into the bauble business.

Favorite items include balloons, miniature plastic footballs, buttons of all sizes, ribbons, flowers, and various sorts of noisemakers. All of these can be purchased wholesale with the name of your school appropriately emblazoned. You probably will need a franchise from the school to sell your wares at the game, the homecoming, or whatever, but no one can prevent you from locating yourself on a convenient street corner and hawking "Trivia!" at the top of your voice.

To display your goods attractively, simply cover a large piece of plywood with some inexpensive bulky fabric such as burlap. Pins, ribbons and the like can then be attached to the cloth, while balloons are filled with helium and tied down.

If you can wangle a monopoly from the administration, hire an army of vendors. Most students and alums will stroll blithely past the first half dozen displays they see, then finally succumb and buy something—so figure about one vendor for each 500 potential customers. You can pay them $1.50 an hour plus a tiny commission or put them on a straight commission basis.

Souvenir sales depend on crowds of people and the "crowd spirit." If you start with 10,000 fans, 500 will quickly buy a banner or a button. Another 1,000 will see the 500 with their new toys, and decide to pick up something for themselves. Pretty soon, just about everybody will have bought himself a souvenir. If you only have a crowd of 500, on the other hand, the 25 people who buy immediately will just look a little silly, and the other 475 will not follow suit. So confine yourself to campus events which attract large masses of people. When such an event comes along, get your gee-gaws ready and start hawking.

20. COURSE MATERIALS

It is possible to make a little change peddling paper, pens, pencils, notebooks, binders, and other everyday school supplies, particularly if they have the college emblem on them somewhere. But for the most part the co-op and local stationery stores meet the demand for these goods on their own leaving you with scant likelihood of earning a fortune.

But specialized student supplies are another matter entirely. Bandage scissors and thermometers sell well to nursing students at Saint John College in Cleveland. Laboratory aprons and goggles for chemistry courses are a big item at Princeton University. Drawing paper, paints, pastels, and charcoal attract the money of art students at Williams College in Williamstown, Massachusetts.

A studious entrepreneur at La Sierra College in Riverside, California, has a more unusual sales item. He recently compiled and printed an outline of American history, then peddled it to his fellow students, netting himself a fast $200—and no doubt a greater knowledge of American history as well.

Study guides like the La Sierra outline are dangerous fare for undergraduate businessmen. Most colleges have strict regulations governing such enterprises, fearing that an outline of American history might turn into an outline of Professor McGillicuddy's American history course. Our man at La Sierra evidently avoided this pitfall, but if you plan to follow in his footsteps, check carefully with your college administration first to make sure that they approve of the project.

Other items required or recommended for special courses are safe, and often quite lucrative. The most secure method is to take orders, then buy wholesale, but for things like art supplies you will have to purchase some stock and take your chances on selling it. There is no reason to peddle specialized materials door-to-door. Talk to the men who teach the relevant courses and ask them how much demand they think there will be. Many will cooperate by mentioning your name in class, or even allowing you to take orders during their class time. In any case, a few notices on the appropriate academic bulletin board will do the trick.

21. CLOTHING

College students spend a greater percentage of their available funds on clothing than any other segment of the population. A rather small portion of this money is paid to other students, but the fraction is increasing annually, and the time to jump on the bandwagon might be now.

The grandest way to sell clothing, of course, is to open your own store. We know of two cases of this. An ambitious student at Drexel Institute of Technology in Philadelphia owns a "sweater shack," and two coeds at the University of Illinois run a dress shop called "In Stitches." The Drexel enterprise is strictly commercial, while the Illinois girls design and make their own dresses. Running your own store is nearly as complicated an undertaking as running your own restaurant, and it is rarely worth the candle. Even the girls at Illinois admit that business is slow, but claim that "it's fun, and that's the main thing."

If you're more interested in profit than fun, and you don't want to design your own product or invest your life savings, a more moderate approach is advisable. There are two alternatives.

The first is to buy your own stock wholesale, then sell door-to-door or by some other means. This requires ready capital of at least $500, reasonably good taste in clothing, lots of sweat and lots of luck. We know of a Midwestern student who tripled his initial investment selling shirts on this basis. He started with 15 dozen shirts, half of them sport shirts for men, one-quarter button-downs for women, and the other quarter men's dress shirts. Selling door-to-door in the dorms and fraternities, he managed to clear a $1,000 profit in just a few weeks.

He could have wound up with 15 dozen shirts for himself—in ten different sizes. Whenever you buy a substantial stock of anything, you must recognize the possibility that you will be stuck with it. To avoid tragedy, pick your goods very carefully, taking into consideration the location of your school and the tastes of its students. Besides shirts, blazers and rainwear are good sellers on most campuses. Heavy sweaters and jackets do well in the North, swimwear and light casual slacks in the South.

As with wholesale food buying, you should do a good deal of comparison shopping before choosing a supplier. Your ability to pay cash will be a point in your favor, but a good number of wholesalers who already have outlets in your area will very likely turn you down anyway.

If the worst should happen and your goods are not moving very well, run a clearance sale. Unload what you have—at cost, if necessary—and start over again . . . in some other business.

The second method of making money from clothing sale is to become a campus representative of some major clothing company; they will supply you with free samples or a catalog, and all you will have to do is take orders and deliver the merchandise when it arrives. This is the system used at most colleges. Shirts, socks, jackets, neckties, slacks, sweaters, and nylon hosiery are the most usual items.

The commission on clothing sales is considerably less than on novelty items; 20 to 30 percent is about average. Short-term hosiery sales at women's colleges are almost always successful, netting a quick $75 or so. But more expensive items sell more slowly, and on urban campuses the clothing concession is rarely one of the big money-makers. Clothing salesmen at the University of Florida at Gainesville, Georgia Institute of Technology in Atlanta, Georgia, and Trinity College in Hartford, Connecticut, all describe their business as a convenient way to pick up a little extra cash around the frat or sorority—but hardly a steady source of big money.

At rural schools it is a different story. If you're in a part of the country where Sears, Roebuck and the other professional mail-order houses do big business, then a campus clothing concession probably will too. But the work is still hard; you'll know you've earned your money.

22. NOVELTY CLOTHING

Especially in areas where clothing stores are plentiful in town, novelty clothing is far more likely to sell well on campus than the everyday variety. We have already discussed the sale of clothing with the college seal or name on it. A closely related business involves the use of the names of fraternities, sororities, and even dormitories.

Fraternity jackets are a ubiquitous profit-maker, though the profiteer is usually the frat itself. Custom-made sweatshirts and tee-shirts offer a wider scope for your talents, either through a commercial outfit or as a do-it-yourself operation. In the latter case, buy your solid-color shirts wholesale in a variety of sizes. Pick up an assortment of dyes at any fabric store, and you're ready for business.

Frats and sororities will be your biggest customers, but dormitory residents will also be interested in inexpensive made-to-order shirts. Campus organizations such as the newspaper or the debate club may also fall prey to the lure of your colorful gimmick. So should informal student groups and "drinking clubs." Stencil names on the front and numbers on the back, and you're ready to outfit your college's intramural athletic teams.

There are several procedures for applying patterns to fabrics; you can read about them in the local library, or inquire at a nearby store. Whatever your method, the novelty tee-shirts can sell for as much as $3 or $4, the sweatshirts for $5 or $6. Purchased wholesale, the unadorned shirts will set you back less than one-quarter of that amount. If you are outfitting an entire team, dorm, or frat, you can afford to offer a substantial quantity discount and still do very well.

You needn't be confined to names and numbers. If you're something of an artist (or can hire one), try painting designs on shirts to order. Or embellish your merchandise with sketches of the current pop hero on campus. Or work up a batch of "psychedelic shirts."

A junior at Swarthmore College in Swarthmore, Pennsylvania, tried this last method. He dyed plain white tee-shirts with various patterns in fourteen different colors, then put the finished products on sale at $2 apiece, a 200 percent mark-up over his costs. His advertising method was as simple as it was effective: he gave a few shirts away to attractive girls on campus, who served as unpaid models wherever they went. Before long he had a fad on his hands, and had to hire dyers at $1.75 an hour. He sold 300 shirts before he quit.

Swarthmore is a small college; 300 shirts represents more than a quarter of its student body. On a larger campus, you could earn far more than this innovator's $400.

23. JEWELRY

We have already mentioned the sale of college rings, pins, and other jewelry as an excellent student money-maker. Equally as profitable is the sale of fraternity or sorority pins and so forth. In the case of national fraternities, this is invariably handled through the organization itself, but if your school has local social clubs, you may be able to make some money supplying them with distinctive jewelry. Contact a manufacturer and see what you can work out.

Other than college-related merchandise, commercial jewelry is not a popular sales item on the campus today. But there is no reason why it couldn't become one. A student at the University of Detroit is well ahead of the pack in this field. He successfully operates a one-man agency selling diamond rings and pins on behalf of a mail-order jewelry firm. Although he has done well, costume jewelry seems to us a more likely venture, if you insist on selling commercial jewelry at all.

Much more common is the sale of hand-made jewelry. This nets talented students significant profits at LaGrange College in LaGrange, Georgia, Carnegie Tech in Pittsburgh, Rochester Tech in Rochester, New York, and Swarthmore College in Swarthmore, Pennsylvania. Earrings seem to be the biggest seller, possibly because they are easiest to make, possibly because coeds lose them so quickly. In any case, we haven't the slightest idea how to *make* jewelry (if you don't know, don't try), but to *sell* it your best bet is canvassing door-to-door in the dorms and sororities. A satisfactory second-best is a table set up in a prominent location, such as the student union. We will talk more about campus-made jewelry in Chapter Four.

24. BUTTONS

Closely related to jewelry (anatomically if not emotionally) are buttons—not the kind you sew on, but the kind you pin on. There was a time, back in ancient history a year or so ago, when buttons were the tool of political activist groups. They said things like "Freedom Now" or "Stop the Bombing." Today, however, they are more likely to read "Chaste Makes Waste" or "Jewish Power" or "Fuck Censorship." A magnificent gesture of alienation, rebellion, and humor all in one, buttons are earning big money for campus entrepreneurs from Swarthmore in Pennsylvania to the University of California at Berkeley. They are the top campus fad in the country, and hence one of the top campus businesses. Today, that is; by the time you read this book, buttons may have been succeeded by nose rings.

The button concession at Duke University in Durham, North Carolina, is typical. On a trip to New York City, two daring Duke undergraduates visited a store in Greenwich Village, where they picked up three or four copies each of 50 different buttons. Back on campus, they simply set up a table in the middle of the school's main quadrangle, and started selling. When they ran out, they wrote for a new supply. In six hours of work, the two of them grossed $225. Bought at a cost of 10 cents each, the buttons easily sold for 35 cents, three for $1.00. Net profit: $150, or $25 an hour.

Buttons are of course available on a mail-order basis, but experience has shown that sales by this method are much lower. As our correspondent at Duke put it: "Buttons are a Now craze, so students won't buy on order. They see a button they like, they want to wear it, now, while the craze is still on. We had a few competitors selling buttons cheaper than we were on a mail-order system, but they just couldn't compete with us."

Button salesmen quickly discover that the key to success is an unending stream of new buttons. "Students want that button they saw yesterday," we are told, "but they definitely don't want the one they saw the day before yesterday too." A few constant favorites emerge, however. Anything to do with sex does well; Duke's biggest sellers to coeds were "Chaste Makes Waste" and "Cure Virginity." Also popular were "Take a Trip with Jesus" and "King Kong Died for Our Sins."

There are easily a thousand different buttons available, with more coming out each day, but you ought to know your campus well enough to pick the few dozen that will sell easily. Bear in mind that this is not a steady money-maker. Fads go as quickly as they come. Our sources at Duke describe themselves as "activists" (they picked up the first batch of buttons after traveling to New York to march in an anti-war parade), and admit that they entered the business world "mostly for the fun of it—we wanted to play capitalist for a few weeks." Whatever your politics, you had better not count on more than a few weeks of playing with buttons.

25. VARIATIONS ON THE THEME

Any campus fad can make you money. Several students across

the country got just a little bit richer last year by going into the "Batman business"—selling everything from capes to old comic books. Pop Art posters seem to be on their way out now, with Op Art posters on their way in. We won't give any more examples here, because most of the current fads will be obsolete before this book reaches the printer. In general, if you plan on taking advantage of the current craze at your school, do it in a hurry. Find a reliable source of supply, and then buy in small quantities, so you won't be left with a mound of garbage when the fad suddenly collapses. Plan on maximum exposure over a short period of time, and don't take orders for anything. Twenty-five dollars an hour is good money, even if it only keeps up for three weeks.

26. COSMETICS

"Avon Calling!" is the sound of college students making money from the University of California at Santa Barbara to Gordon College in Wenham, Massachusetts. So common is this student business that when a coed decides to peddle a different line of mail-order cosmetics, everyone thinks she's the Avon girl anyway.

Not surprisingly, cosmetics go over best on a campus where there are women. (The men at Princeton, however, have been known to purchase perfume for their dates from a "perfume man.") With the mail-order cosmetics business as well organized as it is, it does not pay to run the agency any other way. But some sort of gimmick to boost sales wouldn't hurt a bit. A sophomore at Georgian Court College in Lakewood, New Jersey, for example, took a short summer course in the proper use of cosmetics. She now gives free demonstrations for her classmates, using the very same beauty preparations she sells. After each demonstration she takes orders. Lots of orders.

27. RECORDS

Any major record distributing house in the country would be more than happy to receive a letter from a college undergraduate offering to represent their firm on his campus. Normally, it is possible to arrange to sell a $5 phonograph record for as low as

$3.95, with the student salesman receiving a commission somewhere between 10 and 20 percent of his price. At a college with large numbers of audiophiles, half a dollar per record can quickly build into real money.

The nicest thing about this business is its tendency to develop dedicated repeat customers. "Records Unlimited" at Carleton College in Northfield, Minnesota, for example, undersells not only the local record stores, but also the professional discount "clubs." Once your bargain prices become known on your campus, students will keep coming back to you whenever they want a record. All you have to do is send in the order and wait for your commission; in most cases, the company mails the record directly to the customer.

It is not necessary to peddle your service in the dorms or frats. A little judicious advertising in the campus newspaper and some strategic bulletin board announcements will get you started, and returning customers and word-of-mouth recommendations will keep you going. In all, record selling is one of the easiest ways known to make money at college.

28. RECORD EQUIPMENT

We may as well mention in passing that the sale of sophisticated audio equipment is a highly lucrative business on a few campuses. Throughout most of the U.S., of course, listening to records takes only a phonograph and a needle, and you've had both of those since you were twelve. But wherever a significant part of the college population has the erudition to know a woofer from a tweeter and the money to care, some fellow-student with equal erudition is collecting the money. If you happen to be one of the cognoscente, hi-fi equipment is a business well worth considering.

29. MAGAZINES

One of the hoariest student businesses around is the sale of magazine subscriptions. The almost inevitable success of this particular venture stems from two factors: 1) many undergraduates who really want to subscribe to a given magazine just never get around to doing so, and will cheerfully agree to buy when you visit them in their rooms; 2) a large number of magazines offer substantial discounts to students in an effort to obtain lifelong committed readers.

Taking advantage of these factors usually requires no more than a letter to the subscription department of the magazine or magazines of your choice. So long as no other student represents them on your campus, they will be delighted to send you order blanks, sales materials, and whatever else you need. If you want to carry an extensive line of magazines, you can try to affiliate yourself with one of the direct sales companies that already have arrangements with many publishers. The problem with this approach, however, is that you are likely to lose the advantage of special prices for students. In the long run, it usually pays to make your own deal with each individual publisher.

Choose your magazines carefully in terms of their popularity on your campus. Try to stick with publishers who offer special student rates and who have established campus sales programs you can join. These companies will usually supply you with instructions and selling aids designed to make your work easier and more profitable.

The following magazines meet these criteria, and have earned substantial profits for students on various campuses in the past: *Atlantic, Esquire, Harper's, Life, New Yorker, Newsweek, Playboy, Reader's Digest, Saturday Evening Post, Saturday Review, Time.* At men's colleges you will want to add *Sports Illustrated, Popular Mechanics, Argosy,* and other magazines catering to the male animal. Coeds may want to order *Glamour, Mademoiselle, Vogue, McCall's,* and other special-interest publications for women. Politically active campuses will favor the *Nation, New Republic, National Review,* and so forth; engineers will want *Scientific American* and similar journals. Take a look at the magazines local newsstands are moving to get an idea of what would sell on your campus.

Magazine subscription salesmen frequently set up displays in conspicuous locations on campus, with a pile of subscription order cards built into each display. The customer fills out his own card and sends it in to the company, and the "salesman" collects his commission. This is undoubtedly the easiest method of selling subscriptions, but it barely scratches the surface of the market. A much larger number of students will subscribe if you corner them in their rooms, order blanks in hand, and volunteer to handle the paper work for them. At the very least, drop your order cards personally into each student's mailbox; the convenience of a card in hand may well be enough to clinch the sale.

However you organize your selling, concentrate it at the beginnings of terms. For some unfathomable reason, students like to start receiving their new magazines at the beginning of the new semester. September, October, January and February will therefore be your most profitable months.

Commissions vary considerably from magazine to magazine, but generally average between 30 and 40 percent of the selling price. A $5 subscription, then, will net you around $1.75. You can expect to sell at least two or three subscriptions for each hour of door-to-door work.

There is hardly a campus in the country that doesn't have one or two students peddling magazine subscriptions. Large universities can easily support a dozen of them. This is not the most original or exciting student business in the book, nor is it the most fantastically profitable—but the financial return on your effort is substantial and fairly secure. You are your own boss, free to work when and where you wish, and your business will keep reaping profits for as long as you keep plugging away.

30. NEWSPAPERS

Those of us who delivered newspapers in our youth have little inclination, even in our more nostalgic moments, to go back to being a paperboy. Nevertheless, the sale and delivery of daily newspapers is among the most lucrative businesses on the campus today. It deserves a second thought.

Mail subscriptions to out-of-town papers operate just like magazine subscriptions—but there is unfortunately little call for these at American colleges. The demand is for the morning paper of the nearest big city, delivered as soon as the print is dry and before the news is cold.

Contact the circulation department of the paper itself. They will tell you how much to charge, how and where to pick up your papers each morning, and how to enter new subscriptions and cancel old ones. The only satisfactory way to peddle subscriptions is door-to-door, but it only has to be done once, and it is the smallest part of your work. The biggest part is getting up at six every blasted morning, rain or shine, and delivering papers. Just like when you were a kid.

Only the money is different. Your share of each subscription will be roughly one-third of the price. Sell a hundred subscriptions at $30 apiece, and you've just earned yourself $1,000.

You can cut down some on your profits and eliminate almost all your work by employing paperboys. Here is one business where it often pays to pass up student employees and hire town kids to do your dirty work—at the same wages you were paid at their age. Another money-saving possibility is to work through the student newspaper delivery system. This has been successfully arranged at a number of schools. The men delivering the school paper have to make their rounds anyway; they will be happy to add your papers to their pile for a small fee. Of course if the school paper isn't a daily, you'll have to find another way.

The girls at Vassar College have found a simple and effective method for saving work. The *New York Times* sees to it that the right number of papers are delivered to each dormitory. The girls bring the piles inside, mark the number of each room receiving a paper on the top of its front page, then spread out the pile in the dorm lobby. Each student picks up her own paper when she comes down for breakfast.

Another labor-saving device is to sell your papers directly to the frats and sororities. If you can get each house to purchase 20 newspapers for the use of its members, your commission will be as high as if you had sold all the papers individually, and your delivery work will be greatly simplified. The same goes for administrative and faculty offices, which generally pay a higher price than students and may buy in bulk.

Selling and delivering newspapers is a bothersome way to make money. For some reason, students are notoriously slow to pay their bills for this particular item. And whatever your delivery system, you are bound to spend several painful hours a week dealing with complaints of mis-delivery, late delivery and non-delivery.

Only the money is good. Newspaper tycoons on large campuses rake in several thousand dollars a year, and even the smallest college has enough newspaper readers to earn you $500 or more. If you can lick the delivery problem, there is hardly a more lucrative student business to be found.

31. SUNDAY PAPERS

Subscriptions to Sunday newspapers are often sold right along with the dailies, but a sufficient number of students want only the extra-long weekend edition to make this a profitable business in itself. Commissions are frequently higher than for the daily paper, ranging from ten to twenty cents a paper a week. The once-a-week delivery you can usually handle yourself, or with one or two assistants. Once the spadework has been done, you can guarantee yourself a fast $30 a week for a few Sunday morning hours of work.

The main objection to this venture, of course, is that it requires you or your representative to be on campus every weekend—which is a hell of a lousy way to spend one's college years.

32. GIFTS

Considering the number of mail-order gift and novelty distributors in existence, it comes as some surprise to learn that holiday gift agencies are not at all common on the college campus. Where they exist, however, they are usually very successful. Princeton, for example, supports two such businesses, one operated through the Fuller Brush people, the other through Esquire Sales. Both net their managers tidy profits, and Esquire is so lucrative that it has spread to other colleges in the East. The Princeton Esquire line now earns good money for local managers throughout New England.

The secret is entirely in the selection of items. Everything should be just a little unusual. Staple items such as carving knives and table lighters should be a bit different from the run-of-the-mill sort available in local stores. Some purely decorative gifts, such as jewelry or wood carvings, should be included. Mechanical gadgets (rechargeable flashlights, automobile vacuum cleaners) are popular, and so are novelty items; a pen which expands to two feet in length for use as a pointer is a surprisingly big seller at Princeton. Gifts involving the college name or seal are perennial favorites, from beer mugs and sweatshirts to art prints and engravings.

Your salesmen should be trained in the proper use and display of all the gifts on your. list. In addition to a sample of each item, you should provide every employee with a convenient case in which to carry his wares. Pay your salesmen on a straight commission basis, and hire a sufficient number of them to talk personally with every student during the six weeks immediately before the start of Christmas vacation. Evening hours between 9:00 and 11:00 will be your prime selling time.

A persuasive salesman with an attractive assortment of gifts will sell something or other to more than half the students he talks to. And more than a few undergraduates will buy their entire Christmas list from his stock. Remember, what a gift agency is really selling is convenience. Your customers will be students who have not yet started their Christmas shopping and are not looking forward to the experience with any great pleasure. They will buy from you partly because your gifts are attractive, but mostly because you're there, and because you will deliver their selections to them, already wrapped, before they head home for the holidays. That is your appeal. For a good number of your classmates it will be irresistible.

33. CHRISTMAS CARDS

Christmas may not yet be wholly the property of the merchants, but they are certainly one of its principal shareholders. Next to gifts, the most important holiday business on the campus is Christmas cards.

Williams College and the University of Pennsylvania are among the dozen schools that report sale of Christmas cards as an important campus money-maker. Most card houses and

stationery companies fill orders, so no inventory is required, and
hence no initial capital. The commission on holiday cards can
soar as high as 50 percent, and is rarely below 30 percent. Even
so, cards are such a cheap item that a profit of half your gross
may not amount to much. It all depends on your campus. If
you have a lot of students running around who send out 30 or
40 cards every Christmas, then it will certainly pay you to lug
a book of samples over to their rooms. But if it's a question of
one for the folks and one for little sister, you'd better leave the
card concession to the service fraternities. They don't have to
pay their salesmen.

At some colleges ordinary commercial Christmas cards do not
sell well, either because they are easily available off campus or
because they are not popular among students. It is often possible
to earn good money at these schools by peddling special cards
that are connected in some way with your college. At Columbia
University, for example, the Christmas card agency designs and
prints museum-type cards from rare books in the Columbia
library or art museum.

One easy way to make Christmas cards pay off is to add them
to your Christmas gift selection. To the best of our knowledge,
no student has yet combined these two money-makers, though
the union looks like a natural.

It is possible to turn a profit selling greeting cards at times
other than the Christmas season, but it isn't easy. Special interest
groups, international affairs clubs, and the like, have managed
to do it on occasion, when their cards were in some way related
to their activities. And we know of one student at Berkeley who
reportedly made a good living peddling off-color contemporary
cards. But on the whole it hardly pays.

34. VARIATIONS ON THE THEME

Campuses that are really gung-ho about Christmas will grab at
anything connected with the holiday, so if you happen to be
living on one of those, give the following suggestions some
thought. After gifts and cards, Christmas trees are your most

likely seller—if the college permits them. Students in the North-west have been known to go out and lop off a few evergreen branches in near-by woods, then peddle them on campus as undersized Christmas trees. Plastic trees are also a possibility (a much more pleasing one to most college administrators).

If you're selling trees, you might just as well go all the way and sell tree decorations. And on treeless campuses, appropriate window decorations may pay off. So might Christmas wreaths. At coed schools, Christmas "pins" (corsages of plastic holly, plastic leaves, and tin bells) should sell. Mistletoe will turn a profit anywhere.

The important prerequisite for making money from any of these holiday items is spirit. It needn't be the holiday spirit, however. At Princeton, years pass by without anyone bothering to decorate his room for Christmas. But let some enterprising student start a concession, and different rooms and dorms at once begin to compete with each other for the cleverest, most ornate, or most unusual Christmas decorations. The result would be Christmas Spirit, Princeton-style—and a tidy profit for the concessionnaire.

35. FIREWOOD

While we're in a wintry mood, we may as well mention the sale of firewood as a potential business. Not every college has rooms with fireplaces, and not every fireplace is built to accommodate a real, live fire, but on campuses which meet both these con-ditions firewood can become a very hot item.

Whether you chop the wood yourself or buy it out of town, you will find legions of undergraduates willing to pay well for the convenience of log and kindling delivery to their doorsteps. A cheery fire in the hearth, you may remind your customers, will warm the room, melt the snow, and warm, melt and snow a date. You should build up a steady clientele in no time.

We do not recommend this business for women, nor for students in the South—for obvious reasons.

36. FLOWERS

Let us pause a moment to consider the number of proms that take place annually at American colleges. Let us further contemplate the number of students attending each prom. Finally, let us cogitate on the profits accruing to local florists across our country from the prom trade.

The purpose of this consideration, contemplation and cogitation is to come up with a foolproof student business idea that has gone practically unnoticed for these many years: flowers. We say *practically* unnoticed, for two students at St. Mary's College in Winona, Minnesota, earn money selling corsages and boutonnieres to fellow students, and so do students at Clarke College in Dubuque, Iowa, and Ursinus College in Collegeville, Pennsylvania.

Assuming that you have no independent source of flowers, and are forced to work through local florists yourself, the only way to make a profit in this line is to offer convenience and savings. In return for your exclusive patronage, one of the town florists should agree to a discount of 15 percent or so. Armed with that agreement, set up a table outside the dining hall or in some other strategic location, and take orders. Deliver the corsage or boutonniere to the student's room, and collect your fee. Your mark-up will depend on the circumstances. If the nearest florist is five miles away, you can get away with prices of $1.00 or so more than the florist himself charges. If he's right in town, your best bet is to equal his prices, taking your profit from your special discount.

Of course if you're talented, and can create corsages yourself out of the raw materials, then you deserve to do better on the deal, and will. You'll find that flowers cost considerably less than floral arrangements. Your profit will be the difference, plus your discount, plus your service charge, if any.

37. DESK BLOTTERS

A desk blotter is a large piece of colored absorbent paper which goes on top of a desk and could conceivably be used for blotting. Mostly it is used for going on top of a desk.

At several colleges on the East Coast, desk blotters have recently been used for making money as well. Local businesses and stores are the source of this money, but we will include the venture in this chapter anyway, since the beneficiaries of the final product are students.

The idea, of course, is to sell advertising space on the blotter to local establishments which cater to the student market. At Trinity College in Hartford, Connecticut, an enterprising senior successfully sold ads to local restaurants, pizza houses, motels, hotels, barber shops, book stores, record stores and liquor stores. It cost him $260 to have 1,000 blotters printed up. He sold $750 in ads, gave the blotters away to students, and pocketed $490. The whole process took only a few weeks.

Plan on a blotter roughly 24 inches by 18 inches. Your printer can order the paper for you, in any color you like. Set aside part of your space for something useful to students. Our man at Trinity included the football, soccer, lacrosse and baseball schedules of the college teams; a calendar or an academic schedule would do just as well. Divide the remaining space into rectangles, and price them according to size. At Trinity, the prices were $7.50 for a 2"x 2" box, $10 for a 2"x 3" box, and $15 for a 3"x 4" box. These rates are a little lower than usual. On the average, a 3"x 4" space would sell for about $25, a 2"x 3" space for $15. If your distribution will be more than 1,000, your rates should be still higher.

To keep printing costs down, limit yourself (and your advertisers) to one color of ink. At Trinity, dark blue ink on light blue paper was the combination chosen. Try to use your school colors where possible. Remember, there's no reason why the blotter should not be printed on both sides. That ups your printing costs, but it doubles your advertising space, and also doubles the utility of the blotter to students.

Selling ads should represent no problem. Simply explain to the owner or manager of each store that your blotter will be distributed free to every undergraduate. Once he realizes that his ad will spend the whole year right before the eyes of students while they're studying (and therefore at their most vulnerable time), he will be more than willing to pay your price. It might help to show each potential advertiser a copy of your tentative agreement with the printer, just so he'll know you're serious about the project. Trinity's blotter man added an extra incentive for hesitant merchants. "When anyone looked like they weren't going to buy," he explains, "I simply offered them one of the better spots, near the schedules or in a corner."

We know of schools where the blotters were sold to students for half a dollar or so, but this is burning the candle at both ends, and we don't advise it. If you plan to sell your blotters, you have no guaranteed distribution to tell your potential advertisers about, and you lose more in advertising than you'll earn in sales. More important, selling the blotters will more than triple your time investment. Done the simple way, the blotter business is a three-week project, and a reasonably safe way to earn $500.

38. FOOTBALL PROGRAMS

The phrase "you can't tell the players without a scorecard" has been in the English idiom for several generations. We like to think it was first coined by an early student entrepreneur who was selling football programs in the stands. In point of fact, of course, you *can* tell the players without a scorecard, but why should you have to? Especially when the scorecard can be sold at such a bargain price with local merchants paying the bulk of the cost.

Most colleges that have football programs at all put them out themselves. This is unfortunate, for the school rarely has enough time to solicit much in the way of advertising. Often, the resulting product is either prohibitively expensive or sold at a loss.

Occasionally a student gets a chance to run the show. Publishing a football program is a great deal more complicated than printing a desk blotter, and the most frequent arrangement is for the student to work together with the college administration on the project. At Williams College, for example, a student undertook to do the writing and layout, sell the ads, and peddle the programs. The administration supplied the information and handled the printing.

A different program was prepared for each of Williams' four home games. Each was printed on 8½ x 11 sheets, and ran 18 to 20 pages, with an action photograph on the cover. Ads were sold for the four programs simultaneously, at the following rates: $30 for one-eighth page in each program; $55 for a quarter page; $100 for a half page; $175 for a full page. A total of 78 local merchants bought ads; national advertisements were furnished through a professional advertising agency in New York City.

Students were hired to solicit local ads, and others were paid to sell the programs in the stands. One thousand programs were sold for each of the regular games; 2,000 were sold for the homecoming game. The salesmen received a regular commission of 2½ cents per program for the first 125 programs sold, 5 cents per program thereafter. The commission was raised to 5 cents and 8 cents for homecoming. The salesmen averaged a profit of $15 to $20 each per game.

The manager had to split his profits with the college, and was left with $500 for himself for the four games. He wouldn't reveal how much the school's share was, but the experience of program vendors at other schools, plus a little arithmetic, leads us to conclude that a well-run football program concession at a school the size of Williams should net roughly $500 *per game*. At one of the big state universities, the profits should be astronomical.

We want to emphasize that putting out and selling a series of football programs is a major undertaking, with numerous arrangements to be arranged and decisions to be decided. Once you have a go-ahead of some kind from the administration, the first step is to get estimates from a printer. The second is to hire an assistant; promise him the concession after you graduate as the major part of his compensation. Keep your layout identical for the whole season, and sell ads for the whole season only. Find an advertising agency that can get you a few national ads, at least enough for the three covers and the center-page spread. Unless you can get enough ads to cover all your expenses (printing, salaries, commissions, and payola to the college), you had better drop the project. Once you reach this break-even point, though, all additional advertisements and all sales revenues are profit.

39. VARIATIONS ON THE THEME

Baseball may be America's national sport, but you wouldn't guess it from counting fans at college games. Football is king at nearly every college in the country.

Rarely does a college print programs for any other sport—and that is your golden opportunity. Naturally we would not recommend trying to eke a profit out of a freshman cricket team that attracts 15 fans per contest. But any sport that pulls in a crowd of more than 300 is a worthy prospect for a mimeographed or multilithed program. Scale down your advertising prices to fit your expected distribution, and you are likely to sell nearly as many local ads as the football program does. For fairly major events (usually basketball and baseball; occasionally hockey), it will pay to sell your programs in the stands. But even a game that attracts only a few hundred spectators can be made to turn a profit. Hand out the programs free of charge; your guaranteed distribution will justify an advertising price sufficient to meet your costs and earn you $50 or so for each game.

The only school we know of which now takes advantage of this possibility is Rutgers University in New Brunswick, New Jersey. There, a student prints up a Rutgers Rugby Bulletin to be distributed at all games of the Rutgers Rugby Football Club. He does pretty well for himself—and so could you.

An athletic program concession could easily be combined with a souvenir agency, since both items are sold or distributed in the stands. At Columbia University in New York, New York, the souvenir-program agency works all home football games, then spends the late fall peddling Christmas gifts door-to-door, just to keep in shape.

Another golden opportunity in the program business is missed every time an important speaker visits your campus and gives his speech without a program. To eliminate this waste, simply talk to the person in charge of the event and offer to print and hand out programs without charge. Then find two or three local businesses (who are not in competition with each other) to underwrite the cost of the program. One sheet of paper folded and printed on both sides will give you a four-page program. Include the date, time, place, and title of the talk, a description of the speaker and his background, a note on the sponsoring organization, and a message from each of your advertisers. Have your program run off or printed, and distribute copies at the door.

Your profit on a venture of this sort should range between $25 and $100—which isn't bad for a couple of days work. A string of programs for a series of campus speakers will begin to run into a lot of money.

The same procedure can be employed for school plays, dances, concerts, or any other event where a program would be useful.

40. STUDENT TELEPHONE DIRECTORY

Wherever students are permitted to have telephones in their rooms, a student phone directory is a sure way to make money. As with programs and blotters, local merchants provide most of the profit.

A Williams College student worked out an arrangement with his administration whereby he produced the directory and they paid for the printing in return for 800 free copies. His advertising revenues were for himself. Selling space at rates ranging from $10 for a sixth of a page to $30 for a full page, he quickly collected $1,500 worth of ads. Twelve hundred copies of the directory were printed; those that were not given to the administration were sold to students and others for 75 cents apiece. After paying off his ad salesmen and his distributors, the manager had a clear $1,200 profit left over for himself—not bad for two months' work.

A student phone book cannot fail, even when the administration does not pay printing costs. A thousand directories will cost about $800 to print; 3,000 will set you back around $1,500. This means that you can sell your directories to students for 75 cents or a dollar and come away with a profit on your sales—not to mention the big money, which comes from advertising.

Besides containing names and phone numbers, your directory should include the address of each student, and possibly his major or his fraternity as well. A special list should be compiled of administration phone numbers, and other numbers frequently called by students. The easiest way to collect your information is to drop a postal card into each student's mailbox, with spaces to fill in his name, address, phone number, etc. Most undergraduates will want to be included, so most of your postcards will be returned. Of course if the college keeps a list of student phone numbers and is willing to lend it to you, so much the better. Selling advertisements should be no trouble at all; very few local tradesmen will want to be left out of a book that students will use every day. Be sure to start early, though. The book will be good for one academic year only, so it should be out in October, not March.

41. VARIATIONS ON THE THEME

At colleges where students are not permitted to have telephones, the directory idea can still turn a profit. Alphabetical lists of student dormitory addresses sell well at Avila College in Kansas City, College of the Holy Names in Oakland, California, Ferris State College in Big Rapids, Michigan, and more than a dozen other schools.

The procedure is the same as for telephone directories, only it is far easier to get your information. The college administration undoubtedly has its own list of student addresses. You need only borrow a copy and turn it over to the printer, along with the text of your advertisements.

Not every college needs an address list. If all undergraduates are grouped into one or two central buildings, a directory may be superfluous. You yourself know how often you have needed to know the address of a fellow student; if the answer is very often, a student directory should go over well on your campus.

When the academic year ends and students return to their homes for the summer, there is customarily a last-minute struggle to scribble down the home addresses of friends. College yearbooks often include a complete list of student home addresses, but if your school has no yearbook, or your yearbook has no list, then home addresses may be a possible profit-making business for you.

At the College of Holy Names, a mimeographed holiday address list earns the campus International Relations Club money to carry out its year's activities. It could help you carry out yours too.

The procedure is the same as for campus directories, but your advertising rates and sales prices should be lower, commensurate with your lower printing costs and the smaller amount of use the booklet will have. Few advertisers will turn down a chance to be included for a $5 charge, and even fewer students will begrudge you a quarter for a copy of the list. The college will provide you with your list of addresses, and can probably lend you the use of a mimeograph machine as well, so your only expenses will be paper and stencils. Sell 50 small ads for $250, and 800 copies of the list for another $200, and you will have earned yourself some ready spending money.

Freshman directories are another common source of funds. They should include the name and home address of each new freshman, and his photograph. Send out a mailing to all incoming students over the summer, asking them to mail you a snapshot of themselves. The finished books will sell readily to freshmen, parents of freshmen, and campus organizations interested in attracting freshmen (some fraternities buy them by the dozens). You can sell the books for $1.00 apiece and make back your printing costs. Local tradesmen, anxious for a crack at the new market, will pay exorbitant rates for advertisements, and their payments are your gravy.

Radcliffe and Vassar Colleges, among others, include dormitory phone numbers in their freshman directories, thereby creating an additional demand for them at nearby men's schools. No self-respecting Harvard man is without his very own picture directory of the new crop of Cliffies.

42. BINDER INDEX

U.C.L.A. used to have a student who sold advertising space on heavy manila cardboard binder indexes, then gave the indexes away free in the University Store, for use in students' loose-leaf notebooks. To the best of our knowledge this business idea has not been utilized in the past few years, but it certainly could be.

The cost of the indexes and printing is small enough to enable a student to earn several hundred dollars from the advertising. The only proviso is that loose-leaf notebooks should be popular at your college.

43. DAILY BULLETIN

On campuses with only a weekly or monthly newspaper, students miss out on a large number of campus events because they never hear about them. Even at schools with a daily paper many events are forgotten because the paper did not consider them worthy of announcement. A daily bulletin can help meet this problem.

The bulletin should be a single sheet of paper, mimeographed and delivered to students each morning. There are several ways of handling distribution. One is to sell subscriptions to students for $5 or $6 a year, then deliver the bulletins to the subscribers' rooms. An easier method is to sell subscriptions to dorms, fraternities and sororities, as well as administrative offices. A third possibility is to leave piles of the bulletins at strategic places on campus, such as the dining hall, allowing students to pick them up without charge. In this last case, your profit will come entirely from advertisements, but even if you sell subscriptions, you should solicit local ads as well.

Do not accept advertisements for a single issue, of course. Local merchants should be enthusiastic about the chance to contract for one or two ads a week throughout the year. In the weeks before an important campus event, such as a prom, a play, or a major speech, the event's publicity chairman will doubtless want to insert large, frequent ads.

A bulletin would be of tremendous value to your college administration, and it will definitely be worth your while to talk to them about working with you. At the very least, they will provide a daily list of official activities. At the most, they may offer a secretary to do your mimeographing for you, and supply your stencils, paper, and mimeo machine. The student government and the administration might agree together to split the cost of subscriptions for the entire student body, on condition that you accept no advertising. With that kind of arrangement, who needs advertising?

On a campus where fewer things are happening, a weekly bulletin might be more appropriate. The subscription rate for a weekly sheet would be too low to be worth selling; a weekly bulletin must depend entirely on ads or administration support for its profit.

44. CALENDARS

Calendars have frequently been used for advertising purposes, but for the most part college calendars have made their money on sales, not ads. Most school calendars run from September to August to parallel the academic year. They normally include the dates of vacations, examinations, and important academic, social and athletic events. Illustrate your calendar with appropriate photographs or engravings of the campus, and you will have a finished product that students will buy for themselves and as gifts.

Just about every college town has a local businessman who is producing this sort of calendar and cleaning up on it through sales to students. Columbia University, the University of Pennsylvania and Princeton University are the only schools we have heard about where students do the job and the cleaning up. Why not add your school to the list?

45. STORES

As a rule, every college has room for one general store—and it's owned and operated by the college. Those few schools with enough demand for more than one store normally have more than one store—owned and operated by the college.

This doesn't leave much of an opportunity for student-run stores.

Nevertheless, we must admit that a general store at the University of Delaware in Newark, Delaware, is still alive and kicking. And "Nick's Nook" at Massachusetts Institute of Technology in Cambridge, Massachusetts, actually earned a $250 profit last year.

Aside from the two clothing stores we mentioned earlier, these two are the only student-owned stores now in operation. Considering the massive amount of work involved, $250 should not be much of an incentive to follow their example.

The day some college lets a student take over the management and ownership of its school store, that's the day we'll recommend that students consider entering the business. Meanwhile, there are easier way to make more money.

46. ARTS AND CRAFTS

We have already mentioned the sale of home-made jewelry earlier in this chapter, and we will have a good deal more to say in Chapter Five about how to sell the work of campus artists and craftsmen. What we want to mention now is the possibility of selling professional works of art on campus.

As far as we know, Princeton University is the only school which has ever made a student business of selling non-student art. At one time, the sale of professional prints, engravings, etchings and paintings for room decorations and gifts was a major money-maker on the Princeton campus. Art agency managers visited New York art centers several times a year to purchase works, and door-to-door peddling supplemented frequent exhibits as a sales method. But even Princeton's art agency has been moribund for a few years now. Art prints are today on sale in many department stores, and travel posters are free. Still, if you want to give it a try. . . .

47. MISCELLANY

Back when pipe smoking first became the cool thing to do, students at several colleges started pipe and tobacco agencies which did good business peddling their wares door-to-door. If pipes are the thing at your school, you might try it.

The University of New Hampshire has students who sell small appliances, notably toasters and irons, to other students. They buy their goods wholesale of course, and seem to be doing pretty well.

At Carleton College in Northfield, Minnesota, a student agency sells photographic equipment at discount prices.

A wine-skin agency on the Princeton University campus sells plastic inflatable containers to students who consider beer mugs just a bit passe.

A student at the Georgia Institute of Technology buys wholesale washable rugs, and sells them to incoming freshmen at the start of each academic year. A student agency at Princeton University does the same thing with refrigerators. Particularly if your school lacks a student second-hand furniture exchange, either of these businesses (or any of the hundred or so similar ones which are possible) should prove profitable to you.

Sales of sporting goods to students and fraternities net an energetic Ursinus College student more than $600 a year. If you can find a wholesale outlet that enables you to undersell local stores and still make a profit, this business is a snap at any men's college.

The campus chapter of A.I.I.E. at Lamar State College in Beaumont, Texas, pays for its various activities by selling miniature diplomas to graduating seniors and graduate students. If it works for them, it could for you.

Girls at Vassar College sell each other pottery and knitting yarn.

A Rutgers University student has developed a unique type of chess game which is now sold, not only to undergraduates, but also to the surrounding community.

Take a good look around your campus. Ask yourself what it needs, what it could use, what it might want. We have listed some of the products which have sold well on various college campuses in the past. It is up to you to decide what would sell well on your college campus in the present. It might be shoe polish or sausages, Bibles or bathing caps, frisbees or firecrackers. Your job is to choose the right product—and then sell it.

48. POSTSCRIPT ON ADVERTISING

Several of the money-makers discussed earlier in this chapter depend for their success on the sale of advertising to local merchants. Anyone interested in the student market is a potential advertiser, but the most likely prospects are tradesmen who compete with each other. The only record shop in town does not have to advertise for student attention (unless there's a student record agency in competition with him). The three liquor stores in town, on the other hand, badly need to attract the eye of students.

One possible way to take advantage of this competition is to offer a local tradesman an exclusive advertising contract for his line of merchandise. To go back to our three liquor stores, suppose you informed Varsity Liquors that only one liquor store would be permitted to advertise in your medium. In other words, Varsity Liquors takes an ad, the Main Street Liquor Store and the Collegeville Liquor Store will be out of luck. The chances of Varsity's taking an ad are extremely high. Your rates can be correspondingly high.

In setting advertising rates, the crucial fact to remember is that a smaller number of ads at a lower rate adds up to the same amount of cash, makes your work easier, and keeps your advertisers happier. The three covers of your book should be the most expensive, costing roughly 50 percent more than a full inside page. Half pages should cost a little more than half the price of a full page, quarter pages a little more than half the price of a half page, and so on. As many ads as possible should be located near copy, so that the student's eye will fall on the ad while he is reading. A good plan is to alternate a page of ads with a page of copy throughout the book. If you are forced to "bury" an ad (to place it in a location where it is surrounded by other ads), it should sell at a lower price.

Before trying to sell any advertisements at all, you should prepare a "dummy." Map out where your copy will go, and divide the remaining space into various size "holes." Each hole should then be given a price. As a matter of advertising ethics, these ad prices should not be varied to accommodate an individual advertiser. Once a price is set, in terms of the size and location of the hole, it should be adhered to.

Armed with your dummy, drop in at a local store and ask to see the manager. Tell him your name and the nature of your business. He will want to know what administration officials have given you their okay, what your expected circulation is, and when your book, blotter or whatever will be published. He will also ask for information about your sales plans. Most of these questions will be aimed at assuring himself that you are responsible, well-organized, and serious about the project. Explain to him why your product will be valuable to students, and in what ways it will help sell *his* products on campus.

Once he agrees to take an ad, find a suitable location in your dummy and mark it with the name of his business. This lets both you and him know that that space is reserved for his ad. Offer to help him write his ad now, or to come back and pick it up (along with his check) at a later date. Be sure to promise to bring him a copy of the ad when it appears in print—and be sure to keep your promise.

The first few ads are the hardest to sell; thereafter, the presence of familiar names on the dummy reassures the potential advertiser that your idea is a good one. It is therefore an excellent idea to make your first approaches to the most likely prospects. These could be tradesmen you know well yourself, or men who customarily advertise a great deal in student publications. You may even offer your printer an advertisement as part of his payment, and put it down as the first reservation in your dummy.

Wherever possible, try to point out to potential advertisers why your medium would be especially appropriate for their merchandise. If you're publishing a program for a speech, book stores might well mention in their ad that they have books by the speaker in stock. Restaurants should want to use your prom program to announce that they will be serving late-night snacks after the dance. A student telephone book is a natural advertising medium for any business that accepts orders by phone.

The knack of selling ads comes easily to some people; for others it is always a tremendous ordeal. If you find you have trouble selling yourself and your plans to local merchants, hire a glib classmate to do it for you. The additional ads will more than make up for his salary or commission.

49. POSTSCRIPT ON THE CAMPUS REP

In the days when cigarette companies aimed a great deal of advertising at college students, lucrative jobs were available to students across the country as campus representatives. They were paid by the manufacturers for passing out free samples of cigarettes. Unless dope pushers have gotten into the act, this particular business is no longer with us—but the term "campus rep" is still used to describe a student who represents a certain company on his campus. These days, however, campus reps have to work for their money. Some of them—airline representatives and laundry agents, for example—offer services; they will be discussed in the next chapter. But the vast majority of campus reps sell their company's products to fellow students, and receive a commission on their sales.

The distinction between running your own business and being a campus rep is a blurry one at best. If you buy your goods wholesale and hope to sell them, you're in business for yourself. If you're paid a commission for taking orders, you're a campus rep, at least as far as the company is concerned. As far as you're concerned, you are still in business for yourself. A full-fledged campus rep pledges to take orders for no competing company, in return for which the company pledges to accept orders from no other student on that campus.

It should be clear by now that many of the business ideas discussed in this chapter have been based on the campus rep model: you contact a manufacturer and take orders for him in return for a commission.

The number of companies with campus representative programs is in the hundreds, and more firms join the ranks every week. If you are interested in becoming a campus rep and are unable to find a suitable manufacturer of the products you want to sell, write a letter to the National Association of Direct Selling Companies. NADSC is a trade association, and most major direct sales companies are included on its membership list.

CHAPTER 3

Service with
a Smile

1. LAUNDRY

All people—even students—need clean clothing once in a while. There are three possible ways of maintaining a steady supply. The first is to buy new clothes every week, and throw out the old ones. The second is to wash your clothes yourself, with a sink, a washboard, and a lot of knuckles. The third is to utilize some sort of outside help, either a washing machine, a maid, or something in the middle.

Until paper successfully replaces fabric as the principal material in clothing, the first alternative will not be a practical one for students, even on the wealthiest campuses. The second possibility is workable, but it is also work—too much work, too hard work, and too inefficient work for the average student to bother with it. By a process of elimination, the third method is the one that most students eventually settle on.

The unavoidable conclusion to be drawn from these facts is that somebody in every college community stands to make a great deal of money from student laundry. Only one thing can impair the validity of this logical deduction: the intervention of the college administration. At many schools, clothes washers and dryers are installed in dormitory basements for the free use of students; at many others, the administration operates a non-profit laundry. Despite the fact that they eliminate a potential source of student revenue, we must commend these two developments. Both save students money, and the latter has the additional advantage of providing a number of on-campus jobs for needy undergraduates. If your school currently meets the laundry needs of its students in either of these ways, you can only mutter a polite thank-you and look around for another business.

But if your college makes no provisions for student laundry, or if its provisions are inadequate, then some form of laundry business has the capacity to earn you tremendous profits. There are a number of approaches to choose from. The days when college students literally "took in washing" from their classmates are nearly over, but an occasional coed can still be found laundering the silk underwear of her better-heeled sisters. This "business" is not only unpleasant—it is downright unprofitable. If you insist on a one-man (or one-woman) operation, take a cue from a student at Bowdoin College in Brunswick, Maine. This enterprising young man simply looked up a manufacturer of coin-operated washers and dryers, and arranged to handle the company's franchise on campus. He easily convinced the administration and fraternity houses of the desirability of letting him install his equipment in their respective basements. He now does his rounds every week or so, seeing to it that the machines are working properly and emptying them of their accumulation of dimes and quarters. For this light labor, the company pays him a substantial commission.

A more usual (though not necessarily more profitable) procedure is to become the campus representative of a local laundry company. Typical of this system is the business of a student at Middlebury College in Middlebury, Vermont. Twice each week he visits each of Middlebury's ten fraternities, picks up his customers' laundry, and carts the mess to the local cleaning establishment. On his next bi-weekly trip, he returns the clean clothes to the frats. Each month he sends out his bills, deducts 25 percent of the total as his commission, and forwards the rest to his employer.

His profits average around $80 a month. When you consider that the business takes him only an hour and a half a week (part of two lunch hours), that's pretty fair compensation.

To be successful at a small college like Middlebury, a laundry concession of this sort must be a monopoly. Otherwise, every man and his roommate will be lugging his weekly laundry down to the shop to get that 25 percent discount. It is usually not very difficult to get the laundry company to agree to an exclusive franchise, in return for your promise to solicit vigorously all possible business on campus. But that still leaves room for other students, representing other local laundries, to muscle in on your domain. At a big university there may be plenty of room for everybody, but at a small college competition can cut into your business to the point where it no longer pays to make the rounds and do the billing. The usual solution to this difficulty is to talk the college administration into authorizing and enforcing a monopoly for your concession. At Middlebury, for example, the student we talked to is guaranteed the fraternity business, while a classmate of his has a monopoly on dormitory laundry. The college does not, of course, force students to utilize either laundry service, but it does in effect force them to choose between the available student laundry and washing their own clothes.

Nothing is sweeter than having a monopoly on an essential service; if you don't believe it, ask the telephone company. Of course, the college will undoubtedly see to it that you don't abuse the privilege by charging exorbitant prices (just as the government watches over the utilities), but even at reasonable rates your profits will be large and secure. In such a situation, advertising becomes almost unnecessary. Our friend at Middlebury simply posts notices in each fraternity, then visits the frats to explain his service and take down names. The same procedure will work in the dormitories.

Things are different at a school like the University of Chicago or the University of Pennsylvania, where a student body of many thousands represents a prize which admittedly could be shared among a number of laundry concessions. In such a situation, a division of the spoils is occasionally imposed by the university administration. More often an informal or tacit agreement develops among students to the effect that one resident of each dormitory and each fraternity will handle the laundry concession for his house.

Neither of these solutions is particularly stable. They are unsatisfactory to student entrepreneurs who wish to spread their wings and pyramid their profits more than a single dorm or frat permits. They are even more unsatisfactory to professional laundry companies; in any city large enough to support more than one of these, there will inevitably be annual attempts to take over the whole college market. A strong-willed administration can enforce a monopoly if it works at it, and if the school operates its own laundry service you can bet your boots it will. But at many large colleges and universities, the student laundry picture is one of cut-throat competition.

That's when it gets to be fun. If you plan on starting a laundry concession at a college that already has a few, our main piece of advice to you is to talk to your company and work out a collection of snazzy offers. Systems vary. Some like to keep it simple, on the theory that students will select the laundry plan they can understand. Others like to make it as complicated as they can, in the hope that students will assume that there must be a bargain in there somewhere. Special offers and bonuses are customary. "Eight pounds for only $1.37, and your handkerchiefs ironed free," advertises one concession. "Only 27 cents a shirt and no charge for sewing on buttons," ballyhoos a competitor. Service is also important. Some concessions operate on a set schedule, picking up laundry at a given dorm or frat one day each week. Others check every day and pick up whatever's there. Some take as much as four or five days to return the clothing. Others offer next-day or even same-day service. Given this kind of choice, most students will naturally select the faster and more convenient concession— if the prices are comparable or if, as is more often the case, nobody can figure out whether they're comparable or not; how many shirts are there in a pound?

Whatever prices and system your company decides upon, *your* main job will be to talk your classmates into them. You will have to be one of the first students back on campus in the fall, ready to give your spiel to incoming freshmen and returning upperclassmen. You may even want to solicit customers by mail during the summer. Set up tables all over the campus, and hire the most prestigious salesmen you can; members of the football team seem to have the best sales records. Try to get your customers to commit themselves in some way, possibly by buying a book of 25 laundry tickets, each good for so many pounds of wash. This is no time for the soft sell. Every member of your student body is going to decide about a laundry service within a week; you want as many as possible to settle on yours.

In some cases the job of the student representative is over once he has obtained all the customers he can. He receives a substantial commission for each customer, and from then on it's up to the company. More often, however, the student's work continues throughout the year. You may be asked to handle all the collection and delivery yourself, or to work together with a company employee. You may have to take charge of the billing, or deal with customer complaints. The extent of your responsibility is up to you and the laundry company you represent. The more you do, of course, the higher your commission will be.

Profits range widely, depending on the amount of competition, the size of the college, the number of customers, the sort of service, and the extent of the student's responsibility. The $80-a-month figure we mentioned for Middlebury College is about average for a non-competitive concession at a small school. Laundry czars at large universities can easily earn five times that amount. Would-be czars who don't make it can just as easily earn next to nothing.

Colleges which encourage student business through a student agencies system sometimes set up a full-scale laundry and turn it over to an undergraduate manager. In such cases, the manager may be paid a salary, but more often he receives a percentage of the take. He is unlikely to earn as much as the independent laundry czar, since college-operated laundries try to keep their prices low, but he will do okay, and he's safe. Columbia University and Princeton University are among the schools which have set-ups of this sort.

Occasionally a student will try to start his own campus laundry; much more occasionally, one will succeed. We know of one student-owned, student-run laundry now in operation, located at St. Louis University in St. Louis, Missouri. The profit potential of such an enterprise is fantastic, but so is the profit potential of breaking the bank at Las Vegas. Most people who try either lose their shirt, which in this case is peculiarly appropriate.

2. DRY CLEANING

Most college students have far less need for dry cleaning than they have for laundry service. On the other hand, every college student needs *some* dry cleaning, and if he doesn't bring his soiled slacks home to Mother, he might just as well let you handle them. Moreover, it is a rare college that runs its own cleaners, so the field is wide open for student entrepreneurs. A dry cleaning concession will not bring you astronomical profits, but it will provide a substantial, steady, secure income.

Many professional laundry companies do dry cleaning as well as washing, and campus representatives of such companies normally merge the dry cleaning and laundry concessions into one. We have heard from ten colleges where the two are handled separately, often because the college itself is in the laundry business, but not the cleaning business. The ten are: Carnegie Institute of Technology in Pittsburgh; College of the Holy Names in Oakland, California; College of Idaho in Caldwell, Idaho; La Sierra College in Riverside, California; Randolph-Macon Woman's College in Lynchburg, Virginia; Rutgers University in New Brunswick, New Jersey; St. Mary's College in Winona, Minnesota; Ursinus College in Collegeville, Pennsylvania; Whitman College in Walla Walla, Washington; and Yankton College in Yankton, South Dakota.

Running a dry cleaning concession is not very different from managing a laundry agency. Once you find a cleaning company to represent, and work out with them the prices and services to be offered, your first job is to acquaint all the students at your school with your service. It is generally impossible to force a commitment from your potential customers. Your best bet is to explain the procedures to every student, then pass out huge stacks of "cleaning cards." The cards are to be attached to the dirty clothing and left in the hall or dorm lobby on the appropriate morning; they notify you or your pick-up man that the clothes are meant to be dry cleaned. There should be space on the cards for the name and address of the customer, so that you will be able to return his clothes and send him your bill.

The remainder of your job consists of pick-ups, deliveries, and possibly billing. Every two months or so you should drop in at the rooms of students who are not using your service to find out why. Pay particular attention to those who gave you their dry cleaning for a time, then stopped. Your commission will depend on the volume of dry cleaning you collect, so anything you can do to build up business is to your own advantage. Dry cleaning agents on campus can earn anywhere from $300 to $3,000 a year, depending on the number of customers they serve.

3. LINEN

Roughly half the college students in the country annually purchase enough sheets, pillow cases and towels for two weeks, see that they get washed and ironed every week or so, and replace them when they begin to disintegrate. The other half subscribe to a linen service.

At colleges where linen services are available, the only students to choose the former method are those who already own cot-size sheets anyway, those with plenty of spare time and access to a free washing machine, and those who don't believe in changing their linen. Anyone who changes his linen weekly and has to use a coin-operated washing machine or a laundry service will quickly discover that it's more economical to sign up with a linen agency. It might just as well be your linen agency.

There are two ways to organize such a concession. The first is more difficult, more profitable, and less usual. Contact a manufacturer, wholesaler or professional rental agency and arrange to rent enough linen for your customers for the academic year. Then start talking to the laundries in town and try to set up a special rate to have your loads washed and ironed each week. Now you are in a position to operate an independent linen rental service. Charge your customers a single fee for the entire year, and establish one day each week when you will pick up their dirty linen and leave them a clean supply. Once you have collected your bill from all your customers, all you have to do is see to the weekly pick-up, laundering, and delivery. If you have enough volume to get a good quantity discount from your supplier and your laundry service, you should be able to make a $15 to $20 profit on each customer and still save him money.

The safer way of operating a student linen concession is to become the campus representative of a professional linen rental company. Your responsibilities still include sales, pick-ups, deliveries, and possibly billing, but your employer will take charge of the cleaning—and most of the profit. Still, you risk nothing by this method, and stand to earn up to $1,000 during the school year.

The simplest linen services supply one sheet and one pillow-case each week; the customer is expected to re-use one of his sheets for another week. A more usual arrangement is two sheets, one pillow-case, and three or four towels. If you want to get fancy, you can offer extra towels, fitted sheets, pillows, blankets, bed spreads, bolsters, washcloths, and diapers. Your best bet is to have half a dozen different plans, and let each student choose the one that best fits his needs.

Getting your linens back at the end of the year can be something of a chore. Some agencies require a deposit of $15 or $20 at the start of the service, returnable only when all bills have been paid and all supplies returned. Others emblazon the name of their agency on all articles in the hope that this will deter thievery. (Any hotel can tell you that it won't.) Still others make use of a college rule which prevents students from graduating until all accounts have been settled. And a few simply rely on the integrity of their classmates.

4. VARIATIONS ON THE THEME

Laundry, dry cleaning, and linen services are closely related, and all possible combinations of them have been successfully set up on one campus or another. We have already mentioned the frequency with which laundry agencies handle dry cleaning as well. It is equally usual to find a dry cleaning concession operating a linen service on the side. Somewhat less often a laundry company will rent linens, and occasionally a single business will perform all three services.

College administrations tend to feel a greater responsibility for overseeing laundry, dry cleaning, and linen agencies than most other campus businesses, since the three are almost essential to the well-being of students. On more than one campus, the result of this concern has been a total take-over of the three businesses by the administration. Those schools which are not equipped to run their own laundry, cleaners, and linen rental company frequently contract with local establishments themselves, then hire scholarship students to run the concessions. The result is to transform three excellent business opportunities into salaried jobs.

If you plan on going into any of these three businesses, it will be necessary for you to reach an agreement with your administration. They will want to know the details of your arrangement with local laundries, cleaners, or whatever, and they will want to be certain that your prices are reasonable and your services adequate. You will have to be very convincing indeed to talk them into letting you run your agency as a profit-making business instead of a job.

On some campuses it may just not be worth the effort. Laundry concessions are the most profitable of the three if the competition is weak. But if your school operates its own laundry, forget it. If there are washing machines in the dorms and frats, forget it. If there are laundromats in town and these are popular with the majority of students, forget it. No student laundry agency can offer prices competitive with these. Of course you can offer faster, better, and more convenient service, but you'd better ask yourself just how much your classmates will be willing to pay for speed and efficiency. Similar problems may confront a dry-cleaning agency, especially if there are good, inexpensive cleaners in town, and "town" is only a block from the campus. Only the linen service concept is foolproof—and it's the least profitable of the three.

We're not trying to discourage you from entering these three fields. The profit potential is there, all right. But the work is hard, and the special problems associated with gaining administration approval are painful. Look into it by all means, but look carefully before you leap.

5. TYPING

There was a time, not very long ago, when all class papers were handwritten. That was the way things were, and your myopic history professor could like it or lump it. Alas, times have changed. The percentage of students who know how to type has climbed, and so teachers have gotten a little spoiled. The number of research papers required has also climbed, and so teachers have got a little desperate. The result is that many professors require that papers be typed, and nearly all recommend that papers be typed. Moreover, it has been proved time and again (and most faculty members will admit it) that the easier a paper is to read, the higher grade it is likely to receive. A typewritten paper is the easiest to read, and it looks neat, competent, and professional to boot.

All of which provides an ornate introduction to the assertion of a fact that everybody already knows anyhow: Typing is far and away the most common student business on the campus.

It's not much of a business. The going rates are between 30 cents and 50 cents a page, depending on local supply and demand. A nickel extra per carbon is customary, and a dime surcharge is usually tacked on for pages involving charts, formulas, or other "displayed matter." Total earnings come to $1.25 an hour tops, not counting the time you spend waiting for a customer to finish his rough draft. Since everybody else's papers generally are due at the same time yours are, the work is always heaviest when the time is least available and most valuable. And you can't afford to turn down many jobs if you want to keep your following.

Still, if you're a fast typist and have lots of free time, the typing business can keep you in spending money. Start small, with your roommates and the other fellows or girls in your dorm, frat, or sorority. Word will spread quickly enough on its own, but you can always help it along with a (neatly) typed notice on a few centrally located bulletin boards. You will very shortly have more customers than you know what to do with. There's not much money in it, and certainly no future; but it'll keep you off the streets, and you might learn something from the papers you type.

Of course if you're really serious about this thing, and there's enough demand at your college, you can start a typing agency. Typists should be willing to work for you because you can provide them with jobs when and only when they have the time and need the money. Students should be willing to use your service because you always have typists available, even if it *is* a big football weekend or the middle of exams.

All you have to do to get started is find a dozen or so student typists who'd like more jobs than they're getting. Make up a list of the phone numbers and preferred working hours or days of each typist. Then advertise your service in the school newspaper and on-campus bulletin boards. Your ads should stress the advantages of your business over individually arranged typing: "guaranteed reliable service," "special emergency overnight typing," "one service for all your typing needs," "available all day every day," and so forth. As each student brings you his manuscript, you find one of your typists who wants to work that particular day and turn it over to him. Your fee of 5 cents a page should be charged to the typist, not the customer.

Typing agencies do not work on every campus. You need a fairly substantial volume of business to make the arrangement pay. You also need a large stable of typists who for one reason or another think it's worth a nickel a page to work through you instead of looking around for their own jobs. Princeton University used to have a very active typing service, but its volume of business has dwindled considerably in recent years, due to competition from free-lance students and secretaries in town. On the other hand, Harvard and Columbia's typing agencies are still going strong. Once you get a typing concession going, it very nearly runs itself—and your profits for a little telephoning each day can run as high as $30 a week.

6. COPYING

Copying is what you weren't supposed to get caught doing in

high school. Strangely enough, it is an eminently respectable—and profitable—business on the college level.

We quote from the financial aid director of Swarthmore College in Swarthmore, Pennsylvania: "The student concession that is closest to the heart of student life is the duplicating (copying) service. Approximately twenty percent of the student body at Swarthmore participates in the honors program, which involves writing a paper nearly every week. These papers must be mimeographed so that each member of an honors seminar has a copy of every paper, for discussion purposes. Therefore, a large segment of the students find their lives centered around getting their papers to the 'ditto office' in time, or finding the concessionnaires when they are late."

You don't have to be in an honors program to have some use for a duplicating service. Swarthmore's operation is not unique; Williams College in Williamstown, Massachusetts, has its "mimeograph service," and the University of Pennsylvania has its "Cyclops Copying Service." The principal customers of these agencies are student organizations that want to announce a speaker or an event, issue copies of a constitution, send out questionnaires on one or another topic, and so on. Other student businesses employ the copying service to run off their ads, handouts, and announcements of special bargains. And occasionally a student (he doesn't even have to be an honors student) needs mimeographing help in connection with his academic work.

To decide whether there is any need for a duplicating service on your campus, simply count the number of mimeoed letters, announcements, and offers that are stuffed into your mailbox or shoved into your hands in the average month. Add in the number of academic papers that must be mimeographed at your school, and the number of questionnaires, tickets, postal cards, forms, and other junk that gets copied by this method each month. Divide the sum by the number of mimeograph machines on campus which are available for student use. Then subtract the number of days each machine is out of order. Take the square root of your remainder and look it up in a table of logarithms. Then flip a coin to decide whether there is any need for a duplicating service on your campus.

All you need to set up a copying agency is a mimeograph machine, a typewriter, some stencils, a few reams of paper, and a couple of assistants. Considering the value of your business to all those honors students, your administration may donate some of these supplies, possibly all of them. If they won't lend you a mimeo machine, contact those student groups on campus which have their own, and offer to pay them a nominal amount each month for its use. They have nothing to lose, the damn thing just sits there in the corner all day long anyway, so they'll probably accept. Then put up the usual posters and notices in the usual places, place the usual ad in the campus paper, and wait. A neatly lettered sign over your door, reading "Honors Students Line Up Here," might help control the chaos. You'll have no shortage of customers—assuming you did your calculations correctly.

Your profits will of course depend upon your volume of trade. Figure about 50 cents a page for typing the stencils, plus a penny a copy over and above the cost of paper, stencils, ink, etc. Collating (that's copy-business language for stapling) should cost extra. And then you'll want to offer a special bargain price for honors students. . . .

7. TUTORING

It must be a significant commentary on something that more American college students need typing than tutoring. Perhaps it's a tribute to student intelligence, or possibly it's an indication that the appearance of a term paper counts for more than its content. In any case, though tutors are less in demand than typists, they are still active enough to deserve some attention.

More than any other student business, tutoring deals with an aspect of college life of primary interest to administrators: education. Understandably enough, most colleges consider it their responsibility to supervise the conduct of this particular business scrupulously. Many schools require all would-be tutors to register with the dean of students. Some demand that they obtain permission from the chairman of the relevant department. Others establish minimum grade point averages for college tutors. As an extreme position, more than a few administrations operate their own tutoring service. Students in need of academic help must apply to the dean of students, who then appoints an eligible (and worthy) fellow student to do the job. Payment comes directly from the dean's office, which either charges the tutee or absorbs the cost itself.

Even if the administration manages to keep hands off, there is usually an honorary fraternity, an honor society, or a student government committee doing volunteer tutoring on campus.

All of which makes life rather difficult for the plain, ordinary, free-lance tutor, and even more difficult for the aspiring tutor czar. Individual tutoring still flourishes right out in the open at Clemson University in Clemson, South Carolina, College of the Holy Names in Oakland, California, Otterbein College in Westerville, Ohio, the University of Massachusetts in Amherst, Massachusetts, and Waldorf College in Forest City, Iowa. And it undoubtedly survives underground at hundreds of other schools. But for the most part the concept of an informal, personal tutor is dying. Which makes the concept of a profit-making, organized tutorial service stone dead.

Still, if you're one of the fortunate few who happen to go to a backward college, tutors customarily get paid $5 an hour, which can add up to pretty good money. And there may be a need, theoretically, for a profit-making tutoring service. At those schools where free-lance tutoring is still popular, tutors and tutees spend a great deal of time and effort looking for each other. That is where you come in. A student in academic trouble won't object to paying a bit more to get same-day service on his urgent request for a qualified tutor in Indo-European philology. Your college's one student expert on that subject will be equally happy to charge a bit less in return for having every troubled Indo-European philology student guided to his doorstep. It will be your pleasure, and profit, to accommodate them both.

The procedure is nearly identical to the one we described for typing agencies. Build up a list of tutors, with the preferred subjects and working hours of each. Then advertise your service. Every time a student calls you for a tutor, take down his name and phone number, and the subject he wants help in, then find him a suitable classmate from your list. Once you have put the two in touch with each other, your job is over—except for collecting your fee.

If the demand is sufficient, it is also possible to organize tutoring groups. One upperclassman could take on a "class" of a dozen students, charging them 75 cents apiece for an hour's instruction. This approach doesn't work for all subjects, but it's fine for science, math, and Indo-European philology. The reduced cost attracts a larger number of tutees, and the tutor still comes out with a greater profit per hour. A tutoring system similar to this one was tried about ten years ago at Rutgers University in New Brunswick, New Jersey. It worked for a while, so it might work again.

All this is highly theoretical. We do not know of a single successful profit-making tutoring service now operating within a college or university. There is usually a campus organization or an administrator willing to do the job for free. And making money on a large scale off the academic difficulties of your classmates seems a little sleazy even to us. Still, the possibility is there, and we pass it on for whatever it's worth.

Off-campus tutoring services for high school or primary pupils are very common in college towns, and are an accepted way of earning money. These will be discussed in Chapter Four.

8. BOOK EXCHANGE

The need for an efficient campus used book exchange system is one that colleges are just beginning to appreciate. It has developed in recent years as the amount of reading required in the average course and the cost of buying course books have soared ever higher. At some schools this need is met by a book exchange service operated through the college co-op. At some, the student government or an honorary fraternity operates a non-profit exchange. At most schools the need simply isn't met.

A used book exchange requires a great deal more time, effort, and dedication than a tutoring service—which explains why non-profit exchange set-ups rarely last more than a year or two. Somebody has to keep track of all the books; somebody has to be around to sell them to interested purchasers; somebody has to see to it that their original owners are paid. The college co-op could handle the job if it wanted to, but it's in the *new* book business, so we can hardly expect it to waste much time or shelf space on second-hand ones. And individual book-selling and book-buying are more trouble than they are worth. By the time you've found someone who wants (or has) books for the course you have (or want) them for, the year is over, the course is no longer offered, the books are obsolete, and everybody's graduated. Occasionally someone manages to make a connection, by dint of unceasing labor posting notices all over the campus, but that happens just often enough to let you know how nice a student book exchange would be.

Wellesley College in Wellesley, Massachusetts, has had a student-run, profit-making used book exchange for a number of years. Figuring that if the girls at Wellesley could do it, anybody could, a group of Princeton students started a similar venture last Spring. In the Princeton procedure, students set their own prices for their books, then deliver them to the exchange office, where they are arranged according to the course for which they are required. When a book is purchased, its owner is advised that he should drop by and pick up his money. An owner may reclaim an unsold book at any time, or lower its price to help it sell faster. Students are encouraged to submit requests for books they need, and requesters are notified when their desired books come in.

The Princeton exchange recommends 65 percent of the original sales price as the appropriate charge for a course book. The buyer pays this amount. The exchange deducts 10 percent of the reduced purchase price as its service charge, and pays over the remainder to the book's former owner.

To start a book exchange, simply distribute mimeographed leaflets describing the service and telling students where to go to leave off old books and look for new ones. Your dormitory room will do fine as an "office" if college regulations don't forbid putting it to such use. The best time to start is several weeks before the beginning of a new term. This is the period when students are beginning to resent their useless stock of last term's books, and when they're beginning to wonder how they'll ever be able to pay for next term's books. The response to your hand-outs should be immediate and overwhelming.

Your expenses in this particular business are negligible, so computing your profits is simply a matter of arithmetic. If 500 students bring you ten books each, with an average resale value per book of $2.50, your stock is worth $12,500. If you eventually manage to sell 80 percent of it ($10,000 worth), your profits will be $1,000. You should be able to repeat the feat every semester.

9. VARIATIONS ON THE THEME

When a college co-op or a professional book store goes into the second-hand book business, it doesn't hold the books for customers and deduct a service charge if and when they are sold. Instead, it buys outright those books it expects to be able to sell, and refuses to buy any others.

If you have an ample supply of capital, shrewdness, and courage, you can run your book "exchange" the same way. The fact that you pay at once for the books you want is an advantage to students who want to sell their books, and should enable you to offer them a lower price than a genuine exchange system would set. Since you can put your resale prices at the same level as an exchange system, your profit on each book you sell will be substantially higher.

But of course your profit on each book you don't sell will be negative. Let us go back to the financial example in the last section. Suppose you buy ten books apiece from each of 500 students at an average price of $2.00 (as opposed to $2.50 on the exchange system). Your total investment in stock is $10,000. If you now manage to sell 80 percent of the books at an average price of $2.50, your gross will also be $10,000. Your net profit is nothing—zilch—unless you consider a load of unsellable second-hand course books a profit.

Based on these rough figures, we may conclude that to turn a profit in the used book business you would have to: 1) buy your books at less than $2.00 apiece, or 2) sell them at more than $2.50, or 3) sell more than 80 percent of the books you buy.

It can be done, and done handsomely, as any second-hand book store will tell you. But it takes a lot of capital, and it's every bit as tricky as LSD. Your best bet is probably to stick to the straight-and-narrow book exchange set-up, except for graduating seniors. These unfortunates can't afford to leave you their books on consignment, and they're sure as hell not going to take them all home with them. The thing to do is to buy their books *very* cheaply. You'll have a nice profit on those you sell, nice enough to let you cheerfully donate those you don't sell to charity and take a deduction on your income tax.

10. HAIRCUTS

From administrators at Dominican College in San Rafael, California, comes the following quotation about student haircutting:

> Oh, the days of the cosmetologist—
> Oh, the days of the scissors' snip—
> Seventy-five cents for a fashionable
>   haircut,
> A dollar gets you a combed-out flip!

There probably is not a girls' college in the country where students are unaccustomed to cutting and setting the hair of their friends, roommates and dormmates. More often than not, the service is performed free of charge. The rest of the time, the 75 cents or dollar fee mentioned in the quotation is pretty standard.

The student haircutting business is by no means limited to women. A young man at Swarthmore College in Swarthmore, Pennsylvania, for example, works as a dormitory barber, averaging six customers a week. His electric clippers, thinning shears, and barber's comb cost him a total of $10, which he earned back in his first week and a half of work. Thereafter, his $6 a week were pure gravy.

It may not sound like much of a business, but this fellow takes a very businesslike attitude toward it. In addition to his professional equipment, he uses a sheet and a safety pin to protect his customers from their own hair. He even has a "specialty"—one which is especially appropriate for his school. "I specialize," he says, "in cutting hair so it doesn't look like it's been cut." His technique enables Swarthmore men to please their parents while staying in stylistic step with their peers.

But any way you look at it, $6 a week isn't a fortune. We suppose that some student barbers and hairdressers make a bit more than that, if they live in a large dorm and their posters are attractive and they happen to be in their room when customers drop by. But you will not be able to pay your tuition or buy a new car on your barbering proceeds.

Nor is there any demand for a student barbering agency, based on the typing agency model we have described. Students rarely have difficulty locating a barber or hairdresser among their classmates, and barbers have equally little trouble spreading the word about their service. No middleman is needed.

The only possible business idea we can think of that might turn student cosmetology into a major money-maker is a student beauty parlor. Most college girls are well beyond the stage where the idea of regular professional beauty treatment seems ridiculous. but have not quite reached the stage where the idea seems natural. At a few colleges small groups of talented student hairdressers have banded together to take advantage of this intermediary period. If you have the knowledge and ability to run a beauty parlor of sorts, and you think your campus has a demand for such a service, buy the necessary equipment, put up a few posters, and see what happens. An agency which is less expensive than the "salons" in town, yet does a more professional job than the average girl could do for herself, might well earn big money at your school.

11. DISCOUNT COUPONS

One of the oldest and most popular collegiate money-makers in the country is the sale of discount coupons on campus. Local merchants are usually happy to work out some sort of special introductory offer for students, and a booklet containing a few dozen such offers sells easily on campus for $3 or $4. The only major expense of the project is printing, and even that is dirt cheap when compared with a blotter or a booklet.

Discount coupons can net big profits on almost any campus in almost any town. They are popular in small college towns like Amherst, Massachusetts (University of Massachusetts), and Morgantown. West Virginia (University of West Virginia). They make it in suburban areas such as Berkeley, California (University of California at Berkeley), and Kent, Ohio (Kent State University). They succeed just as well in cities as large as Atlanta, Georgia (Georgia Institute of Technology), and Cleveland, Ohio (Saint John College).

In the nation's largest metropolis, New York City, the sale of college discount coupons has proved to be fabulously profitable. Students from four colleges in the New York area incorporated themselves a few years ago as College Discounts, Inc. Over a period of several months, they arranged student bargains at scores of New York shops, restaurants, and entertainment centers. The resulting coupon books were tremendously popular on the four campuses, and earned the quartet of entrepreneurs more than enough to pay all their college expenses.

The major impediment to your making a killing in the student discount business is likely to be the fact that somebody else got there first. In this case, "somebody else" may well be a non-profit service organization or a student government committee. On many campuses. discount coupons are given away free to freshmen in an effort to ease their way into the community while smoothing town-gown relations as well. Even more often a Student Senate or an honorary fraternity sells coupon books at a nominal charge, thus building up their treasury a little without losing their amateur status.

Even if nobody else got there first, a discount coupon agency may still fail. Bryn Mawr College in Bryn Mawr, Pennsylvania, has seen the idea fail several times, most recently in 1966. Bryn Mawr is typical of the sort of school at which this business is most perilous. First, the college is small, with a total of fewer than 800 students, all of them girls. Second, the town is small, with very little choice of stores open to someone who wants to buy something. Third, the girls are financially better off than most, with little inclination to think in terms of discount coupons. Fourth, the school is located in a suburb of Philadelphia, close enough so that those with major purchases in mind can make the trip, but far enough (and small enough) so that Philadelphia merchants don't want to bother with special discounts for Bryn Mawr girls.

This is the worst of all possible worlds for the sale of discount coupons. The first and third factors can be gotten around, but the second and fourth are murder. Even one of the two by itself can seriously endanger a discount coupon business. If everybody already knows the only drugstore in town and has no choice but to shop there, its owner will see no particular advantage to offering a discount. Big city merchants will be equally unenthusiastic for a different reason: Trade from your college is such a small part of their business that it just isn't worth the effort to figure out a discount and honor it once every three months when someone comes in with a coupon.

The small town problem is insoluble, unless a lot of students have cars and you can talk merchants in neighboring towns into offering discounts. The big city problem has a few possible solutions. The easiest is to concentrate on stores in the immediate vicinity of the college, in effect transforming a city into a large town. Another way out is to concentrate on business for which the student market is crucial; sporting goods stores, record shops, and inexpensive nightclubs are examples. The third tactic is the one chosen by the four New York City students we mentioned earlier; if you can arrange to have your discount book sold on a dozen campuses in and around the city, you can be sure that most merchants will be interested.

We have stressed the potential for failure of this business because its potential for profit is so great as to make its lure almost irresistible. The smallest profit we have heard about was earned at Massachusetts Institute of Technology in Cambridge, Massachusetts. Cambridge is a suburb of Boston, and is also a good-sized city itself, with several colleges beside M.I.T. within its boundaries. With this handicap to grapple with, M.I.T.'s "Collegiate Sampler" agency still sells $250 worth of tickets per year. Given ideal circumstances—a large campus located in an isolated large town or small city—you should be able to earn several thousand dollars without much trouble.

Figure it out yourself. Suppose you put together a book of 25 coupons, with a total possible retail value (if all coupons were redeemed) of $100. On a campus of 3,000 students, you should be able to sell 1,500 books for $4 apiece. That comes to $6,000 gross. Subtract $1,000 for the salaries of your solicitors and salesmen, and another $1,000 (let's be generous) for your printing costs, and you're still left with a sweet $4,000 profit for your few months' work.

The procedure is laughably simple. When you visit local merchants, remind them that you're not trying to sell them anything. You're offering them a free chance to attract new customers. Even if your plan doesn't work for some reason and no new customers come, they haven't lost a penny.

The sort of deal they should offer depends on the nature of their business. If there are four barber shops in town, one of them should be willing to give 50 cents off the price of a haircut, or even a free haircut; discount-hunting students who like the haircut they get will keep coming back—at the standard price. Similarly, a restaurant which is not a big student hangout can afford to cut a dollar or more off the cost of a meal, in the hope of weaning students from their more customary haunts. Every competitive business, from dry cleaners to drugstores, book shops to beer parlors, should want to offer a coupon of this nature.

Many businesses are non-competitive, but still miss out on a lot of student trade because what they offer is not considered a necessity. Entertainment facilities such as bowling alleys and skating rinks are in this category. Places of this sort should offer a free game or a free hour of play. Some of the students who come to use their coupon will enjoy themselves enough to return many times during their school years. Peripheral "educational" businesses are in the same boat. An ample percentage of those who show up to claim their free dancing lesson, guitar lesson, or speed reading lesson will later sign up for the whole course.

The final category of businesses which should jump at your discount ticket proposal consists of those which stand to make a good profit even at discount prices. A movie theater, for example, has nothing to lose by offering 50 cents off the entrance price of a matinee; the theater will not be filled anyway, so whatever extra they get is just that much to the good. Similarly, appliance stores and clothing shops can well afford a student coupon which allows 10 percent discount on any purchase of more than $30. Their profit margin is great enough to make the deal pay, and an appreciable number of students who don't really need a new suit or a stereo will succumb to the temptation of the discount.

The appeal of your project should be obvious to local tradesmen. Do not dissipate it by involving your coupon book in conflicts of interest. If all four barber shops in town offered a free haircut, the value of the discounts to the shops would be nil. If three shops offered a free haircut and the fourth only a dollar off, the situation would be still worse. One coupon for each type of merchandise or each service should be your rule, and you should stick to it. If you inform local tradesmen of this rule when you visit them, you will rarely have to walk away empty-handed.

Once you have obtained all the discount offers you want, have them printed up in a small book or folder of tickets. Each coupon should contain the following information: the name of your agency, the name and address of the business making the offer, the nature of the offer, and the expiration date. The expiration date for each coupon should be set by the merchant offering it. The date should never be later than the end of the current academic year. Barber shops, restaurants and the like will want to set an early expiration date, since they wish to attract freshmen before their shopping habits are established. Stores offering percentage discounts on large purchases will probably specify a much longer period of validity for the coupon.

Your coupon book should be designed so as to prevent several possible forms of cheating. Mimeographed coupons are definitely out because they are too easily copied; with the profits you're bound to make on this deal, you can afford to pay a printer. Choose a fairly distinctive and unusual paper (pastel green with wavy-line watermarks would be nice) as a further protection against duplication. Bind or staple the coupons together in book form, and print a notice on the inside front cover of the book to the effect that coupons are valid only if they are still attached. This will prevent students from selling or giving unwanted coupons to their classmates. Leave a space on the front cover of the book for the purchaser's name. He signs this when he buys the book, and must be able to duplicate the signature if requested when he redeems a coupon. This procedure will make it very difficult for students to lend their books to one another.

All these precautions are aimed at protecting participating businesses. Together, they make certain that each coupon will be used only by its owner. But the precautions become meaningless unless you see to it that no student buys more than one book. Your "one book to a customer" rule should be inviolate, and you should keep lists of purchasers to insure that it remains so. The lists will also help prevent non-students from buying your coupon books (unless you have agreed with participating merchants that they will be permitted to do so).

Selling the books will take time, but it shouldn't take very much sales pressure. Add up the approximate value of all the coupons in your book. It should easily come to more than $100. Make use of this fact in your ads and your sales pitch. Describe some of the everyday items for which you have discount coupons, and show how a student could make his purchase price back in savings in a week or two of normal buying. Just thumbing through your coupons once should be enough to convince most students that they ought to buy a book. Hire salesmen to peddle the books door-to-door. Nearly every freshman and roughly half of all other students will cheerfully hand over the $4 or $5.

A very successful method for boosting sales is a money-back guarantee. Inform prospective customers that they may return the coupon books at the end of the academic year and receive a full refund if they have saved less than their purchase price on the coupons they used. This offer is perfectly safe. The only students who will fail to make back their purchase price in savings are those who misplace the book or forget about it. Very few of these will be able to locate it by the end of the year, and fewer still will have the effrontery to return it.

12. VARIATIONS ON THE THEME

The student discount business is so profitable that it has been attempted on a national scale. Varsity International Sales Association has local representatives all over the country. Each representative is empowered to sell VISA cards, as well as booklets listing the stores and other places of business which offer VISA discounts. We will discuss this giant student business in some detail in Chapter Six, but the opportunity to represent VISA in your area is one we want to mention now. The University of Pennsylvania and Dartmouth College are among the schools which have reported substantial incomes for VISA representatives on their campus.

One other aspect of VISA deserves comment here. The group conceives of itself as a liaison between the merchant and the college student. It therefore considers it appropriate to charge both sides for its service as a middleman. The student pays for his VISA card and booklet; the businessman pays to be listed in the booklet.

An organization as large as VISA can get away with this. Merchants are willing to pay the price for the same reason resorts are willing to pay to be listed in popular guidebooks. For operations on a smaller scale, however, charging at both ends is not a good idea. Your goal is to offer the widest possible range of premiums, to sell as many coupon books as you can. Losing even one or two local tradesmen because they did not want to pay the price would probably cost you more in sales than you would gain from the other tradesmen in fees.

VISA is not the only national organization interested in student discounts. The United States National Student Association has for years distributed books of bargain coupons for use in Europe. USNSA has the contacts abroad and the campus reps across the country to make this a paying proposition. We would not advise you to try it yourself.

13. TICKET SERVICE

More than 50 of the colleges we contacted in connection with this book mentioned ticket selling as a significant business on their campus. Many others probably meant to mention it, but didn't think of it. Yet the strange fact is that we have yet to hear of an organized comprehensive, student ticket agency operating on a college campus.

This isn't so remarkable at some schools. A tiny college in a tiny town has slight use for a ticket agency. Tickets for campus events can easily be distributed by the sponsoring organization, and off-campus events are non-existent.

But at a large university, or a college of any size in or near a big city, it's a different story. Here the absence of a well-organized middleman is sorely felt. Promoters of off-campus sports events, plays, shows, concerts, etc., have no convenient way of reaching the student body. Organizers of on-campus plays, concerts, proms, and athletic contests face a similar difficulty. And the individual student who wants to attend one of these affairs is forced to go out questing for the appropriate ticket salesman. He may or may not bother; if he does, he may or may not find the guy.

Independent free-lance ticket salesmen pick up small amounts of money as representatives of this or that organization. A small agency may handle the tickets for on-campus sports events. One student represents a nearby opera house. Another sells tickets for the city's boxing arena. An understaffed committee tries to move junior prom tickets. An overworked publicity manager tries to push tickets for student drama club performances. A sympathetic enthusiast tries to unload a few seats at the city's philharmonic concerts. And Americans are supposed to be the world's greatest efficiency experts!

Occasionally things get a bit better organized than the picture we have painted. At Bethel College in St. Paul, Minnesota, tickets for various St. Paul concerts are sold through the Student Senate. A Residence Hall Cultural Committee distributes tickets for several off-campus groups at the College of the Holy Names in Oakland, California. A Cultural Committee of the Student Association does the same at Saint John College in Cleveland. The Union Activities Committee does it at Luther College in Decorah, Iowa. Alpha Kappa Psi does it at St. Mary's College in Winona, Minnesota. And—O Infamy!—the job is very well handled on the campus of the University of California at Riverside by a professional Mutual ticket agency.

All these groups (except the last) are non-profit service organizations. All of them (except the last) have other responsibilities which occupy the bulk of their time. Thus all of them (except the last) fail to meet adequately the need for a comprehensive ticket agency on campus.

Why couldn't all the tickets for all the events on and off campus be available in one central location? We visualize an agency which would charge campus organizations from the athletic department to the drama society a set fee for peddling their tickets. We visualize an agency which would stock, in addition, tickets to all major off-campus events, and would charge the promoters of these events for each ticket they sold. We visualize an agency which would take orders for tickets to less usual or less popular events, and would charge the student who placed each order a reasonable fee for its work. We visualize an agency which would prepare a weekly sheet listing the names and prices of all events for which it has tickets in stock. And we would bet our royalties that such an agency would earn huge profits at any fairly large, fairly sophisticated college in or near a city.

14. DISTRIBUTION SERVICE

While we're on the subject of badly needed businesses that don't exist, we'd like to put in a plug for a student distribution agency.

The most widely used method of distribution is the postal service. It is a fairly efficient way of reaching people who are spread across the country, or the state, or even the county. But when it comes to reaching people who are spread across a campus, then the mail is a very wasteful method. A student distribution service could certainly afford to deliver ads, notices, or handouts on campus for considerably less than what the post office charges.

Many organizations already use student distributors when they want to reach campus residents. But they are forced to hire students specifically for the one job, or in the case of on-campus groups, to do the job themselves. The resulting expenditure of money or time is nearly as inefficient as the postal approach. An organized distribution agency could provide inexpensive, fast on-campus delivery on behalf of any organization—student or professional, commercial or non-profit.

To set up such a service, simply enlist one student employee from each dormitory, fraternity, sorority, and other student residence. Every employee is then responsible for showing up at the distribution office at certain specified times and picking up his allotment of handouts. On a very large and busy campus, you will want to schedule a delivery every evening. At smaller schools, once or twice a week might be enough. However often you deliver, you should always be delivering for more than one customer at a time. It is this multiple delivery, plus your organization of residence representatives, which enables you to charge a rate so low that it would hardly pay anyone to distribute by any other method.

Once you have your representatives lined up, all you need do to start things rolling is to notify all major campus organizations of the existence of your service. Suppose you charge 75 cents per student for delivery. At a college with 4,000 students, your price for individual delivery to every student's room is $30. If on a given delivery night you have five customers, your gross for that night is $150. Assume that you have 20 residence representatives, each covering 200 students. You could pay them $3 apiece, and still be left with a net profit of $90 for the night's work.

Once you have things organized, all you have to do is divide each distributing job into piles with the proper number of copies for each representative. If you like, you can shuffle the piles into small packets containing one copy of each item, and make your employees' work easier. Your only other responsibility is to solicit new customers.

On-campus organizations will provide a good deal of your business, but by no means all of it. Insurance companies, charities, and others will want to solicit from students by means of your service. Even businesses that do not customarily employ a distribution service or send out mailings may be attracted by your low prices. You might visit a few local tradesmen, for example, and point out that their ad in last week's issue of the college newspaper cost them $35. For $5 less than that amount, they could have had a handbill distributed individually to every student.

A student distribution service can conveniently be combined with any of several other student businesses. If you plan daily distribution, then you might as well switch your delivery time from evening to morning and deliver newspapers as well. And of course if you are delivering newspapers, you ought to be selling newspaper subscriptions too. Alternatively, you might want to set up a duplicating agency as part of your business. Your customers could then bring you their ad or notice to have it typed, mimeographed, collated, and delivered all in one operation.

We admit that not every campus needs a student distribution agency such as the one we have described. If all students live in one dorm, with mailboxes in the lobby, it is an easy matter for any group to stuff their announcements into the boxes. If everybody eats in the same dining hall, and on-campus groups customarily hand out their notices there, you may not be able to find enough outside commercial business to keep your business going. But any college with more than two thousand students should have enough action to make a student delivery service a highly profitable venture.

15. VENDING MACHINES

Machines which swallow coins at one end and spit out goods at the other are an accepted part of our environment today, the ultimate in impersonal, efficient salesmanship. It is hardly surprising that many students find the installation and maintenance of such machines a highly profitable campus business.

There is a wide variety of products to choose among. The campus of Rutgers University in New Brunswick, New Jersey, is dotted with newspaper vending machines, which are kept full of papers and empty of coins by a Rutgers student. The Columbia University newspaper agency has a machine in the lobby of every residence hall. Students at Pennsylvania in Philadelphia and Bowdoin College in Brunswick, Maine, supply dormitories and fraternities with coin-operated clothes washers and dryers. Bany College in Miami, Florida, has a student-run automated food canteen. Upsala College in East Orange, New Jersey, abounds in soft drink machines, courtesy of one of its fraternities. Cigarette machines, of course, are ubiquitous at every college, and even pin-ball machines have been known to earn money for college students. The only existing money-eating monster that has yet to turn a profit for undergraduates is the coin operated telephone, and some imaginative young entrepreneur will no doubt eliminate that exception any day now.

The first step in the vending machine business is to talk to the people who own the places where you want to put the machines. The second step is to talk to the people who own the machines you want to put in the places. The third step is to keep them from talking to each other—or they'll talk themselves into a deal and you out of a commission.

The usual method for earning money from vending machines is to act as the agent of the machine company. You arrange for installation and handle servicing in return for a percentage of the take. All sorts of variations abound. The company may undertake to keep the machines stocked and in working order itself, in which case you earn your commission simply by arranging the original installation. Or they may lease you the machines for a set amount each month, leaving you to worry about keeping them stocked and in use. Finally, it is possible to buy vending machines outright in the hope of recouping your purchase price and going on to make top profits. This last method is not practical for a college student unless he is sure he can resell the machines to an underclassman before he graduates.

Profits from vending machines vary with the arrangement with the company, the kind of machine, and the amount of use it gets. On the average, you can expect between $5 and $10 per machine per week. That is your compensation for keeping the machines filled and handling the financial paperwork. If you employ a service to refill the machines, your profits will be smaller, but so will your work load. In any case, the major problem in this business is keeping the frats and the college administration from noticing that they could be raking in the dough as easily as you. If you can lick that one, you're bound to make money out of vending machines.

16. INSURANCE

When you start thinking about buying life insurance, man, you have entered the Great American Adult Middle Class. The GAAMC is not such a bad place to be, but not every college student wants to get there so fast. Which is why the sale of life insurance is not a big business at every college.

But if you have a large number of GAAMC-hungry students at your school, you couldn't do much better than selling life insurance. Policy-holders tend to stay with the same insurance company for life, so the company can well afford to give you a generous commission on each sale. Life insurance is a big business at the University of California at Santa Barbara, the University of New Hampshire at Durham, Williams College in Williamstown, Massachusetts, and St. Louis University in St. Louis, Missouri. Profits of more than $1,000 a year are not unusual at these schools.

In order to sell insurance in most states, you must be licensed by your state government. Requirements vary from state to state, but they nearly always include an examination, and very often a minimum age. If you think you might qualify, write to the home office or local representative of one of the major companies. If they think life insurance could sell on your campus and you could be the man to sell it, they will help you study for the state test. Once you are licensed, they will brief you on the terms of their policies, and then turn you loose on the campus.

You're not going to sell any insurance without personal contact, but at most colleges it hardly pays to talk to every student individually. The best method is to distribute a folder describing your company's policies (the company will usually supply these). Enclose a letter with the folder identifying yourself as the agency's campus representative, and ask students who are interested in hearing more to get in touch with you. Then make your personal visits where they will do the most good.

There is an additional gimmick that occasionally earns campus insurance agents mountains of money. Most colleges try to enlist seniors in some sort of long-term pledge of contributions, to be managed by class officers and presented to the school as the "class gift" at a major reunion or homecoming. We know of at least one college where these pledges have traditionally taken the form of insurance policies, with the class as beneficiary. At the end of the term of the policy, or after the death of the insured, the money is put toward the class gift. If you can interest your class officers and administration officials in such a plan, your commissions should total to a handsome sum indeed.

17. TRAVEL AGENCY

Fairleigh Dickinson University in Rutherford, New Jersey, St. Edward's University in Austin, Texas, and Simmons College in Boston all list "travel agent" as one of their most profitable student businesses.

A student travel agent normally works as a representative of a professional travel agency that is too far from the campus for students to visit themselves. He notes the travel needs of each customer, works out a suitable arrangement with his agency, and then reports back to the customer. He sees to it that reservations are made, tickets are delivered, and baggage is properly shipped. Normally, he also handles the billing of his customers, and advertises heavily in order to attract more students to his service. For all these jobs he is paid a percentage by the agency he represents.

Instead of or in addition to the work described above, a campus travel agent may specialize in travel services of special interest to students. These include charter flights, student tours, bus chartering, automobile rentals, etc. It is not necessary to work through a professional travel agency to provide these services; a student may negotiate tours, charters and rentals directly with the companies involved. As a result, these matters are often handled independently not only of travel agencies, but also of one another. We will therefore treat each in turn.

18. STUDENT TOURS

As European travel gets cheaper and American students get richer, student tours get less and less popular. Today, the cool way to travel, whether abroad or in the United States, is alone—or, better still, with a friend or two. Nevertheless, student tours still comprise a sizable chunk of the student travel business, especially in the Midwest.

The American Express Company (main office in New York City) is the country's largest promoter of student tours, but hundreds of smaller groups are in operation. Copy the names of a few from the travel section of your Sunday newspaper, and write to them. Most companies offer a variety of summer tours through Europe, South America, and even Asia and Africa, as well as shorter vacation jaunts to Bermuda, Hawaii, Nassau, Mexico, Florida, etc. Select a tour you think will be popular on your campus, and ask the company for permission to organize a group. Then start looking for customers.

The company will give you plenty of help. Brochures and folders should already be available, and most tour services will reimburse you for the cost of supplementing these with posters, flyers, and campus newspaper advertisements. Once you have talked a classmate into joining the tour, he makes his booking arrangements directly with the firm's headquarters.

For most overseas tours, campus organizers receive their payment in the form of free passage. The number of paying customers you must enlist to get your own free tour is usually about 15. If you are not interested in taking the tour yourself, financial remuneration can generally be arranged, though it will of course be less than the retail value of the tour.

19. CHARTER FLIGHTS

For students who have obtained summer jobs in Europe, or who want to travel on their own there, charter flights are the accepted means of transportation. Essentially, the procedure is to find a planeload of students who can agree on a time and place of embarkation and disembarkation. The agency charters the plane for a set price, sells seats on it to students at a savings of up to $100 under commercial rates, and pockets the difference.

Charter flight agencies are popular throughout the country,

especially on large university campuses where it is comparatively easy to find enough interested students to fill a plane. Since Europe is the preferred destination for nearly all charter flights, and the East Coast is closest to Europe, the charter flight business is particularly remunerative in that section. We know of no Ivy League or Seven Sisters school without one.

Negotiating with the airline is the most difficult part of operating a charter flight agency. Agreements are highly complex, involving such arcane questions as insurance, type of airplane, and scheduling—as well as high finance. At a fairly small college, it is often simpler and more sensible (though less profitable) to work through an established travel agency.

The charter flight agency at Middlebury College in Middlebury, Vermont, is typical of a small-college operation. Working through a Boston travel agency, its student manager successfully signed up 25 customers—15 from Middlebury and 10 from Simmons College in Boston. His price was $333.00 for a round trip, Boston to London, on a TWA jet. The departure date was in early June; the return flight left London in early September.

Bear in mind that a charter flight agency needs a lot of time and effort to be successful. First, there's the matter of making arrangements with the airline or travel agency. Then you have to advertise, and begin trying to sell your flight. Our friend at Middlebury mimeographed and distributed 1,700 leaflets to get his 25 customers. He also made use of bulletin boards, left folders and pamphlets at strategic information desks, and talked about his flight to everyone he could. Once you have your passenger list completed, there's still a lot to be done. Paperwork is high on the list, with schedules, tickets, reminders, baggage transfer, payments and bills to worry about. Your biggest headache will undoubtedly be the perennial procrastination of students. As our contact at Middlebury put it: "College students seem to think last-minute plans are the thing to do." Many students will try to sign up three days before flight time, and nearly as many will try to drop out at the same late date.

Your remuneration for all this work can vary greatly. Because his concession was small and because he worked through a travel agency, the manager of the Middlebury charter flight service earned only his own free trip. Even this $333 value is not bad, when you consider that his business grossed less than $8,500. The Massachusetts Institute of Technology charter flight service grosses roughly $80,000 a year on a variety of summer flights to Europe and Christmas flights to the West Coast. Its annual profit (in cash) comes to about $2,300. Even the M.I.T. agency is not particularly big compared with some. In Chapter Six we will discuss a giant charter flight business run by a student at the University of Texas. Managing flights for 63 different Texas colleges, the agency grosses $350,000 a year.

Don't try to start a charter flight service at your college unless a substantial number of students have the money and the inclination to travel to Europe. If you do start one, try to get the administration to give you a monopoly. Offer to open up the flight to faculty members and college employees in return; they like to save money too. If you have the demand and can get the monopoly, go to it. You'll have to work hard, but your profit should more than justify the work, particularly at a large school.

20. BUS SERVICE

Not everybody at Middlebury has the requisite bank account for a European junket, but a good number can afford a trip to New York, or even Chicago or Washington. To accommodate these students, another Middlebury entrepreneur serves as a campus agent for the Vermont Transit Corporation. His job is selling bus tickets, and he is paid a commission on each ticket sold.

Bus services are common on many campuses across the country. In addition to selling tickets, bus agency managers generally arrange chartered trips for special occasions. At the Carnegie Institute of Technology, for example, there are a large number of students who live in the New York City area. Carnegie Tech is in Pittsburgh, Pennsylvania, a good day's bus ride from New York. At the start of every vacation period, a Carnegie Tech student charters a bus for the New York run, and sells tickets to classmates who want to go home for the holidays. A few days before classes resume, the bus makes the return trip.

Bus chartering services are not limited to holiday travel. At

Wittenberg University in Springfield, Ohio, for instance, the bus service sells tickets for trips to athletic contests at other schools, social events in the area, and so forth. Weekend pleasure jaunts to nearby cities are another possibility, particularly if your college is in an isolated small town with fairly poor public transportation connections with the outside world.

Chartering a bus is not a big deal. All you do is call up the bus company, name your date, time, and destination, and find out how much it costs. The rates are low enough to enable you to sell tickets at a reasonable price, and still make a tidy profit. And students do not have to be wealthy to make use of your service; they just have to have a little wanderlust, and no car.

21. EUROPE BY CAR

"Europe by Car" is the name of a campus agency which exists at a select few colleges and universities on the East Coast. The purpose of the agency is to arrange for the summer rental of European sports cars for students who plan to travel abroad during the holidays. Customers using this agency have the option of purchasing the car at the end of the summer. Most of them exercise it; a European sports car is even cooler here than it is in Europe. It then becomes the job of the agency to arrange for the importation of the car and its delivery to the customer's door.

It should be clear from this description that not every college can support a Europe by Car agency. As a matter of fact, not even every college that has use for a charter flight service needs this particular luxury. But at those few schools with a demand for such a service—and Princeton, Columbia, Swarthmore and M.I.T are among them—the income of its manager is usually substantial.

The big headache in this business is the long-distance negotiations that are necessary to rent a car in Europe and later to bring it over to this country. The customary solution is to work through a major automobile import-export firm, with representatives on both sides of the Atlantic. Once you have found a company that can help you see to it that the Porsche gets to Amsterdam and the Saab gets to Philadelphia, you are ready to go looking for classmates who can afford to rent or buy the Porsche or the Saab.

Your profits in this business usually come out somewhere around four percent of your total sales volume. At M.I.T., for example, the Europe by Car agency netted $2,000 on $50,000 in sales. It won't work everywhere, but where it works, it works nicely.

22. RENT-A-CAR

The domestic equivalent of the Europe by Car agency is the rent-a-car agency. There is no particular evidence that they try harder.

The only college that has mentioned a campus rent-a-car agent to us is St. Edward's University in Austin, Texas. There would seem to be some room for expansion in this line of work. Of course if a car rental service already exists in town, there is no need for one on campus. By the same token, if the nearest agency is 60 miles away, there is no chance for one on campus (unless you happen to own a lot of cars). But in that large middle zone where the nearest rent-a-car is too far for a student to walk but not too far for an agency employee (or you) to drive, there we think a student car rental service would succeed. In return for drumming up business on campus, you would be paid a percentage of the agency's charge to each student you sent them. Of course, you'd have to figure out a way of getting the car to the customer or the customer to the car. But it works at St. Edward's.

23. AIRLINE REPRESENTATIVE

Just about every college has an airline representative. Fortunately, there is more than one airline in the country, so you still have a chance to enter the field.

To become the campus representative of an airline, all you have to do is write the company's main office and offer your services. Your principal responsibilities will be to arrange for advertisements in your school newspaper, sell discount tickets to students under 22 years of age, and give advice on how easy it is to get to———(fill in customer's destination) via———(fill in name of your company). Occasionally you will be asked to do something special, like recruiting classmates for stewardess jobs, or picking up a misplaced piece of baggage at the nearest airport and delivering it to an irate former customer.

Most airlines pay a small salary in addition to commissions on sales. The two together come to around $500 a year. Considering the amount of work you have to do, that's not bad money.

24. RAILROAD REPRESENTATIVE

A few colleges have campus representatives of railroad companies. They do pretty much the same thing as the airline representatives (with special emphasis on student discounts for holiday travel), but they don't do it as much, and they don't get paid much for doing it.

25. MOTORCYCLE RENTAL

Students usually rent cars because they want to get someplace. That is also why they buy airplane tickets, train tickets, and bus tickets. And we have never heard of a student who joined a charter flight just for the hell of it. A nice change from this utilitarian emphasis in the campus transportation business is a motorcycle rental agency. Two students at the University of Connecticut in Storrs, Connecticut, started one last year. Their name gives a good indication of their function; they are "Just For Kicks, Inc."

Just For Kicks owns seven bikes—six Suzukis and a Honda. They are open for business from noon till dusk weekdays, nine till dusk on Saturday and Sunday. Their bikes rent for $3.50 an hour, and most of them are out on the road most of the time, at least on weekends.

This business has more problems than most. For one thing, it is absolutely essential to carry liability insurance, so that if a student is hurt or hurts someone else while riding one of your bikes you are covered. As an additional protection against liability, it pays to incorporate; that way the most you can lose in a lawsuit is the assets of the business. Even after you are fully protected, you will want to take all possible safety precautions. This means showing inexperienced students how to ride the bike, permitting only one person at a time on each vehicle, and refusing to do business with students who show signs of intoxication. It also entails a lot of maintenance and repair work—so if you can't do it yourself make sure there's someone around who can.

Another problem is the likelihood of damage to the bikes, or even outright theft. Our contacts at Connecticut take down the name and address of each customer, and also require a $10 deposit, to be returned when the bike comes back in good condition. A second insurance policy, this one on the motorcycles themselves, is also a good idea.

In compensation for these difficulties, a motorcycle rental agency affords more than the usual ration of pleasure. Your customers are swinging kids out for a good time, so they are good company. In the words of one of Just For Kicks' managers; "The students who rent bikes are all vibrant and young and fun to be with. Nobody could like their customers more than we do." As a fringe benefit, you can take a free motorcycle ride on the job whenever you feel like it.

Starting a motorcycle rental agency requires a good deal of capital. The bikes cost upwards of $200 apiece, and the insurance costs an additional few hundred. It will take you awhile to make that back and start earning a profit, so you shouldn't attempt this business unless you have a few years of school left. Even then, you had better like people and risks, and both you and your classmates had better like motorcycles.

Your college administration is highly unlikely to like motorcycles. At your school this may be enough to kill the project, but the Connecticut enterprise simply went off campus and the administration, we are told, "couldn't do a thing about it."

26. VARIATIONS ON THE THEME

A number of other student businesses involving the rental or servicing of transportation equipment exist on various campuses. The most common is of course the car wash. This is a traditional means of earning money for fraternities and service organizations. It seems to depend on a widespread spirit of charity and togetherness, however, and we have never heard of a student car-washing service which made money on a day-to-day basis. But there's a first time for everything.

Automobile repairs are a much more reliable business venture. If you have the equipment and the know-how to do minor repairs, you need only advertise your name and your service a few times to be deluged with jobs thenceforth and forever—always assuming that there are plenty of students with cars on your campus. Just about your entire gross is profit so you can well afford to charge considerably less than service stations in town and still make a killing.

Utica College in Utica, New York, has an interesting variation on the auto repair racket. A student there operates what he calls a "student car-starting service." It's not quite clear what he does, but he makes money.

Vassar College in Poughkeepsie, New York, is known for its rolling hills and its legions of bicycles (and of course its girls). So popular are the bikes that the college supports a "bicycle exchange." Essentially, the student manager's job is to hold onto the bikes of graduating seniors, then sell them to the new crop of freshmen in the fall. At Vassar the entire purchase price is sent on to the original owner, and the manager collects her salary from the administration. But the business could just as well be run on a service-charge basis, similar to a book exchange, without administration support. Alternatively, the bicycles could be bought outright and sold at a profit in the fall.

Bicycle rentals can also earn good money on a campus where bikes are popular. A collection of second-hand bicycles costs a lot less than motorcycles, and you don't need any insurance. Students will rent them for picnics and pleasure rides of all sorts.

A student at Reed College in Portland, Oregon, noting the popularity of bicycles on his campus, decided to start a repair service for them. If you know or can learn how to fix bikes, you might try the same thing.

Princeton University has had a canoe rental agency since 1962. Students may rent the canoes by the hour or the day, for use on picnics or trips, for exercise, or for getting a front-row view of the Princeton crew races.

In 1958, an imaginative Princeton sophomore opened a new transportation agency, known as the Princeton Livery Service. For $5 an hour, students or alumni could rent his horse, buggy, and driver, and take a leisurely tour of the campus and environs. The carriage and formal attire were turn-of-the-century models; the horse was reputed to be nearly as old. Throughout its experience, the livery service was booked solid on weekends. Its originator has long since graduated, but the idea is still good, and waits patiently for an ambitious student somewhere to revive it.

A student at Ohio University in Athens, Ohio, has purchased several house trailers, and rents them out to classmates for use on weekends, during holidays, and sometimes in the middle of the school week as well.

27. PARKING

At large colleges and universities, where visitors hit the campus by the thousands for football games and homecoming weekends, few student businesses are as lucrative as a parking agency.

The job of a parking squad (as the agency is usually called) may actually involve parking the cars, but usually it means no more than collecting the parking fee and pointing the way to the nearest space.

At many big schools the administration manages the parking concession itself. This means that some unfortunate administrator must spend hours advertising for student employees, seeing that they get to the right parking lots at the right times, paying them, and so on. Schools which arrange to award the parking concession to one student, and let him do the advertising, seeing, and paying, are usually much happier about the deal. If your college is still using the former method, you might try being the first on your block to suggest the latter instead.

Campus parking fees for special events are rarely less than 50 cents, and can go up as high as $3. The average is about a dollar. If 5,000 cars converge on your campus to park, your gross will be $5,000. Of course the administration will take the giant share of that; after all, it's their football game or homecoming, and their parking lots. Still, they can well afford to give you 5 percent of the take, which in our hypothetical example comes out to $250. After paying your student employees for their day's work, you should have about $125 left. All you will need to net $1,000 a year is eight big campus events.

28. CATERING

This section really should have been entitled "Almost Catering," for the genuine whole-hog student caterer, equipped to prepare, transport, and serve an entire banquet, is a rare bird. Not an extinct one, however. The University of Texas at Austin has a full-scale student catering service, which handles banquets, dinners and parties off campus as well as on. This is a very time-consuming enterprise, nearly as complicated as managing a restaurant, and we would not recommend it to the student who wants a good financial return on a part-time commitment.

Far less difficult (and far more common) is the student "catering" agency which really does no more than serve the food and clean up afterwards. No special skills or capital investment is necessary to start such an agency. Simply round up a few classmates who look like they won't drop too many plates, offer them two bucks an hour for their help, and start looking for customers. The college administration itself is the biggest customer at small schools like Luther College in Decorah, Iowa. At somewhat larger institutions, campus organizations also have frequent need for this sort of service. Your fee for "catering" an event should be enough to permit you to pay your employees and still have $20 left for yourself. Once your agency gets a reputation for doing a good job, you ought to be working nearly every weekend. With luck, you can net up to $1,000 for the year.

Midway between a genuine caterer and the sort described in the above paragraph is the "party rep." This is a student who not only serves the food for a party or banquet, but also orders it and makes sure that it gets delivered. The procedure here is to approach the person in charge of an up-coming social event well in advance, and offer your services. He tells you his budget and the sort of food he wants, and you take it from there. Working through delicatessens, grocery stores, restaurants and even professional caterers, you work out a menu that is within his price range. Your fee for the job should be between 15 and 20 percent of the cost of the food. This covers ordering and delivery; if a sit-down dinner is planned and you are asked to do the serving and cleaning up, an extra fee should be charged.

If your campus has a large number of parties, banquets and similar social events, you should be able to parlay an agency of this sort into a highly profitable enterprise. Your customer list should pyramid nicely, since the more customers you get the greater discount you can demand in your food purchases, and therefore the better menu you can offer for the price. Before long you will be able to assure prospective customers that they can get more for their money through you than they could on their own—even with your 20 percent commission. The average delicatessen-style feast for 50 people runs to about $125, which means $30 for you, plus your fee for serving the meal if they want it served. You should have no trouble earning $50 a week throughout the school year.

29. VARIATIONS ON THE THEME

Affairs large enough to be catered are usually large enough to require a variety of other services as well. Any or all of these can be supplied as part of a catering agency or party rep business; some of them are remunerative enough to be made the basis for independent agencies.

We have already discusssed parking concessions for football games and other giant campus events. It hardly pays to set up a parking agency specifically for parties of 50 or 60 people, but such parties often could use a few students to park cars or to direct traffic in the parking lot. Either a parking agency or a catering agency could handle this chore as a sideline.

Once the guests have arrived a coat checking service is often required. Generally this is managed by the catering agency, but it needn't be. The University of Pennsylvania, for example, reports a group of students who earn substantial incomes through this service alone. They work not only at parties, but also at plays, concerts, and other events where catering is not required, but coat checking is. Customarily, the manager is paid by the organization which hires him, while his employees receive their payment in the form of tips. If tipping is not permitted or not customary on certain occasions, the manager must pay his employees, and must therefore charge his customers more.

Another supplementary service which catering agencies may offer is bartending. Since this requires more skill and often more men than coat checking or car parking, it is very often organized as an agency in its own right. A bartending service is not limited to dinners; it can also work cocktail parties, fraternity dances, and so forth. Your college administration undoubtedly gives a number of small cocktail parties for visiting dignitaries and the like, and it will be among your biggest customers. So will campus clubs, organizations in town, and even individual faculty members and townies when they plan a large party.

To organize a bartending agency, you must find a group of students who know how to tend bar. At many schools this is no problem. At some, it may be nearly impossible, and you will have to get hold of a few good books on mixing drinks and teach your men their business—after you learn it yourself. Your bartenders should wear a distinctive jacket of some sort. You may purchase these for them or require that they do so; in either case, the responsibility for laundering them is theirs.

For most affairs, all you will need is your men and their jackets. Some customers however, will want you to come equipped with the necessary glasses, openers, and other paraphernalia, and some might even want to give you the responsibility for buying the liquor and mixers. If so, so much the better. You can buy everything wholesale, and double your profit.

Dartmouth College in Hanover, New Hampshire, and Cornell University in Ithaca, New York, are among the schools which have independent student bartending agencies. If liquor is permitted on your campus, a bartending agency is bound to gross more than $2,000. Your profit should come to roughly half that amount.

30. BOOKING AGENCY

Fraternities, sororities, student organizations, faculty and community groups, and even college administrations often find themselves in need of a student combo, dance band, or entertainer of one sort or another.

A student booking agency does not make book on their chances of finding what they want. Instead, it finds it for them.

College booking agencies come in all sorts and sizes. Most of them concentrate on supplying campus and community groups with student bands. Others include a wide assortment of student entertainers, including magicians and puppeteers for children's parties. A few work through professional talent agencies and booking services to furnish big-name performers for important campus social events. In Chapter Six we will discuss an agency at Brigham Young University in Provo, Utah, which does all of these, and much more, handling nearly all the college and high school entertainment booking in the Southwest.

A campus booking service may operate in one of two ways. Either you act as an agent for several campus entertainment groups, finding them as many gigs as you can, or you work on behalf of organizations which frequently need entertainers, providing them with what they want when they want it. The distinction is tenuous. The former situation does not prevent you from having steady customers, nor does the latter arrangement rule out using the same entertainment groups many times. But the difference is important in determining where you make your money. If you consider yourself a talent agent for performers, you collect your 10 percent from them; if you view your service as a booking agency for organizations, you bill them for your time and effort. It is not considered kosher to do both.

In practice, however, it is often difficult to tell which function you are filling. If a fraternity agrees to pay you $100 for a three-piece combo for the evening, it hardly matters whether you take out $10 and pay your performers $30 apiece, or hand them the full $100 and ask for $10 back.

As a rule, it is better to establish yourself as a free-lance booking agent for organizations. This enables you to call on whatever entertainers you need to meet the particular demands of your clients. It also lets you branch out into related services, such as booking a big-name professional, hiring a hall, renting whatever equipment is needed, and even catering a dinner-dance. For all your services you should render one itemized bill to your client.

A booking agency can go further still. College Forum Enterprises at Ohio University in Athens, Ohio, frequently takes charge of all aspects of an evening's entertainment on behalf of a campus organization. They will not only hire the entertainers, they will also see to the printing and distribution of tickets, handle the publicity, and so on. From here it is only a short step to producing your *own* entertainment. We will talk about this business in the next section.

If your college has only a few student combos and only a few organizations that ever hire them—and the two groups already know about each other—then there is no good reason to start a booking agency. Like all businesses which function as a middleman, a student booking agency flourishes best on a large, loose-knit campus. Talk to the presidents of a few fraternities and other clubs, and ask them whether they usually have much trouble finding the sort of entertainment they want. If the answer is yes, you've got yourself a business. On some campuses booking agents provide entertainment for a dozen fraternities each weekend, in addition to supplying other organizations from time to time during the year. Their annual profits frequently exceed $2,000.

31. PARTIES AND SUCH

Student entrepreneurs supply entertainment for social events. They also supply catering, car parking, coat checking, and a raft of other services. It is surprising that they so rarely think to run an event themselves, and collect their profits directly from classmates who come to have fun.

Campus organizations woke up long ago to the money-making

potential of a well-run social event. A successful dance on a large campus can easily net $3,000 or $4,000; all it needs is good entertainment, good food, good publicity, and good luck. A feature movie earns less, but it is easier and a great deal safer. There are hundreds of companies that rent out first-rate movies of five or ten years ago for a fee of $100 or less. The college will probably lend you a suitable room and a movie projector and screen. Use posters and newspaper ads to publicize the event, sell tickets in advance and at the door, and count your profits during the second reel. You can even sell candy and popcorn in the lobby if you like.

Several large colleges and universities have agencies that bring big-name entertainment talent to the campus at their own expense, publicize the event themselves, and hope to earn a profit from ticket sales. This is a dangerous business, but potentially a very profitable one. If you have a knack for gauging public demand at your school, you can easily net $2,000 in a single evening this way. If your knack goes bad, you can just as easily lose $2,000, and watch the Warsaw Symphony Orchestra or Johnny Mathis play to an empty auditorium.

The list of potential one-time entertainment money-makers is endless. Bridal shows, carnivals, variety shows, mother-daughter or father-son banquets, hootenannies, scavenger hunts, and hundreds more have been used to earn profits for organizations on various campuses. An individual student businessman should be able to do the job just as well.

32. CLOTHING RENTAL

Every now and then a banquet, dance or party comes along which requires students to put on the dog. The invitation may read "black tie requested" or "formal dresss" or whatever euphemism is popular on your campus. Whatever it reads, its meaning is clear: men who want to come have to go out and get themselves a tux, and the women they invite need a long gown.

There are campuses where formal affairs are so common that a tuxedo or a long gown is an essential part of every student's wardrobe. There are campuses where formal affairs are non-existent, tuxes and long gowns unheard of. But most campuses are squarely in the middle; students occasionally have need for formal clothes, but the need is too infrequent to justify buying them. This is where a rental service is bound to succeed.

Tuxedo rental agencies already exist at most colleges. Unfortunately, it is rarely students who are running them. For some reason, the tux rental business has been left almost entirely to the local clothing stores, who are perfectly glad to have it. This is perhaps inevitable at schools where the town store actually has its own complete stock of tuxes for hire. But in the vast majority of college towns, the local clothing store takes orders and measurements a few days in advance, then sends to the nearest big city for the tuxedos. If they can do it, so can you.

All you have to do is get in touch with a large clothing rental agency in the nearest city. They will tell you what measurements they need, how far in advance to order, and how much each tux will cost you. Then get yourself a tape measure, put a few ads in the school newspaper, and you're in business. Charge each student a few dollars more than you pay, and you should be able to earn $300 or $400 per formal dance. To the best of our knowledge, Rochester Institute of Technology in Rochester, New York, is the only school where students regularly run their own tuxedo rental service. Considering how ridiculously easy the business is to manage, there should be similar agencies at every college.

Rental of formal gowns for coeds is a trickier business. For one thing, female students are likely to be attending formals on other campuses, which makes rental a little harder. For another, there are only a couple of different kinds of tuxes, but *every* gown is different—and women care about the differences. Most important, many college girls look on a formal dance as a good excuse to buy a gown; as likely as not, they would resent a gown rental service for removing the necessity to do so. Despite all this, professional gown rental agencies do exist, and a campus version might do all right at some schools.

Formal wear is the most obvious example of a clothing item students often need and rarely possess, but it is not the only example. If costume parties or amateur theatrics are popular on your campus, you should consider starting a costume rental service. If school tradition requires freshmen to wear a certain article of clothing for the first few months, you might try renting that. Give some thought to the specialized clothing needs of your campus, and see what you come up with.

33. COMPUTER DATING

The computer dating business is a newcomer to the college campus, but it is already one of the biggest money-makers around. To run such a service on your own, you have to know something about computer card punching and sorting. But even a technical ignoramus can get a job as a campus representative for one of the multi-campus computer dating services. These services require students to fill out a questionnaire about themselves and their "ideal date," and send this information to a central office with their payment. Several months later, they receive in the mail a list of "matched" date prospects in their area. The job of campus rep is simply to publicize the venture and distribute question-naires. In return for this, he receives a percentage of all fees collected from his college.

If you're interested, simply write one of the giants and give them your name and college. They'll send you all the necessary information and forms. The biggest of the big in this game is "Operation Match," a major business enterprise originally started as a joke by a few Harvard University students. We will talk further about Operation Match in Chapter Six.

34. ROOMS

All this dancing and dating and entertaining raises a special problem for the student at a men's or women's college: once he or she has invited somebody down or up for the weekend, where does he or she quarter him or her? A few kindly college administrations provide inexpensive rooms for weekend dates, and a select few even provide enough rooms to go around. But by and large it is up to the individual student to search out and pay for a room for his guest. Of course if your town has a plentiful supply of clean, cheap, convenient hotels, this presents no problem; but if your town has a plentiful supply of clean, cheap, convenient hotels, it's the only town in the country that does. Usually, the choice boils down to getting a room at an expensive hotel, or spending three days in search of a reasonable rooming house not too far from the campus.

On the other side of the coin, consider the predicament of poor Miss Priss, a sweet old lady with an upstairs room she'd just love to rent out on weekends. She's only eight blocks from the campus, but she can't very well go hawking her room from door to door, and she doesn't know any students. The result: while dozens of students have to settle for a room across town or an expensive hotel, Miss Priss's upstairs room goes untenanted.

A student rooming agency solves all these problems. At the beginning of the school year, canvas the entire area around the campus in search of homeowners with empty rooms they'd like to rent to students' dates on weekends. Also place an ad in the town newspaper asking people with available rooms to get in touch with you. Interview each landlord or landlady to be sure the rooms meet minimum standards. For each room that does, fill out an index card with the name, address and phone number of the owner, the number of beds in the room, the price per night and per weekend, and any other relevant facts (private door? private bath? curfews?). Each landlord should agree to pay you 10 percent of the money he collects through your agency.

Once all this has been arranged, advertise your service on campus. Establish one evening each week when you will hold "office hours," doling out rooms on a first-come, first-served basis. The student pays the landlord for the room; you keep a record and collect what is due you each month.

If rooms are very scarce in your town, you may want to reverse the procedure. Offer your service to landlords free of charge, and collect your service fee from your classmates.

Either way, a rooming agency should bring you between 50 cents and $1.00 per room per weekend. With 50 rooms on your list, that averages out to $37.50 a week. And once your list has been compiled, the job is easy, requiring only one night a week for room distribution and one day a month for bill collection. We know of eleven schools at which successful student rooming agencies are now operating. There should be one at every all-male or all-female college with a rooming problem, which means just about every all-male and every all-female college.

Arranging special hotel rates for students over vacations is a potentially profitable sideline to the room business—but it is also potentially dangerous. Several years ago a Harvard student worked out an arrangement with the Hotel Commodore in New York City for student-rate rooms over the Thanksgiving vacation. At his own expense, he printed 15,000 circulars advertising the deal, and had them distributed at all the Ivy League colleges. He received only one reply, and that from an Amherst College student. His total loss on the project was $2,500.

35. NECKER CHECKER

At coed colleges the big problem is not rooms for visiting dates, but behavior of resident dates. According to *Newsweek* magazine, Hunter College in the Bronx, New York, is rumored to employ a "necker checker," whose job it is to patrol campus lawns and benches with an 18-inch ruler. Couples closer together than that get whacked with the ruler, and bare toes lying in the grass without shoes get stepped on. The job is probably apocryphal, and if it exists it no doubt goes to someone like Miss Priss, not to a student. But if you're really hard up for money, you might give it a try.

Similar services on other campuses will be discussed when we come to skilled work in Chapter Five.

36. POOL HALL

At Upsala College in East Orange, New Jersey, the boy-girl problem is apparently less critical. It is kept successfully under control by the existence on campus of a pool hall, operated for profit by one of Upsala's fraternities. If you can borrow a room and rent or buy the tables and equipment, perhaps you too can earn money from your classmates while earning the gratitude of your administration for concentrating the male student's attention on the holes on the table.

37. FURNITURE EXCHANGE

Princeton University in Princeton, New Jersey, Vassar College in Poughkeepsie, New York, and Wellesley College in Wellesley, Massachusetts, have at least two things in common. All three are Ivy League or Seven Sisters schools, and all three have student furniture exchange agencies.

The business involves nothing more than the purchase of used furniture from graduating seniors in the spring, and the sale of same to incoming freshmen in the fall. It is highly profitable, and bound to succeed on nearly any campus.

The first problem to be met is financing. You will have to pay out a great deal of money the first year to build up the stock which will bring you your profits the second year. Your college administration may be willing to advance you the money, if you can convince them of the merit of your scheme. Alternatively, they may put in a good word for you at a local bank, which will then arrange a standard commercial bank loan for you. If neither of these methods works, you will just have to risk your own money, or find a few wealthier classmates willing to invest in your plan. It hardly pays to go into the furniture exchange business if you can't build up a stock worth at least $500, and for top profits you'll have to purchase several thousand dollars' worth of furniture.

Your next difficulty will be storage space. Again, your administration may be willing to lend or lease you a basement somewhere. If not, it shouldn't cost much to rent an unused garage in town.

Once you have solved these two problems, the rest should be easy. Very few graduating seniors want to lug their moth-eaten sofas, thread-bare rugs, and scratched-up desks home with them. They want to sell. All you need do is drop in at each senior's room and offer to buy. He's not about to lug the junk around town for purposes of comparison shopping, so there's no need to offer top prices. The very fact that you will take care of hauling the stuff away is worth a good deal to him. For a fairly new armchair you should pay $10, for a beat-up one, $5; lamps, mirrors, and assorted small pieces go for $2 or $3; a good sofa. desk or bed might be valued as high as $20. Don't haggle. If he doesn't like your offer, shrug and walk away. He'll call you back.

Attach a tag to every article you buy. Each tag should include the name and address of the original owner and the price agreed upon. After school lets out, your movers will know to take all articles which are tagged. A separate list of all items bought from a given room should be drawn up, with the price of each noted. One copy of this list goes to the customer to remind him how much money you owe him; the other you retain to check against the furniture you pick up before sending the customer his money.

Once all the moving has been done and your movers have been paid ($3 an hour is an appropriate wage), inventory your stock and send out checks to your original owners. Then go home for the summer.

Be back on campus before the freshmen arrive, and start advertising. Use posters, notices, ads, handouts—the works. Your selling price should be at least double what you paid. It will still be cheaper than commercial used furniture prices. As each freshman visits your warehouse and picks out his furniture, collect his money and attach a tag with his name to each purchase. He may pick it up himself, arrange for someone else to pick it up for him, or pay you something extra to deliver it to his room.

A furniture exchange business requires an unusually great amount of work over a fairly small period of time. Buying and inventorying will take you about three weeks; selling will take another two. During these five weeks you will have time for little else. Your profits after all expenses have been met should come to at least half of your capital investment, more if you mark up some items more than 100 percent. Thus, for example, if you buy $1,000 worth of furniture in the spring, and sell it for $2,500 in the fall, your gross will be $1,500. Roughly $700 of this will be paid out in wages and other expenses; the remaining $800 is your profit.

Do a good deal of thinking and talking before you commit yourself to a furniture exchange agency. Does the college administration furnish incoming students with essentials such as a desk, bed, and bureau? Do many students arrive on campus with furniture of their own? Are off-campus furnished apartments popular at your college? Any of these factors will cut down on your volume of business, and therefore on your profits. Consider them well before starting to buy.

When you do buy, buy carefully. Pay as little as you can, and only buy what you are confident you can resell. Some items do not pay to handle at all. A battered sofa that you couldn't sell for more than $10 is not worth buying at $5 since it will cost you more than the other $5 to move and store it. If worst comes to worst and you're left with a lot of old furniture in the middle of the fall, unload it for whatever you can get—to students if possible, to a junk dealer if not.

There are safer ways to run a furniture exchange agency, if you don't mind accepting smaller profits. Vassar's exchange, for example, is managed by a student, but run by the school administration. Each graduating senior tags her own furniture, marking down the price she wants to sell it at. At the end of the spring term, the dorm janitors deliver the tagged items to the exchange office. Freshmen visit the office in the fall, choose the articles they want, and pay the price marked on the tag. The original owner is mailed the full purchase price, and the administration pays the manager a salary for her work.

The Vassar system could easily be modified to function without the administration's active participation. Movers would still have to be hired to get the furniture to the exchange office, but money could be withheld until the article was sold. The original owner would then be sent 80 percent of the purchase price; the agency manager would keep the other 20 percent as his commission. This method would be far less profitable than the one we outlined above, but it would also be far less dangerous, and probably more pleasing to your administration.

38. HAULING

Seniors have to move out of their rooms. Freshmen have to move into their rooms. Sophomores and juniors often have to move out of one room and into another. All of which means a lot of trunks, crates, armchairs and refrigerators to be lugged across campus.

If you can get hold of a small truck, a few handcarts, and a lot of husky underclassmen, there's money in doing the lugging. Where they exist, student hauling agencies charge something like $12 an hour for a crew of three. That comes out to $3 apiece for each of your movers, plus $3 for you. The procedure is simple. Advertise for advance commitments, then spread your employees all over the campus while the moving is being done to pick up informal jobs where they can.

A somewhat more complex hauling agency has existed for many years at Princeton University. A representative of the agency visits each non-graduating student in the spring, and offers to move his furniture and baggage for him after the term ends. Few students can resist the opportunity to have their goods all set up in their new room when they arrive back on campus in the fall. A tag giving the customer's name and his new room is placed on every article to be moved. The size and difficulty of the job is estimated and a single charge made.

A hauling agency can easily be combined with a furniture exchange service, since both operate at the same time of the year and both employ moving men and equipment. You should charge for the two services separately: "X dollars for the armchair and Y dollars to get it to your room."

39. STORAGE

A student at the University of Chicago operates a trunk and furniture storage service during the summer holidays. This business is ideal for combination with a hauling agency, where one bill can be rendered for picking up, storing and delivering a student's belongings. At some colleges a hauling agency has no choice but to go into the storage business as well. If the dormitories are in use over the summer, it will not be possible to do your moving directly from one room to the other in the spring. Nor will you be permitted to let all the moving wait until fall. Summer storage is the only answer for a hauling agency in this position.

Since a furniture exchange business already has storage space for its own stock, it might just as well go into the storage business, and hence the hauling business too. Princeton's "Express-Reunion Agency" has parlayed these three activities into one of the most profitable student businesses on campus, grossing over $80,000 a year.

Another reasonable supplement to the hauling-storage businesss is the sale of packing materials. Students moving into or out of the college, or from one room to another, badly need boxes, crates, cord, and other packing materials. As long as you're going to do the moving, why not sell them the wherewithal?

40. ADVERTISING

Most campus-directed advertising is done not on behalf of student groups, but on behalf of stores and businesses in town. We will therefore reserve our discussion of student advertising agencies for the next chapter.

We do know of one campus business, however, which made its money solely as an advertising service for students. Run by an undergraduate at Dartmouth College in Hanover, New Hampshire, the business was a weekly classified sheet. The student manager of the agency (known as KIASK) collected money from classmates who wanted to place ads, mimeographed his accumulation each week, and distributed copies on campus. His weekly profit, for a bare minimum of work, was around $12.

41. MONEY-MAKING

Dartmouth's classified ad sheet is an example of a fairly unusual kind of student business, one which makes its money by helping other students to make money. We know of only two other examples.

The first example is a mutual fund sales agency. The idea here is to invest the contributions of fellow students in an assortment of stocks, bonds, and other securities. The manager decides where the money is to be invested, and takes an established percentage as his cut. Each of the other "members" receives a percentage of the fund's annual profits proportional to the amount of money he originally invested. Of course, if there is an annual loss instead of an annual profit, everybody loses money—except the manager. If you are an up-and-coming financial wizard, and can convince your classmates of your financial acumen, this is a good way to earn some money while learning your trade. Several colleges and universities have mutual funds organized along these lines, or as cooperative stock investment clubs. To the best of our knowledge. the one at Harvard University is currently doing best—which seems to refute the maxim that eggheads never prosper in the stock market.

Our second example is a bit harder to imitate, for it depended on outside help for its success. Just before Christmas of 1965, a radio station in St. Paul, Minnesota, sponsored a "cookie contest," offering a money prize for the heaviest Christmas cookie entered in the competition. An enterprising Bethel College student heard the contest announced, and decided to enter. He solicited contributions of one dollar from classmates, on a double or nothing back proposition. With the money collected he baked a two-ton cookie, assembled it on the back of a truck, and drove it to the station. "Naturally he won!" recalls a Bethal administrator. "I am not certain what the profit realized was, but we all had a good time." The student cookie-baker later appeared on national television, on the quiz show "I've Got a Secret." No doubt he won there too.

42. ANSWERING SERVICE

Ten years ago, a student at Princeton University founded a student answering service. The agency installed three telephone lines, and for an annual fee of $5 it received and delivered telephone messages to students who did not have their own phones. The business failed, largely because many students *did* have their own phones, and were willing to take messages for their dormmates for nothing.

On a campus where students are not permitted to have telephones in their rooms, a student answering service could be successful today—if the business could talk the administration into an exception for its own phones. Instead of an annual fee, however, we would suggest a set rate per message. The rate should be fairly low for subscribers, very high for non-subscribers. If you can convince your administration to refer all calls for students to your service, the difference between the rates will soon force every student to become a subscriber.

43. MISCELLANY

An agency at Massachusetts Institute of Technology in Cambridge, Massachusetts, operates a hi-fi equipment rental and exchange service. On a total sales volume of $70,000, the agency nets roughly $4,000 a year.

The Model United Nations organization at the College of the Holy Names in Oakland, California, makes money ironing academic collars just before graduation.

A Dartmouth College student used to operate a speed-reading course for his classmates, guaranteeing to triple the reading speed of any student who took the course. Undergraduates at other schools occasionally serve as campus reps for professional speed reading companies. They advertise the service and explain its value and methods to interested students, receiving a commission on every classmate who signs up.

A student at Swarthmore College in Swarthmore, Pennsylvania, repairs shoes in his room. He has built up a steady clientele of fellow students, who pay him well for his skill.

A typewriter repair service is the part-time business of a student at La Sierra College in Riverside, California. He fixes machines for students and faculty members, and also does a good deal of business with companies and individuals in town.

Princeton University requires a long research paper (thesis) from nearly all undergraduates, and further demands that the theses be bound. A thesis-binding agency has developed on the Princeton campus to meet this need.

At Harvard University, not all students buy refrigerators. Instead, many rent them from Harvard's refrigerator rental agency. The agency earns a substantial profit each year on its stock of old-but-usable refrigerators.

Raffles, wagers, and chain letters are three very common though somewhat frowned-upon collegiate money-makers. Raffles are a favorite way for charities to raise funds, and should be left to charities; when tried as a business proposition they often fail to sell enough tickets to equal the cost of the prize, and therefore lose money. Wagers contribute more than a little to college frivolity, but they are hardly a regular source of profits. (Still, we know of a Princeton student who made nearly $100 betting that he could bicycle to Yale in under 22 hours.) Chain letters frequently skirt and sometimes fail to skirt the borderlines of illegality, but they persist anyway. Some are quite complicated, involving sales of "contracts" to get on the list, and similar devices aimed at legitimizing the procedure.

We will not mention the source of our last two ideas, except to tell you that both come from fairly small, very wealthy colleges. We know of one lad who engages in the work of shoe-breaking, softening the corners of shoes for the tender feet of his more wealthy classmates. He charges $1.00 a pair. A young lady at a nearby exclusive women's college works as a professional trunk packer. Half her fellow students would never be able to leave school for the year if she happened to quit.

Ask yourself what services are needed by students at your college. Then go out and do them, and collect the proceeds.

CHAPTER 4

Ambassadors
Extraordinary

1. BABY-SITTING

Baby-sitting is the high school girl's principal source of extra cash. In many parts of the country, it is an important money-maker for college coeds as well.

Rates are standard and nearly unalterable in any given town, though they vary considerably from area to area. Seventy-five cents to $1 an hour is average for the early evening. Afternoon hours bring between $1 and $1.35, since they usually involve playing with the children as well as sitting with them. Extra charges are usually made for more than two children, for infants, for preparing and serving dinner, or for staying into the wee hours of the morning. Special rates may be established for long-term or regular sitting. A girl at Barat College in Lake Forest, Illinois, for example, charges a new customer $10 for overnight sitting. Regular customers for whom she sits on a scheduled basis get the same service for $6 a night.

The most anyone can expect to earn from baby-sitting is $20 a week—and that's pushing it. Most girls are happy to locate and fit in enough jobs to earn half that amount. The big appeal of baby-sitting is not the money, but the rest and relaxation. Not that a coed would do it for nothing—but there's a special delight in collecting $4 for hanging around all evening doing your home-work between snacks. College administrators approve of baby-sitting work for the same reason. "Having a few uninterrupted hours of study time in a quiet house several nights a week is bound to improve a student's grades," notes one Midwestern dean.

Whatever the reasons for its attractiveness, there is no doubt about the popularity of baby-sitting among college women. Of the 600 girls at Barat College, roughly two hundred baby-sit regularly, and an additional hundred take an occasional shot at it. Several years ago, Bryn Mawr College in Bryn Mawr, Pennsylvania, conducted a survey to gauge the extent of its student baby-sitting business, and found that it produced more than $15,000 annually in student income. Administrators there have little doubt that the figure has increased in recent years, and will continue to increase. Baby-sitting is the single most profitable student business at Barat and Bryn Mawr, and also at nearly every other woman's college we contacted.

Since baby-sitting is a big business, we expected to find it organized like one, but on the vast majority of campuses it is not. A dean at Flint College in Flint, Michigan, told us: "Any of this type of activity (baby-sitting) is done strictly on an informal basis between student and customer. There is not any organization providing central service." His comment reflects the situation, not only at Flint, but also at hundreds of other schools across the country.

Very often, a modicum of organization is imposed on the student baby-sitting business by the college administration. This happens more or less by accident. In the absence of a baby-sitting service, families in need of a sitter wind up calling administration offices, which then feel obligated to do something about the calls. Informal clearing houses begin to emerge, operated through the Dean of Women, the financial aid office, the student employment office, the dormitory office, or whoever seems to get stuck with most of the phone calls.

To be sure, it occasionally happens that these involuntary administrative middlemen face up to the task at hand and begin operating well-organized referral services. In such cases, you should leave well enough alone and look for another business. But as a rule, administration activities of this kind are haphazard and inefficient, operated by a secretary who has better things to do and knows it.

Only once in a while does a student suddenly see the light and organize a baby-sitting agency. It happened at Appalachian State Teachers College in Boone, North Carolina, where a student club took over the chore, earning, as well as money, the heart-felt gratitude of administrative officials. It happened at Chatham College in Pittsburgh, Pennsylvania, where a student-run "baby-sitting bureau" has been in operation for several years. It happened at West Virginia University in Morgantown, West Virginia, where one of the sororities now operates a busy baby-sitting service. And it happened, strangely enough, at all-male Princeton University in Princeton, New Jersey.

Princeton's highly successful "Tiger Tot Tenders" agency proves a point which is often overlooked. Baby-sitting money will buy men as much as women. In a town with a men's college and no women's or coed school, it should be very easy to invade this usually feminine domain. Your only competition will be high school girls and older women in need of work, and both are considered less than ideal as baby-sitters.

Establishing a baby-sitting agency is child's play, baby. Make a list of classmates willing to work, establish hourly rates, and advertise. Faculty families will provide much of your business, but by no means all of it, so be sure to publicize your service in town. As your list of customers starts to grow, it will pay you to set up some system of regular responsibility for your employees. Perhaps you could have five students on call every weekday afternoon, ten every weekday evening, and twenty or more on weekends. Any student could of course be on call more than one day; your purpose is only to insure a minimum number of available sitters at all times. As each request is phoned in to your office, you simply relay the name and address of the customer to one of your on-duty employees.

There are two frequent situations for which special provision should be made. The first comes up when a family requests a sitter on a regular basis, perhaps every Tuesday night. They will want to have the same sitter each time, and this should not be difficult to arrange. A reduced hourly rate is appropriate here; your employee might accept a small cut in his fee for the job, and you should definitely demand a smaller commission. The other situation arises when a special event takes a number of your regular customers away from their children at the same time. Faculty meetings, parties, and big football games are among the occasions which may produce this problem. Particularly if the event occurs in the afternoon, you should capitalize on the situation by offering to take charge of all the children affected. On a sunny day two or three of your employees can keep a large flock of children occupied outdoors, and their parents will be happy to pay a reduced "group rate" for the service.

A baby-sitting agency acts as a middleman, and is of value to both the parents and the baby-sitters. Your commission should therefore be split between the two. The correct proportions could be determined according to local supply and demand. If sitters are scarce, hit the parents for 20 cents an hour and your employees for a nickel. If jobs are in short supply, charge each parent only a nickel an hour, and collect the other 20 cents from the sitters. Whatever the division, your quarter-an-hour commission will soon add up to real money. An agency that supplied sitters to 60 customers a week for an average span of five hours, for example, would be earning a neat $75 a week.

2. VARIATIONS ON THE THEME

The term "baby-sitting" is usually reserved for low-paying, occasional arrangements which call for little more than the mere presence of the sitter as a precaution against possible emergencies. Sometimes a college girl will strike a more permanent bargain with a family to serve as a regular companion to a child or several children. Such jobs are difficult to get and even more difficult to schedule, but they are not impossible. We know of coeds who have contracted to "mind the children" of a busy family every weekday afternoon; others take charge for their clients all weekends or several evenings a week. A few years ago a student in such a position would have been referred to as a nurse, a governess, or a nanny. Today the job is known as "child care."

A baby-sitting agency can and should handle whatever requests of this nature come its way, finding a suitable employee for each job. There is no need for an agency devoted solely to long-term child care assignments. For one thing, the demand is too small; more important, families in search of a "surrogate mother" want to make their own choice. But the possibility of taking a child care job yourself is one you should not overlook. The pay is considerably better than what baby-sitters are used to getting. And the opportunity of coming to know one family intimately can make this "business" one of your most richly rewarding college experiences. It's not for everyone, heaven knows, but if you like to work with children, you will find child care infinitely more satisfying (and more remunerative) than baby-sitting.

There is a tendency for the responsibilities of student child care to begin to stretch to include cooking, housework, and so forth. This is when you cease to be a "nursemaid" and become instead a "mother's helper"—which is another cup of dishwater entirely. We will take up this alternative later in the chapter.

3. TUTORING

Long before children are too old to need a nursemaid, they are old enough to need a tutor. It wasn't always that way. Not too many years ago, only pupils in danger of failing resorted to tutoring, and only high school pupils were ever in danger of failing. Today, the parent of a second-grader with a 'C' in spelling worries that the kid won't get into college, and hires a tutor to help bring that spelling grade up to a 'B,' with a special bonus if Junior pulls an 'A-minus.'

One result of this trend has been an increased laxity in college rules governing off-campus tutoring. A few old-timers like Vassar still require that the tutee have his teacher's permission and the tutor her department head's approval, but by and large high school and primary tutoring is unrestricted.

Another result of the expanded demand for tutors is that service organizations have begun to specialize. Ten years ago most honorary fraternities and the like, if they were engaged in tutoring at all, would take on any pupil who asked. Now most concentrate their efforts in the slums, working with disadvantaged children who are *not* worried about a 'C' in spelling.

This leaves the paying customers for you. Rates vary, depending partly on the age of the child, the extent of his problem, and the experience of the tutor, but mostly on the section of the country. The going price in New York City is $5 an hour. Pittsburgh, Pennsylvania, reports an average fee of $2.50. Two dollars or $3 is about right through most of the South and the Midwest. In the big cities it gets up to around $4, and it goes just a little higher than that in the giant urban areas on the East and West Coasts.

A free-lance tutor has much the same trouble finding jobs as a free-lance baby-sitter. It can be done via student employment offices, academic deans, or department heads, but it's a pretty haphazard business at best. If there is any real demand for paid off-campus tutors, someone should organize a referral service.

Columbia University in New York City has the only profit-making off-campus tutoring agency that we have heard about. Known, sensibly enough, as the Columbia Tutoring Agency, the group serves the entire New York metropolitan area.

A tutoring agency is a bit different from a baby-sitting service, since every job that comes in will be a long-term job. A tutor who has been working with a child for some time will be justifiably reluctant to hand over a percentage of his pay every week, merely because you put him in touch with the kid's parents last year. The parents will be equally unhappy about paying good money to a now-superfluous middleman.

There are two possible solutions to this problem. One is to charge your tutors a single commission for each customer you find for them—$5 would seem about right. This money is due you regardless of whether the contact lasts for two lessons or two years. The other method is to act as the manager of a cooperative enterprise, with each tutor paying you a set percentage of his earnings in return for soliciting new customers, taking phone calls, making appointments. billing, and whatever other chores you can think of to justify your commission. Neither method is wholly satisfactory, though both have been known to work successfully. If you can think of a different approach which would succeed at your school, more power to you. We would not be surprised to learn that tutoring referral services earn less than the individual tutors they employ—but there's nothing to keep you from doing both.

Non-profit tutoring of children from disadvantaged families is one of the most satisfying and worthwhile things a college student can do. Profitable tutoring of children from advantaged families is not the same experience at all. But if you need the money, the demand is certainly there.

4. HOUSEWORK

We have already mentioned the fact that many coeds who thought they were being paid for wrestling with a family's children find themselves wrestling with its pots and pans, its vacuum cleaners and steam irons, its dirty windows and unpolished silver as well.

If that's what you had in mind, fine. You can become a "mother's helper," and learn all about housekeeping in someone else's house. The money isn't very good—usually a dollar an hour or slightly more—and it's hardly entertaining, but it's a job.

Actually, the days when college coeds jumped at a chance to do housework are past. There are too many other opportunities for women today which are better paying, more educational, more fun, and easier. Most college girls would rather take one of these and postpone the drudgery until they get married.

Housework survives as a more-or-less popular money-making alternative for coeds in one form only: the room and board maintenance arrangement. A college coed going to school away from home can often save as much as $1,000 a year by receiving her food and lodging in a private home in return for light housework, cooking, and baby-sitting. At many colleges, these arrangements are supervised by the school administration, which sees to it that the student is not made to work more than 20 or 25 hours a week, that ample time and room for study are provided, that the health conditions and food in the home are adequate, and so forth.

A recent survey at 43 teachers colleges in five Eastern states found that roughly one percent of the students at these colleges participated in home maintenance arrangements. Nearly all of them were girls, and most were freshmen. The majority of the students interviewed said they didn't mind the work and appreciated the quiet study atmosphere of a private home, but many felt unhappy about missing out on the "collegiate experience." The disadvantages of this "business" are as apparent as its benefits, each student must decide for herself which factors weigh most heavily.

5. YARDWORK AND HEAVY HOUSEWORK

Mowing lawns, gardening, heavy housework, and the like offer male students a much more substantial source of income than light housework provides for coeds. For one thing, heavy work pays better, often as much as $2 an hour. For another, men are permitted to be more aggressive. We know a graduate student at Michigan State University who spends his free time wandering through wealthy neighborhoods near the campus until he spies a home where the lawn needs attention. Then he simply knocks on the front door and offers to attend to it. In addition to numerous one-time jobs, this approach has led to regular, scheduled arrangements with many homeowners. His income from mowing lawns, he claims, amounts to more than his graduate assistantship at the university.

There is even a masculine counterpart to the coed's maintenance arrangement—though it is a good deal less common. Each year, five students from the Los Angeles area are given room and board in a giant Bel Air neo-Tudor mansion (five acres; thirteen bathrooms) in return for occasional work on the estate as gardeners, window-washers, car-attendants, watchmen, and butlers. Exulted one lucky freshman from San Fernando Valley State College: "I knew college would be a new experience, but I never expected this!"

6. VARIATIONS ON THE THEME

Students have been known to offer a tremendous variety of additional home services to local residents. But many of these, such as car-washing, butlering, and chauffeuring, are not sufficiently in demand to support an independent agency.

Among the home services which *are* popular enough, catering is probably the most common. The University of Texas at Austin has a full-fledged student catering agency, capable of preparing, transporting, and serving a complete banquet. A less ambitious but equally profitable enterprise is the Harvard University catering agency. Though it will supply butlers and waiters for affairs of any size, the Harvard enterprise limits its food preparation to hors d'oeuvres. Despite this restriction, a large number of Back Bay hostesses are delighted to have their guests served by Harvard men, and pay well for the privilege.

Another popular home service is bartending. Dartmouth College in Hanover, New Hampshire, and Columbia University in New York City are among the schools which have student bartending agencies operating off campus. The Columbia agency goes so far as to offer a free course in bartending techniques. Graduates of the course are paid $2.50 an hour for tending bar; the managers spend their time soliciting engagements, and receive substantial commissions for their work.

House-painting agencies are somewhat less common, but they earn good money on several college campuses, and could do as well on many others. Harvard has the largest agency of this sort, handling both interior and exterior painting, paper-hanging, masonry work, and some carpentry. The business operates in the summer as well as during the school year, and pays out more than $80,000 a year to students.

7. ODD JOB AGENCY

The big problem with all home services, from housework to house-painting, cooking to car-washing, is finding your customers. Most local residents do not need student help on a regular basis, yet several times a year many of them run across a chore they'd like to hire a student to do—if they only knew where to get in touch with one. The best solution to this difficulty is a student odd job service. Swarthmore College in Swarthmore, Pennsylvania, has one, known as the Student Employment Service. It is the only college we know of that does.

Your principal responsibility as manager of such an agency will be to solicit jobs from town residents. You might put an advertisement in the local newspaper, or distribute handouts, or hang a few posters in strategic locations, but the cheapest and most effective way to start an odd job agency is by telephone. Simply call every homeowner in the neighborhood of the college and explain who you are and what you are doing. Point out that you can supply students for a wide variety of household chores, and ask each customer to keep you in mind next time he needs to have his windows washed, his garden weeded, or his fence painted. Suggest that your potential customers write down your name and phone number where they will be able to find it when a suitable job comes up; they will be surprised how often that is—and so will you. Each time a request for help is phoned or mailed to you, find a student to do the job. Before long you will have a good list of reliable student workers, and a much longer list of steady customers in the community.

You should agree on an appropriate hourly wage with your customer in advance. Have the customer pay the student worker, who in turn will hand over 20 percent of his wages to you. This 20 percent figure is not unreasonable, since it is your efforts that will keep your workers supplied with jobs.

At present, most college administrations act as a referral service for odd jobs. This is not only a nuisance for them; it is also woefully inefficient. Since administrators are in no position (and have no time) to solicit odd jobs from townspeople, the volume of student odd-job work is not nearly as great as it should be. Contact your school's employment office and tell them about your plan to start an odd job agency. They should be very enthusiastic about its potential, and may even supply you with an office and a telephone. In any case, your dormitory room will do for an office, and if you don't have a phone, you can operate the whole business by mail. However you work it, an odd job agency is a good bet to succeed in just about any college community.

8. CURB-NUMBERING

A student at the University of Illinois at Urbana has come up with an original and highly profitable business idea which could easily be copied in other college towns. It is a home service—but hardly one which a homeowner would be likely to think of for himself.

The business is a curb-numbering service. The first step was to hire a number of classmates, equip them with brushes and outdoor luminescent paint, and instruct them to walk through the streets of Urbana's residential areas, painting the correct street numbers on the curbs in front of houses. Then, several days later, the manager did the rounds. He knocked at the door of each house, informed the owners of what he had done, and collected "donations." The business operated for 18 weeks, and netted this inventive entrepreneur nearly $2,000.

It is a rare homeowner who would not appreciate the convenience of having his street number clearly marked on the curb in front of his door. Few would think of doing it for themselves, but when an entire street has been done, most are both amused and grateful. Many are happy to show their amusement and gratitude with a small contribution.

The local police department, however, may not be amused or grateful. Be sure to check with them before you start.

9. ADVERTISING

A home service business may be the most obvious way of making money from the community which surrounds your college, but it is by no means the only way. A fair number of student agencies on various campuses have been organized to provide one or another service to the local *business* community.

One of the most profitable ways of helping a local merchant is through his advertising. We have already talked about desk blotters, telephone directories, discount coupon books, and several other business possibilities which afford local tradesmen an excellent campus advertising medium, while providing something of value to students as well. We come now to a different sort of advertising business, one which provides a service only to the merchant, not particularly to his customers.

The simplest case of this sort of business is the student advertising representative. More than one undergraduate has managed to convince a group of small local tradesmen that he would do a good job handling their modest advertising budgets. Several years ago a student at the University of Pennsylvania accumulated six such clients, each paying him a moderate commission for planning and inserting their ads, both on campus and off.

For many merchants near your college, the greatest single advertising problem is the college itself. Particularly at schools where the college newspaper appears infrequently or is not read by the majority of students, local businessmen may have great trouble finding a way to reach the student market. A campus-oriented advertising agency can help them out.

Massachusetts Institute of Technology recently organized such an agency. Known as "Advertising Design," the group plans advertising campaigns, prepares brochures, handouts, and ads of all sorts, and works out promotional stunts for its clients. The agency is still in its organizational stages (it netted only $200 last year), but it expects to expand greatly in the next few years.

Meanwhile, a student at Northeast Louisiana State College in Monroe, Louisiana, has already discovered an advertising gimmick with fantastic profit potential. For $40 he purchased a broken-down, battered hearse from a nearby funeral home. A do-it-yourself car wash and a three-dollar battery put the limousine in shape for business. He marked off the surface of the car into fifteen available areas, then sold advertising space for up to $15 per area per month. The ads were painted on with shoe polish, and nearly all were based on themes connected with the hearse. Examples are: "Had to Use This Because I Didn't Buy from Medical Arts Pharmacy"; "You Will Not Need This If You Eat at Ray's"; "You Are Dead Right at. . . ." And so on.

The advantages of the Hearse Advertising Company were immediately clear to local tradesmen. Complicated college regulations governing on-campus advertising did not apply to the hearse, which was private property. And since it was registered as its owner's official business car, it could be parked anywhere on campus. The novelty of the vehicle added to the cleverness of the ads written on it, guaranteed that every passer-by would take a look. By moving the hearse from place to place a few times a day, the agency also guaranteed that nearly every student would be a passer-by nearly every day. These factors, combined with low monthly rates, made the hearse a uniquely desirable advertising medium. In a very short time the agency had to invest in a second limousine, this one for $25.

The Hearse Stunt Company was formed to take the cars where the crowds were—pep rallies, ball games, even drag strips. Dressing up as monsters, a student group known as "The Undertakers" won a local drag race in the agency's 1953 Cadillac hearse. The act was so successful that the group has since contracted the stunt to other drag strips. With a few modifications, it served as an ideal promotional gimmick for drive-in theaters featuring horror movies.

But even without these sidelines, a hearse advertising agency should net a few thousand dollars a year on just about any college campus. Fifteen dollars a month per ad is a very low figure for this unique mobile billboard; in most parts of the country you could get $20 or $25 without much difficulty. Fifteen ads at $20 a month comes to $300 a month—for each hearse. With two cars in operation, you can clean up $600 a month, minus the cost of shoepolish. Even for a hearse, that's quite a killing.

10. PUBLIC RELATIONS

A close relative of advertising is public relations. But unlike advertising, PR work is generally considered a highly technical, professional activity, well beyond the competence of college students. Two undergraduates at Brown University in Providence, Rhode Island, disagree. They have formed a PR firm which they call Community Relations Associates, and they already have half a dozen clients, including two suburban police departments and a labor union. Their efforts on behalf of one of the police departments were sufficiently extensive to attract the attention of the Providence *Journal,* which published a story on the cops' attempt to project a less fuzzy image. Naturally the agency has done well financially, and the outlook for the future is good: It will never run out of police departments with unflattering reputations. If you're good at projecting images (we never got past shadow bunnies ourselves), you might give this unique student business idea a try.

11. PROMOTION

One very promising way in which college students can serve local tradesmen is by devising and running promotion campaigns. The possible range of promotional stunts is limitless, running the gamut from conventional contests and give-aways to outlandish mysteries, ceremonies and the like.

One of the simplest and most common forms of promotion is the exhibit. Banks, hotels and similar institutions often like to arrange various displays to attract the attention of customers and passers-by. Normally, these displays are conceived and set up by a regular employee of the institution, but college students have been known to take over the chore simply by offering. Government agencies and large industrial concerns will be more than willing to supply you with exhibit materials, and you can supplement these by borrowing from your college. Anything from a famous local author to recent research in the geology department can serve as the basis for a display. Your fee for each exhibit will depend on how long it is to be on display, but $30 would not be an unreasonable estimate.

Another common promotional gimmick is the premium ticket. Suppose a local movie theater has trouble attracting customers for weekday matinees. You offer to try to unload large numbers of tickets at a discount rate. Once your offer has been accepted, approach a shopping center, a new supermarket, a car dealer who is scheduling a "grand opening," or some other merchant, and convince him to use your movie tickets as a premium. The merchant buys the blocks of tickets to give away to new customers, customers purchasing more than a certain amount, or whatever. You collect your commission from the movie theater.

Premiums and exhibits are established, run-of-the-mill promotional methods. To gain a local reputation as a genius in this line, you will have to think of some gimmicks which are a bit more unusual. Don't try to sell your ideas until you have a few, but once you come up with something you think would sell a lot of shoes or jewelry or flowers, bring it to a few merchants and see what they think. After one or two resounding successes, you will have no trouble talking other local businessmen into utilizing your service. Your fee in each case should be roughly 20 percent of the total budget for the promotion.

Imagination and time are two commodities that college students usually have more of than local merchants. Advertising promotion is one of the very best ways to turn these commodities into cash.

12. INFORMATION GATHERING

One of the most successful student agencies aimed at helping businessmen is Harvard University's Information Gathering Service. Started in 1964, IGS already has an annual payroll of over $100,000, and has done work for the Xerox Corporation and the First National Bank of Boston, as well as many smaller companies.

As its name implies, IGS collects information of various sorts for its clients. Its jobs have ranged from testing the marketability of a new product to researching a company president's speeches. Its techniques have ranged from personal interviews to questionnaires to library research to computer analyses. With the help of foreign students at Harvard, IGS also operates a translation service in 35 languages.

The service is ideal both for students and for their customers. Underclassmen are hired by the hour (and by the hundreds) to handle the routine side of the operation; upperclassmen oversee each project and write the reports. Companies pay anything from $6 to $12 a man-hour for IGS help. Considering what they will be paying the same people for the same work after graduation, it's cheap at the price. Meanwhile, the managers can afford to pay wages as high as $5 an hour, and still pocket a tidy profit for themselves.

13. PROTEST

Last spring three George Washington University students founded a unique service agency, and dubbed it "Proxy Pickets." For as little as $17, the group will put five sign-carrying protesters in front of the White House for an hour—for any cause. A mere

$79 will set 25 students marching, $154 will buy you a crowd of at least 50, and "larger demonstrations and additional services" are available on request. GWU is located in Washington, D.C.; we doubt whether a free-lance protest business would fare as well in Oshkosh or Albuquerque—but you could always try.

14. LANDSCAPING

A student at Flint College of the University of Michigan operates a somewhat more practical business. Known as "Jack's Lawn and Landscaping," the company specializes in sod laying. It earned a net profit of nearly $10,000 last year.

The enterprise started when the student got a job mowing lawns for a building company. He went on to sod work and, once he had learned the necessary skills, decided to go into business for himself. He now owns his own tractor and other equipment, and does finished grading and landscaping as well as sod-laying. He bids for major jobs, advertises for smaller ones, and hires other students on a full or part-time basis as he needs them.

In essence, the business is simple. The manager buys his sod for roughly 65 cents to 75 cents a yard, contracts with builders, lays the sod, and collects his profit. But there is nothing simple about a $14,000 contract to landscape a new apartment building. Whatever it is in essence, the business is highly complex in operation. It involves legal problems, purchasing problems, insurance problems, salesmanship problems, and all the myriad of other headaches that give businessmen ulcers. But when the headaches are gone, $9,000 a year is left in the bank. That goes a long way toward relieving the ulcers.

The Flint landscaping agency is of particular interest because it illustrates a crucial point about off-campus student businesses. With rare exception, they are outgrowths of a common, routine, run-of-the-mill student job. They develop because some student just wasn't satisfied with the common, the routine, and the run-of-the-mill.

Roughly one-third of all working students hold off-campus jobs. This is fine; jobs are certainly more secure than independent businesses, and many jobs are rewarding, exciting, and reasonably well-paying. But turning a job into a successful business, as our sod-laying friend from Michigan did, can mean greater rewards, more excitement, and higher profits. If you have the ambition and courage to make the switch, look around a bit for a job that could become a business. With a little imagination, you will discover hundreds. We will give just a few more examples here, to illustrate the variety of salaried jobs that are capable of undergoing this metamorphosis.

15. SECRETARIAL WORK

College coeds who are proficient at typing and shorthand frequently seek part-time jobs as secretaries for local business concerns. More often than not, because of their inability to work a full day, they have great trouble finding regular secretarial positions. Most have to settle for occasional part-time work—and the occasions are few and far between, depending on a company's overload coinciding with a girl's schedule.

The business department of Bany College in Miami, Florida, has solved this problem for its students, by operating a secretarial pool for local businesses. Girls sign up for the hours and days they are free to work, and nearby businessmen call the department office when they need extra help. The result is more work for the students, and more help for the businessmen.

The Bany program works like a collegiate version of professional secretarial employment agencies such as Office Help Temporaries. It would be a simple matter for qualified students at any college to organize a similar service, with or without administration help. All you need to do is inform local companies that the college is now ready to supply competent part-time office help of all sorts, by the hour, the day, or the week. Screen your girls to make sure they *are* competent, and before long you should have a monopoly on all the part-time secretarial work in town. If you are running the agency yourself, assess each girl 10 percent of her wages as your commission. A more convenient approach might be to set up the service as a cooperative enterprise, with each would-be secretary taking her turn at the telephone, running the agency. In either case, a student secretarial pool is a very practical way to turn an unsatisfactory part-time job into a highly satisfactory part-time business.

A similar agency could be established to do typing for local businessmen. The difference between a typing service and a secretarial pool is that free-lance typists do not work at the office of their employers. They pick up the material to be typed, do the work in their own rooms, deliver the finished product, and collect their fee. A typing agency can be run on a commission basis, or as a cooperative with the typists themselves taking turns running the business.

In Chapter Three we described a typing agency aimed at student customers. There is no reason why the two businesses should not be combined. Faculty members with a book or a research paper to be typed comprise a third potential source of work. Put the three together and you will have a service of value to the entire college community. You are bound to wind up with more business than you know what to do with.

Even an individual student can turn her proficiency in shorthand and typing into a business venture, by becoming a public stenographer. A public stenographer is, appropriately enough, a stenographer who is available to the public. There is seldom enough demand for one in a small town, but in any good-sized city you should do nicely if you can get yourself a desk in the lobby of a hotel or large office building. We know of one coed who arranged with a hotel manager to help with his secretarial work for a few hours each week in return for office space in the hotel and a desk in the lobby. She soon had a steady clientele of visiting salesmen and businessmen who needed letters typed. When she wasn't working, she studied.

16. JANITORIAL SERVICE

A substantial number of college men take part-time jobs doing janitorial work for local stores and businesses. The work generally includes sweeping and mopping floors, emptying waste baskets, and straightening up desks and counters; it may also involve cleaning and polishing heavy equipment, vacuuming carpets, dusting, swabbing out bathrooms, and so on.

There is very little you can do with this sort of work to make it more fun, but at least you can make it more profitable—by organizing a janitorial service for a number of local establishments. Visit as many nearby stores and businesses as you can handle, and offer to take on the janitorial chores of each for a monthly fee. A few potential clients may hesitate to hand you the key to their office, but most will be willing to trust a college student that far—and nearly all will recognize the value of your service. Start with just four or five jobs, and keep at it until you have proved both your competence and your reliability. Then slowly begin to expand, hiring other students to do some of the dirty work. Eventually you could become the director of a far-flung student janitorial empire, pocketing a sizable monthly commission without ever having to get your hands dirty.

An enterprising student at La Sierra College in Riverside, California, operates a janitorial service of this sort. He's a lot happier than the run-of-the-mill student janitor, and he makes a good deal more money.

17. MODELING

College coeds who are lucky enough to be well-endowed with beauty and poise often get part-time jobs as models, showing off clothing for department stores or large clothing shops. Those with energy and imagination as well as charm forget the job bit, and organize their own fashion shows.

All you need to run a fashion show is a bunch of pretty girls and a clothing store. A shop which is about to introduce its new seasonal line is your most obvious customer, but you needn't be confined to that. A fashion show will also help get a sale moving, or break a midwinter slump. Approach any local clothing merchant and offer your services on a commission basis—the more clothing he sells during the show, the more money you earn. A few well-placed advertisements are all you need to attract a crowd to the show, and the beauty of the girls will take care of the rest. Once you're organized, you can go from store to store in and around your community, and earn up to $300 or $400 at each stop.

Another way to turn modeling into a business is to organize a fashion show on your campus. Contact manufacturers and distributors of low-cost collegiate clothing, and explain that you are planning a fashion show at your college and would like to include their line. Your fee for modeling each outfit will of course depend on the size of your school, but $25 to $50 should be the right range for most colleges. You should also arrange to take orders at the show for each article of clothing; your commissions on these orders will provide an additional source of income. Once you have 20 or 25 ensembles signed up, set a date for the big event. Publicize it as much as you can, but don't worry—most girls will be more than willing to attend a free fashion show.

You can add a third source of profit to your set-up by charging local department stores and clothing shops for a plug. As you introduce each outfit, you announce first that it is manufactured by the Zilch Company (that nets you your initial $25 to $50), then that it is available at Griselda's Clothing Store (that nets you another $10 to $20). By the time you've gone through 25 outfits and taken orders for them all at the end, you should have a gross profit of nearly $1,500. That will leave you with nearly $1,000 after all your models have been paid and other expenses taken care of.

If you're really ambitious, you can turn your campus fashion show into a traveling business, going from college to college at a thousand bucks a shot. A Princeton student tried this routine and failed (see Chapter Six), but there's no reason why you shouldn't improve on his mistakes.

18. WATCHMAN

Offices, warehouses, banks, factories, and college buildings all require the services of night watchmen. Students have frequently been known to hold such jobs, but they inevitably suffer the results. A night watchman has plenty of time to study, but no time to sleep, except the daytime—which is generally class time. The obvious solution is shorter shifts, but what company wants to bother to hire four college students when it can hire one non-student who will sleep days?

The best way around the problem is to organize a student night watchman agency. The company can hire one agency, the agency can schedule four watchmen, and everybody's happy—especially the manager of the agency, who can sleep all night and collect his commission in the daytime.

19. BOOKKEEPING

Accounting, auditing and bookkeeping are skills, and not every student has them. If you're one of those who does, you can choose between two ways of turning your skills into money.

You can get a job. Since you can only work part-time, the job will be as an assistant in the bookkeeping department of a large company. It won't pay very well, and it won't be much fun—but it's a job. This is what most students do.

Alternatively, you can start a business. There are scores of small companies, stores, and restaurants in every college town which have neither the need nor the funds for a full-time bookkeeper—so they have none at all. You could offer each of these establishments your services on a part-time basis. Visit each customer for a few hours a week or a few hours a month (whatever is necessary to keep his books in order), and charge a fee commensurate with your work. Before long you will have as much bookkeeping as you want. If you have more than you want, hire a few assistants. When the business gets big enough, you can stop going the rounds yourself and concentrate on keeping your own books, and counting your profits.

20. JOBS

Bookkeeper, watchman, model, janitor, secretary, landscaper—we have shown how these six common jobs can be turned into profitable student businesses. We could easily go on to list a hundred more. A student who works for a television repair shop can start his own repair agency. One who services swimming pools on salary can start servicing them on commission. A computer programmer for IBM can become a free-lance programmer. A bus driver or taxi driver can start his own bus or taxi service. And so on, and so on, and so on.

But there are jobs, we must admit, which do not easily lend themselves to student entrepreneurial endeavor. A waitress can hardly start her own restaurant, a tax examiner his own tax department, or a student pastor his own religion. Some jobs just have to remain jobs.

Moreover, there is a great deal to be said for jobs. At least six advantages can be enumerated: 1) Economic security—you need no capital when you start, and can lose no capital when you finish. 2) Economic stability—you know how much money you are earning, and unless you lose your job, you can count on earning it. You can make plans for your money, even spend it in advance, without danger. 3) Regular hours—you know when you're scheduled to work and how long you're scheduled to work, and can budget your time and plan your day with these facts in mind. When you're not at work, you're not working, and you don't have to worry that you should be. 4) Relaxation—you know what your job requires, and one thing it doesn't require is overwhelming dedication. As Charles Dudly Warner once wrote: "Nothing can move a man who is paid by the hour; how sweet the flight of time seems to his calm mind." 5) Simplicity—your job may be easy or difficult, but in either case its scope is prescribed by your employer. You needn't worry about purchasing, selling, insurance, legality, labor problems, or anything else; your boss worries about them, and tells you what to do about them. 6) Friendships and contacts—you are one of the crowd at the office, and your friendships get warmer with every coffee break. Your employer may not be a friend, but he is a useful guy to know. If he's happy with your work, he may give you a job after you graduate, or a good recommendation if you want to work elsewhere.

There is a seventh advantage which ought to be mentioned, though it is in a sense a combination of several others. Many college students look on off-campus work as an opportunity to develop new skills and test career objectives by training on the job. Most training of this sort is impossible in an independent student enterprise. Even when it would be possible, a salaried job allows you a better look at the sort of business you're interested in, and lets you make your mistakes at the company's expense rather than your own.

If you are looking for a job, pretty much the only advice we can give is just that: look. Check the want ads of nearby town newspapers and the classifieds of your own college paper. Drop in at your school's employment office and see what they have on tap. Visit the local chamber of commerce and ask if they have a list of companies that hire part-time workers. Check with the nearest offices of the state employment service and the Civil Service Commission. Ask around. Keep your eyes open for help wanted signs in store windows, and your ears open for talk of available positions.

In most college communities, you shouldn't have too much trouble finding *a* job. The difficult task is to find *the* job—the one that best fits your skills and your interests, your academic schedule and your financial needs. If you're going to throw away the bulk of your free time for nothing but pay, the pay had damn well better be good. Since it's not likely to be, you would be well advised to look for a job which is enjoyable and instructive, as well as remunerative.

A list of all the jobs currently held by college students would fill a thousand pages, and would be pretty useless, since most of them require special skills and a special situation which you are not likely to duplicate. A list of the jobs held most frequently by college students would fill only half a page, and would also be valueless, since these are the opportunities you already know about and would like to avoid if possible. In the next few pages we shall present a compromise list, including selections from both the above categories, but concentrating on the middle ground, on jobs which should be available in many college towns but which are frequently overlooked by student job-hunters. The list is in random order, to encourage browsing.

A. SALES CLERK

Every variety of store except the self-service supermarket employs sales clerks. The pay is usually by salary only, but some department, clothing, and appliance stores give their employees a tiny commission on sales as well. Most store employees get a special discount on their own purchases, which is a hidden advantage of this otherwise exhausting and low-paying job. Clerking can be enjoyable and worthwhile if and only if you can get a job at a store which sells something you're interested in. A music student in a record shop or an electronics bug with an electronic supply firm can have a good time and learn something. With that exception, clerking is a job to avoid if possible.

B. HEAD CLERK

Occasionally a college student manages to land a more responsible store job, overseeing other clerks, heading a department, or providing some sort of special customer service. These jobs pay better than the routine clerking position, and they afford more responsibility and more challenge. But they're hard to get without being a regular clerk first—which just isn't worth it. You may be able to force an exception to the hierarchical order if you have some special skill. We know a girl in a jewelry store, for example, who specializes in redesigning new pieces for customers' old gems. She enjoys her work, and is comparatively well paid. A coed at Muhlenberg College in Allentown, Pennsylvania, works as a fashion consultant and part-time buyer for a local department store's "College Corner."

C. CASHIER

If you think clerking is boring, try being a cashier for a week. Unless you have a compulsive need to handle other people's money, this job is better left to the townies.

D. WAITRESS

Our use of the female gender is not meant to imply that college men never get jobs waiting on tables. But proprietors of inexpensive restaurants prefer pretty girls, and proprietors of expensive

restaurants prefer experienced, full-time help—and so student
waitresses are a good deal more common than student waiters.
This is all for the best. Waiting on tables is a hard, long, ill-paid,
messy business, and college men can usually do better. For that
matter, college women can usually do better, and they should
certainly try to. We know a girl who actually enjoys working as
a car-hop at a drive-in restaurant, but to us this is prima facie
evidence of insanity.

E. RESTAURANT MANAGER

Working for a restaurant in a semi-executive position is a different story entirely. A student at Princeton University has a job
as part-time assistant manager of a popular restaurant in town.
He makes up food orders, handles the payroll, keeps the books,
and sees to it that everything runs smoothly while he's on duty.
The job pays him very well, and offers plenty of variety and
challenge. If you can land a position of this sort, with a restaurant or any other local business, you would be well advised to
take it.

F. PLAYGROUND WORK

A number of colleges report students employed as playground
supervisors for local recreation departments or boards of education.
The job usually involves organizing athletic contests and other
events, as well as watching out for the safety and well-being of
those using the playground. The pay is not particularly good, but
the job is outdoors, and affords a chance to work with children
and get a little exercise at the same time.

G. RECREATION WORK

Besides playground work, a variety of other jobs in the recreation
field are open to students. Interest groups of all sorts, from pot-
tery-making to stamp-collecting to play-producing, are among the
principal opportunities in this line. Athletic coaching offers a
similar source of employment. Contact your local government,

nearby private schools, and the closest YMCA and see if they have any openings. A student at Knox College in Galesburg, Illinois, recently earned more than $1,000 serving as youth director of his local YMCA. The Boy Scouts and related groups represent another possibility, but most of this work is on a volunteer basis until you get fairly high up the ladder.

H. TEACHING

Substitute teaching is one of the best possible sources of part-time student income, particularly for undergraduates who are considering careers in education. Salaries range from $18 to $30 a day, averaging around $25 in most large cities and suburban communities. As a substitute teacher, you may be called on at any time to teach anything from Spanish to metal shop—but you don't have to accept every time. If the call comes on a day when you can make it, that $25 comes in mighty handy, and all you're expected to do is keep the kids in line.

Many college students labor under the illusion that substitute teaching jobs are open only to education majors. It is true that the education departments of many colleges act as liaisons with local boards of education for their students, but you can make it without their help. Simply write to the school boards in your area and ask what qualifications are necessary to be put on their list of substitute teachers. In many states, the teacher shortage has forced local boards to accept "sub-standard teachers" not only as substitutes, but also for full-time work. You may find that all you need to get on the list is a couple of years of college, which you already have. At the very worst, you may have to take an education course or two, and go get a chest X-ray. In very large cities, you might be given a test of some sort before being certified for those subjects and age levels you are "qualified" to teach.

Whatever paperwork is necessary, do it. Student substitute teachers earn more money than part-time waitresses, and have more fun, and learn more. There is hardly a better part-time job around, for men or women.

In many communities, regular, part-time school jobs are also available. The most common of these is the "teacher's aide." TA's are not paid as highly as substitute teachers, but they work more hours and regular hours, and the work is usually easier. You may be asked to supervise the school cafeteria, or to monitor pupils during their recess, or to grade papers and tests. Make your inquiries at the nearest Board of Education office.

Local religious schools provide another excellent source of part-time teaching work. In some areas, you may receive as much as $20 a week for teaching religious history or ceremony for a few hours every Sunday. Many churches have a special need for students with a sophisticated religious background, to teach advanced classes in ethics, theology, or modern religious thought. Sunday school teaching rarely conflicts with other college activities, and offers a particularly painless and rewarding way to make money.

I. LIBRARY WORK

Students are often employed in local libraries as circulation librarians, reference librarians, catalogers, or (this last is the most frequent) all-purpose assistants. Library work is now considered a profession, and unless you are studying library science at school, you should not expect to advance very far in the job hierarchy. Still, the work is pleasant, and the pay scale starts at around $2 an hour. And library customers are a lot nicer to deal with than the ones you run into in a restaurant or shoe store.

J. SERVICE STATION

The nearest male equivalent to a waitress, in terms of dirt and low pay, is a service station attendant. The only difference is that very few people tip at a gas station. Nevertheless, part-time service station jobs are plentiful, and one or two desperate job-hunters at every college wind up taking them. We hope you're never that desperate.

Of course if you're a skilled or even semi-skilled mechanic, capable of more than pumping gas and wiping windshields, a service station job can pay very well. But if you don't know a fuel line from a Fallopian tube, keep away from gas stations except when you need gas.

K. TAX EXAMINER

More than 200 students at the University of Texas are employed each year by the Austin office of the Internal Revenue Service. Their principal job is to examine tax forms for computational errors and other . . . errors. If you go to school near an IRS office, and can swallow your red-blooded American distaste for "revenuers," this job has excellent potential. The pay isn't half bad, and the work should be enlightening. If nothing else, it will teach you a great deal about the activities (and ethics) of the average American citizen.

L. HOSPITAL WORK

Many hospitals have job openings for college students, ranging from totally unskilled work like running errands and making beds to more demanding tasks such as taking patients' histories or working in the hospital laboratory. Without professional training you cannot go very far in hospital work. But if you plan a career in medicine a job as an orderly or nurse's aide will give you a sharp foretaste of what you're getting into.

At psychiatric hospitals jobs are occasionally available for student orderlies. As a rule your work will be nothing more than guard duty, but you may be given a chance to help with, or at least observe, treatment procedures.

A student at the University of Pennsylvania has a well-paying part-time job as a subject for hospital-run experiments. Steady jobs of this nature are fairly rare, but you should keep your eyes open for them.

M. KEYPUNCH OPERATOR

With the introduction of computer sorting techniques into the business procedures of many companies and government agencies, the job of keypunch operator has become a favorite of college students. A keypunch is a typewriter-like device which is used to punch holes in computer cards. It takes about ten minutes to master the machine, another few hours to get really proficient at it. From then on, you can earn up to $2.50 an hour any time you feel like a little punching. Nobody ever claimed it was fun, but it beats a lot of jobs.

N. COMPTOMETER OPERATOR

We're not really sure just what a comptometer is, but the want ads of every big-city newspaper are filled with desperate pleas for employees who know how to operate one. A few college students learn how, and earn up to $2.75 an hour thereafter. If your school is located in a big city, why not give it a try?

O. STUDENT PASTORATE

Students who plan to make the ministry their life's work often have a chance to try it out in advance while at college. Bible colleges and Divinity schools have the best records for this sort of student work, but it is not unusual for an undergraduate at a secular college to take over a small rural parish or help out in a large urban one. Payment ranges from nothing to $30 or $40 a week, and often includes room and board as well. If you plan on entering the ministry, we don't have to tell you about the non-financial values of a student pastorate; if you don't plan on entering the ministry, you won't want to (and won't be able to) get this job anyway.

P. DRIVER

Bus and taxi driving is a time-honored source of student earnings. A special driver's license is usually required, and you may need a permit of some sort from the municipal government as well, but the company that hires you will help you through the paper work. Both jobs pay fairly well, especially cab driving, which can add up to $4 or $5 an hour, including tips. The best thing about driving jobs is that your hours are almost completely flexible; whatever your other college activities, you can plan out a working schedule that won't conflict with them.

Q. WAREHOUSE AND SHIPPING WORK

Students are sometimes employed in warehouses as night watchmen, but the most common warehouse job is moving crates from one place to another. This is also the principal chore of student workers in factory shipping departments. This kind of work used to be very popular among college students, but the growth of labor unions and the increased availability of better-paying semiskilled jobs have taken their toll. Very few students regret the trend.

R. UNSKILLED LABOR

The same holds true for other kinds of unskilled work, whether it be in the factories, the mills, the fields, the quarries or the stockyards. Some industries in some parts of the country are still without unions, making it possible for students to earn money at manual labor. But the hours are long and the pay isn't high—and the work is back-breaking. There must be a better way.

S. MUSIC

Most student musicians are paid by the gig, and therefore qualify as independent businessmen; we will talk about their activities in Chapter Five. But a few regular part-time jobs are available for students with musical talent. Foremost among these are church jobs. Students are frequently hired as organists, choir members, choir soloists, choir masters, or even church music directors. Choir members usually receive a nominal fee, unless the choir is very small, very good and composed entirely of professional and semiprofessional singers. The other church positions often pay well, but require a substantial time commitment. A church organist, for example, must play at all services, attend choir rehearsals, practice on his own, and meet regularly with the clergyman in charge to plan for future services.

Student instrumentalists are occasionally successful in landing jobs with nearby orchestras and bands. Very often this requires joining the musician's union, which can set you back as much as $100. From then on, though, you command union-scale wages, which averages around $25 or $30 for two rehearsals and a performance. The big problem is to find enough jobs to keep the money coming in. Most student musicians are lucky if they can get that $30 once a month. Still, however little you make, you're getting paid for doing something you love. Life could be worse.

T. USHER

One of the softest jobs around is that of usher at a theater, movie house, auditorium or stadium. The pay is not much, but neither is the job—showing customers to their seats and refunding their dimes when the Orange Crush machine breaks down. And if you make head usher, whose job it is to see that the other ushers show up, you might even command a decent salary. A girl at Agnes Scott College in Decatur, Georgia, works as an usher at Atlanta Stadium, and even gets to do a little cheerleading for the Braves and the Falcons. Her job isn't as relaxing as that of most student ushers, but she says it's a lot of fun.

Your particular abilities and interests should suggest a few choice job possibilities to you. Investigate these first. A student at William Jewell College in Liberty, Missouri, works as an airplane mechanic. Whitman College in Walla Walla, Washington, has a student employed as a mortuary attendant and another giving skating lessons at a nearby "Ice Chalet." A senior at Southern Methodist University has a job as an investment counselor. A newspaper in Atlanta, Georgia, employs an editor who is also a student at Emory University. At Bethel College in North Newton, Kansas, there is a student working as an assistant probation officer, while one of his classmates gives guided tours through a health museum.

The crucial point is this. The airplane mechanic would not know how to arrange a funeral. The skating instructor could hardly edit a newspaper. The probation officer would be lost in a health museum. The best jobs are the ones that are uniquely adapted to your particular assortment of skills and interests. If you can't find any of these, then start thinking about becoming an usher or a bus driver or a waitress or a clerk. But do a lot of looking, listening and asking before you settle for a job that bores you.

21. ENTERTAINMENT AND BOOKING

In Chapter Three we discussed campus booking agencies that supply student and professional entertainment for college events and organizations. We also talked about the possibility of sponsoring a money-making dance, concert or other campus entertainment event of your own.

Both these opportunities exist off campus as well as on. In Chapter Six we will examine a giant booking agency at Brigham Young University in Provo, Utah, which supplies big-name and local entertainment for high schools, colleges, and civic organizations throughout the Southwest. Smaller off-campus booking agencies are common in many college towns. Usually they specialize in providing nearby high schools and community organizations with student bands for parties and dances, but other areas of specialization are possible. At Princeton University, for example, there is an active Speakers' Bureau. For anything from $10 to $50 per presentation, the bureau sends student speakers to schools and adult groups all over New Jersey. A brochure listing the available speakers and their topics is mailed to more than a thousand organizations each year, and constitutes the bureau's only form of advertising. Illustrated travel speeches and humorous monologues are most popular, but students have been paid to lecture on anything from canoeing to Communism.

Student-sponsored community entertainment events are not too common—but they're not rare either. Dances, movies, concerts and plays are occasionally arranged by students for the benefit of local residents. More often, on-campus events of this nature are opened to townspeople as well as students.

Several large colleges and universities have organizations which produce an annual review for the entertainment of students and townies alike. Some of these reviews have gained substantial fame over the years, and now conduct annual holiday tours throughout the country, earning tremendous profits. Harvard University's "Hasty Pudding" and Princeton's "Triangle Club" are probably the best-known groups of this nature. In a sense, of course, the ordinary college dramatic society belongs in the same category, since it produces entertainment for both students and townspeople. But drama clubs rarely run very much in the black, and none of them earns anything like the profits of the touring collegiate reviews.

Individual students may earn profits of any size as semi-professional or professional entertainers. Since this presumably requires an unusual skill of some kind, it will be discussed in Chapter Five. But there is one sort of individual entertaining that takes no special skills at all—appearing as a contestant on a television quiz show. In New York City, dozens of students have "earned" as much as $700 each for an hour's work on "To Tell the Truth," "Password," "I've Got a Secret," and similar shows. Students in other cities may earn comparable sums on local programs. Often a visit to the appropriate studio is enough to get you a try-out. Nearly as often, a try-out is enough to get you onto the show. Even if you lose, that'll be enough to get you a stereo set or a portable tape recorder or a year's supply of suppositories.

22. SELLING DOOR-TO-DOOR

"I'm earning my way through college selling magazine subscriptions." There isn't a suburban housewife in the country who hasn't stood on her front doorstep and heard this sentence at least a dozen times. She hears it from confidence men, from crooks, from bums, from ne'er-do-wells of all sorts. Occasionally she hears it from a student who is earning his way through college selling magazine subscriptions.

Magazine subscriptions are not the only item which has successfully supported college students through door-to-door sales. The "Avon girl" and the "Fuller Brush man" come immediately to mind, but even these do not exhaust the list of potential peddling profit-makers. The National Association of Direct Selling Companies publishes a directory of its member companies and their products. The list of commodity classifications begins with advertising specialties, animal preparations, arch supports, automobile accessories, bibles, and blankets. It ends with tablewear, toys, uniforms and work garments, vacuum cleaners, water softeners, and women's clothing. All these items, and all the ones in between, have been peddled successfully from house to house. Many of the peddlers have been—and continue to be—college students.

Direct selling has a number of advantages over most other college jobs and businesses. You invest no money, only time, and your time is flexible—you work when you want to work. You are your own boss, yet you have none of the problems that beset most student businessmen—no employment problems, no purchasing problems, no insurance or legal problems, nothing to do but sell widgets. Should you transfer to another college, or go home for the holidays, you can continue your business in your new location.

Earnings depend on how well you choose your product, how good a salesman you are, and how many hours you work. The very top student salesmen for the most popular companies earn annual incomes in excess of $10,000—while carrying a full course load. The run-of-the-mill crackerjack salesman earns at least $5,000 if he keeps at it. Poorer salesmen with less salable products in less wealthy neighborhoods can still manage to net two or three thousand. Students who work fewer hours naturally earn proportionately less. A few companies offer special "scholarships" for their best salesmen, and many run frequent contests as an incentive to higher sales.

Many students, especially coeds, avoid direct selling in the belief that it is very unpleasant way to make money. Students who think that every customer is a cranky old lady are as wrong as housewives who think that every door-to-door salesman is a con man. A few years ago, the National Association of Direct Selling Companies conducted a survey on public reaction to direct selling. Dr. Albert Haring, Professor of Marketing at Indiana University, compiled and analyzed the results. More than 23,000 salesmen were asked what percentage of their customers "react to your calls in a friendly and courteous manner, and seem to welcome you." Nearly two-thirds of the salesmen reported that at least

90 percent of their prospects showed them this warm welcome. Four-fifths of the salesmen noted a warm welcome from three-quarters or more of their prospects. Only 6 percent said they received more cold welcomes than warm ones.

Professor Haring noted that this favorable public reaction to door-to-door selling is a comparatively new phenomenon. "Suburban living, more children per family, shortages of domestic and baby-sitter help, poor public transportation—all of these may make the American public, particularly the housewife mother, more prone to purchase at the home and to give a higher value to the convenience of direct selling."

To get started in direct selling, simply contact one of the hundreds of companies with door-to-door sales programs. They will supply you with a sales kit, samples, price sheets, and other information and equipment. Most direct sales companies ask their salesmen to take orders, then deliver a few weeks later, but a few allow you to sell from stock. In either case, your commission will be a percentage on each item sold. If you choose your company intelligently, in terms of the shopping needs and shopping facilities of your neighborhood, you should earn a minimum of $3 or $4 an hour. Students with a flair for selling have been known to net as much as $10 an hour.

Before commiting yourself to direct selling, you should make a few inquiries about the customer climate in your area. Your college administration will probably be indifferent to your plans, so long as you stay outside the campus and inside the law. The local police department will tell you whether any municipal ordinances control or limit door-to-door peddling. Direct selling is rarely forbidden entirely, but many communities require a special permit, so you'd better look into it before you get started. Most important, check with the nearest office of the Better Business Bureau. The number of complaints they have received from your area should provide a good index of local reactions to door-to-door salesmen. If a crook canvassed your neighborhood last week, you should avoid covering it again next week—especially if you're pushing the same line he was.

For further information and advice on door-to-door selling, read *How to Make Big Money in Direct Selling* by Henry Flarsheim

(Prentice-Hall), or *How Women Can Make up to $1000 a Week in Direct Selling* by Claire Cox (Van Nostrand).

23. SELLING BY TELEPHONE

A number of companies prefer telephone sales to door-to-door canvassing, and students have frequently found it profitable to work for these companies. Payment is usually on a straight commission basis, but some firms offer a small hourly wage in addition. In the former case, you will be handed a telephone list and a description of the article or service you are selling, and can work on your own. If a salary is involved, you will probably be required to do your phoning from a central location. In either case, the profits are rarely as high as those from door-to-door selling, but the work is easier.

Occasionally a student will organize a telephone selling business on his own. Suppose, for example, you approached the manager of a clothing store in your area and offered to conduct a telephone sales campaign for him. Ask him to pick out a number of items on which he is willing to offer a special bargain price. Then borrow his customer file and start phoning. A suitable arrangement might be a fifteen percent commission on all telephone sales, plus a $5 bonus for every inactive account which is reestablished through your efforts. Sell the goods on an approval basis; if the bargain is genuine, very few articles will be returned. Everybody benefits from a campaign of this sort. The customer gets a special bargain at no risk; if he doesn't like what he orders, he can return it. The store gets some extra business through your sales, and reactivates a number of dormant accounts. And you get a commission.

Your profits from this venture will depend primarily on your sales skill. Commissions of up to $6 an hour are common, but so are commissions of less than $1 an hour. Concentrate your calls in the prime evening hours, be clear, concise, and persistent, and stay on the phone. If after a few days of work you're still not doing well, forget it, and find yourself another business.

Telephone sales campaigns of this sort are not, of course, limited to clothing stores, nor are they restricted to direct offers of goods on approval. Anything from movie tickets to restaurant premium booklets to sporting goods to jewelry can be successfully sold by telephone. One of the most profitable methods is to call regular and old customers to inform them of a special, on-going sale. Your commission for this would be a percentage of the purchases of every customer who appeared at the sale after having been invited by you. Alternatively, you could accept a flat fee from the store owner for making the calls.

Telephoning can be a highly profitable student business, especially if you work for several different stores and companies at the same time. If you have a knack for selling by phone, you can assure yourself of a steady income throughout the school year by starting a telephone sales agency.

A valuable sideline for a telephoning business is survey work. A girl at Agnes Scott College in Decatur, Georgia, conducts telephone surveys for nearby radio stations. She has enough business from this one source that she needn't bother about selling by phone. For top profits, though, the two can easily be combined.

Further information can be found in *Successful Telephone Selling* by Merrill De Voe (Prentice-Hall), and *Phonemanship* by William A. Garrett (Farrar, Straus).

24. VENDING MACHINES

An undergraduate at the University of Illinois operates a string of cigarette vending machines throughout the city of Urbana. For negotiating their installation and seeing to it that they are kept stocked· and in working order, he receives a substantial percentage of their gross take. There are very few selling businesses which are more secure, more profitable, and less difficult than the vending machine racket. It is highly unusual for a student to obtain a franchise for off-campus vending machine operation, but if you can do it, more power to you; it's a hell of an easy way to make money.

25. INSURANCE SALES

Most student insurance salesmen sell to their classmates; this business possibility was discussed in Chapter Three. Once in a while, however, a student has a chance to work with an off-campus insurance agency. Commissions and procedures are the same as the ones we have described for the on-campus agency, except that your leads will probably be supplied for you. If you know something about insurance and can negotiate an arrangement with a dealer in town, this is definitely a business to consider.

26. REAL ESTATE SALES

The main difference between selling real estate and selling pots or pans or potato peelers is that the average real estate sale is for $30,000 instead of $3.98. Another difference is that, when you go door-to-door, you take your customer with you.

College students with a glib tongue and a confidence-inspiring manner often work as real estate agents. If you have these two attributes, contact a local agency and see what you can work out. Many agencies pay a small salary even to part-time employees, but your big money will come from commissions. Your job will be to accompany customers on their visits to various properties, pointing out the advantages and obscuring the disadvantages of each. The agency will handle contracts, mortgages, and other technicalities of the exchange.

There is no way to estimate your expected profit as a student real estate agent. You could go for months without making a sale, then suddenly make two in the same day, and pocket a quick $1,000 or so. Profits of $5,000 a year are not unusual for part-time real estate work, but they are by no means guaranteed. If you're not a smooth salesman (a smooth salesman these days is a salesman who doesn't seem smooth), you'd better look around for something else. The "sympathy market" may be important in the sale of small items, but nobody is going to buy a $30,000 home from you just because you're a nice kid trying to work his way through college.

27. STOCK SALES

In most states, the sale of stocks, bonds, mutual funds, and other securities is controlled by a network of laws that would make your college regulations look like anarchy itself. But if you can somehow slip around or between the rules, selling securities is an excellent way to make money. A student in Long Island, New York, recently started peddling mutual fund shares from door to door. He soon became so successful that, as a bemused dean put it, "I think he now earns more than most of his professors." This student had two summers of Wall Street experience behind him. and a wealthy suburban neighborhood around him. The former is a tremendous advantage, and the latter almost a necessity, if you plan to make good money selling securities.

28. YOUR OWN PRODUCT

Every year a small number of college students across the country earn money by selling their own hand-made goods to the surrounding community. The most popular items are candy and cakes. knickknacks and decorations, paintings and drawings, hats, home-sewn clothing, and knitted and embroidered articles. The most usual procedure is to peddle your wares door-to-door, but occasionally commercial outlets can be found for student handicraft. A student in Washington, D.C., for example, used to mold and paint toy lead soldiers, supplying a dozen stores with his popular product.

Since student handicrafts of this sort require special skills, we will discuss the business more fully in Chapter Five.

29. MAIL ORDER SALES

Even at a tiny college in a tiny town, it is possible to earn big money from a student business—simply by selling by mail. To be successful, a mail-order business must advertise on a large scale. It must also have a product that people are willing to purchase by mail.

In the past, college students have successfully sold three sorts of items by mail. The first two, booklets and handicrafts, are discussed elsewhere in this book. The third is postage stamps. Philatelists, particularly amateur philatelists, are quite accustomed to buying stamps by mail, often on an approval basis. Each year several college students who are themselves stamp collectors go into this business. Usually they buy their stamps (by mail) from overseas suppliers, arrange them in attractive packets, and send them out on approval to customers throughout their region. Several years ago a Princeton student earned more than $3,000 in one year by this method. Average annual profits are closer to $1,500.

30. STORES

As we have already pointed out, the successful student-operated store is a rare phenomenon. Still rarer is the student-run store which sells to the community at large, rather than to fellow students. A store is not a part-time responsibility, and to run it as though it were is to invite failure. There are too many easier and safer ways to make money.

31. MISCELLANY

This chapter has been even less comprehensive than the two that preceded it. We have mentioned three ways of making money off-campus: service agencies, jobs, and selling. We have listed a number of examples of each, but we have barely scratched the surface. Student services at various colleges have included everything from television rental to toy repair. Jobs have ranged from traffic counting to tree farming. Sales items have run the gamut from cement mixes to cemetary plots. The ideas and suggestions collected in this chapter should serve primarily as hints, as prods to your imagination. Take a good look around your community. See what is needed, what isn't being done. Then do it.

CHAPTER 5

Talent Was
a Greek Coin

1. ABOUT TALENT

In ancient times, a talent was a unit of money, equal to 3,600 Babylonian shekels, 3,000 Palestinian shekels, or a full 6,000 Greek drachmas. The meaning of the word has altered some over the years, but today's college student would still do well to remember that talent means money.

In this chapter we have collected a few of the ways students at various colleges have turned their talents into cash. Our discussion will be limited to abilities which are possessed by a significant portion of the student population, but not by everybody. After all, tutoring is a talent, and so is typing, and so is selling—but in that sense, *every* business requires talent of some kind. These very common "talents" were therefore treated in earlier chapters. At the other edge of the spectrum, we find highly unusual student skills such as spot welding, psychological testing, and piano tuning. No doubt any of these exotic talents could be turned into a successful business, too, by the half dozen students in the country who possess them. But they are far too specialized to deserve treatment in a book of this sort.

This chapter will deal with the "in-between" talents, ranging from arts and crafts to athletics and computer programming. These skills are common but not ubiquitous, and for the student lucky enough to find one of them in himself, they are a ready-made source of income.

2. BANDS AND COMBOS

Every college campus in the country is seemingly packed full with student musicians, near-musicians, would-be musicians, and non-musicians, all of whom enjoy filling their non-academic hours with musical noise. Every time three or four of them get the urge to take out the old guitar, the old tuba, or the old kazoo at the same moment, another student combo is born. Whenever two combos clash over practice time, a merger is proposed, and a new student dance band is the premature offspring of the forced marriage.

It therefore comes as no surprise to learn that a lot of colleges and universities have nearly as many combos and bands in the dorms as they have books in the library. Many of these play only for fun, and the fun is all for the performers, not for the involuntary audience in the next room. Indeed, as soon as the guys in the next room start to like what they hear, it's time to go professional. More than 1,000 groups go pro every year, and more than a couple make it big. The rest earn profits of $800 or $900 apiece, which is nothing to sneeze through your tuba at either.

The universality of college combos and bands makes it a bit silly to recite examples. The normal ratio is one profit-making group for every 300 students. West Virginia University has 25 combos. Most of the big Midwestern universities have more than a hundred. And tiny Rocky Mountain College in Billings, Montana, with a student body of 500, manages to support three working groups. Only the girls' colleges fall below par, probably because there's nobody to carry the tuba.

Our references to tubas notwithstanding, the average student combo doesn't have one. With that exception, nearly every instrument gets its share of use, with the choice depending in equal measure on the sort of music to be played and the sort of instrumentalists to be found. Trumpets, saxes, clarinets, drums, and pianos are the backbone of most dance bands. Bass fiddles, flutes, trombones and vibes may be added if they are available. Jazz groups draw from the same collection of instruments, while folk music requires guitars, banjos, and similar pieces. The rock band, which is by far the most common student instrumental group, usually contains three guitars, a set of drums, and one other instrument (often a piano, organ, or sax). The really essential instrument in the rock band is the electrical outlet.

Much more important than the choice of instruments is the choice of names. The Harvey Lord Quintet at Pittsburgh's Carnegie Institute of Technology does pretty well, largely because its manager is also in charge of the student coffeehouse where the group usually plays. But really, it is a pretty square name. Much more auspicious are names like The Seventh Seal (Bridgewater College, Bridgewater, Virginia), Lothar and The Hand People (University of Illinois, Urbana, Illinois), The Moon Misters (St. John's University, Collegeville, Minnesota), The Empty Set (Lakeland College, Sheboygan, Wisconsin), or our favorites, The Potted Plants and The Smoke Grass (both at Utica College, Utica, New York).

Aside from finding musicians and finding a name, the only important problem student combos must solve is finding engagements. Sometimes the college music department will help arrange for jobs. At other schools the dean of students' office, the placement center, or the student employment office may lend a hand. A few colleges keep a list of all campus combos and bands at the Student Union, and groups pick up many of their gigs from that source.

Most of the time, however, the choice boils down to one question: Do you solicit your jobs for yourself, or hire a student booking agency to do it for you? The right answer to this query depends entirely on the college involved. On a campus of 3,000 students or less, there is really no need for a booking agency. An ad in the school newspaper, personal contact with frat presidents, and word-of-mouth should be enough to get you going and keep you going. It is even possible to get off-campus gigs without an agent, if you specialize in local high schools and neighboring colleges and have the time and energy to develop the necessary contacts. But if your college has 50,000 students and 100 or more combos and bands, then you'd better work through a student booking agent. Even at a smaller school it may be necessary to use a middleman, particularly if most frats and social clubs are accustomed to depending on an established agency for their entertainment.

Professional booking agencies won't be particularly interested in you until you have gained something of a reputation. But as soon as you're big enough to cut a record, hit a big-city nightclub, or plan a vacation barn-storming trip, you'd better find yourself a professional booker. He'll grab 15 percent of your take, but he'll more than make up for it in engagements you could never have negotiated on your own.

For further help on organizing and running a student combo, let us examine a typical small-time success in some detail. The Nightwatch Band was organized in the fall of 1964 by five underclassmen at Princeton University. Specializing in rock and roll, the group includes a bass guitar, lead guitar, rhythm guitar, electric piano, and drums. When the "Motown Sound" is called for, the bass guitar switches over to saxophone, and the pianist can handle an organ or a tambourine when necessary.

The Nightwatch spent five months rehearsing before playing its first job, a party at Charter Club of Princeton. The debut was a success, word got around, and the Nightwatch was soon booked solid for the rest of the year. In the sixteen months that followed, the band played over 50 dates at colleges, high schools, prep schools and deb parties throughout the Northeast. Nightwatch members attribute much of their success to those first profitless five months. "Before you have your first appearance," they advise, "you should practice for at least five to six months, and build up a repertoire of 50 or 60 songs. You must be sure you are ready before your first appearance, for the first impression can make or break you."

Another important factor in the success of the Nightwatch was organization. They recommend "a special role for each band member, who can be consulted as an authority in his area." In their case, one man handled finances and business another stage appearance, clothing and such; another, musical arrangements; another, transportation and bookings; another, use and maintenance of electronic equipment.

Back in 1965, the Nightwatch charged $125 for a full evening's performance (9 P.M. to 1 A.M.). With success came rate increases, and now the group gets $350 for each engagement. They play nearly every weekend of the school year, grossing almost $10,000 a year. Transportation, clothing, food, accommodations, and equipment have to come out of that, but the proceeds from summer tours (one year through New England the next down in Florida) add considerably to the kitty.

At the beginning, the Nightwatch relied entirely on campus newspaper ads and word-of-mouth for publicity. They played for a number of local teen events, which helped them gain attention and provided a chance for "live practice" at the same time. As soon as bookings started to come in, they agreed on a strict rule never to play free jobs, for friends, roommates, parents, or anybody else. "People will lose respect for you if you do free jobs," they note, "and will expect you to." As the group became popular, the Nightwatch designed a promotional folder, which they sent to nightclubs and other public establishments. The folders did double duty as press-kits after they became better known. A business card was also designed, and handed out in large quantities at every engagement. It wasn't until after they had cut a record for ABC/Paramount that the group found it necessary to hire a booking agency and join the musicians' union.

Stan Rubin, the famous society bandleader, got his start with a student combo at Princeton. Not every successful undergraduate musician goes on to make music his life's work—but most of them agree that there isn't a better-paying collegiate hobby to be found.

3. VOCAL GROUPS

Many rock and roll bands accompany their electronic cacaphony with a human voice or two. Though this may be the most profitable collegiate use of the larynx, some people feel it hardly deserves to be called singing.

College vocal groups are harder to organize than combos, and they usually earn less money. Still, if you don't own a tuba and you like to harmonize in the shower, you might consider forming one. There are two main kinds to choose between. The first and more common is the folk-singing group, composed of four or five voices and a guitar or two. Folk singers are in demand at parties of all varieties, and are frequently invited to fill in the break-time at large dances. Folk groups are also popular as variety show entertainers, but the big money in folk singing, for collegiate groups that make it to the top, is from record sales.

The other sort of college vocal group is the "choral group," usually composed of from 12 to 20 members, singing *a capella*. These are the groups that usually specialize in eleventy-four-part harmony. They work with old favorites, ballads, and college alma maters, and produce a sound that resembles a union between a barbershop quartet and a Bach fugue. Their most devoted audiences are alumni get-togethers, but they have been known to cut records, entertain at private parties, participate in variety shows, and even provide short and sweet relief at a rock and roll dance.

The "G-Stringers" at Vassar College are typical of the fairly successful collegiate vocal group. Despite their name, their specialty is folk singing. They appear in blue jeans, white shirts, and lumber jackets, and they keep their clothes on.

A 20-year-old tradition at Vassar, the G-Stringers hold their size constant at seven girls, scheduling freshman auditions each fall to replace graduated seniors. The girls do their own arranging in three-part or five-part harmony, with a guitar accompaniment. In addition to an assortment of free gigs on campus, they accept local engagements for a nominal fee of $15 for the group. For visits to other campuses (Yale University is a favorite destination), they charge $25 plus all expenses, or $100 flat rate—which comes to about the same thing. They have sung concerts in Carnegie Hall and the Bitter End coffeehouse in New York City for the same price. Their big money, such as it is, comes from their occasional records. In 1966 they cut their newest, "Live the Life," which earned them a total profit of $600.

Because their performances usually last twenty minutes instead of three or four hours, college vocal groups rarely earn more than the G-Stringers—and many earn less. The major appeals of such groups are the chance to travel and the pleasure of rehearsing and performing with a small group of close friends. Says last year's president of the G-Stringers: "I like to sing and I like the pocket money, but the kids in the group are what's most important. We rehearse together for four or five hours a week, and we really get to know each other and like each other. It's a bit cliquey, but it's a lot of fun."

There are of course a few exceptions to the small-profit rule. Elizabethtown College in Elizabethtown, Pennsylvania, has a student folk-singing group which has turned professional and now earns between $300 and $500 a night for a 90-minute engagement. But in general, if you plan on starting a college vocal group, you'd best do it for the pleasure, not the profit.

4. VARIATIONS ON THE THEME

Skilled musicians of any kind have an ample choice of money-making possibilities, besides small vocal groups and dance combos.

Serious choruses and vocal societies on the college campus rarely earn any money, but it can be done. Seattle Pacific College in Seattle, Washington, for example, has a profit-making student group which specializes in religious music. Church choir members and soloists are often well paid, and even college choirs occasionally pay their members at least a token salary. Large college glee clubs never pay, but they make up for it at many schools by providing free transportation to concerts at other colleges. Some of the top collegiate glee clubs take vacation tours through the Caribbean or Europe; the value of the free trip at these schools often exceeds the earnings of independent student vocal groups.

The greatest potential profits in vocal music come from solo nightclub singing. This is one of the most difficult fields to get anywhere in, but if you think you have the stuff, give it a try. Incomes of $10,000 a year and more await the one-in-a-thousand student who makes it to the top.

Instrumentalists have college orchestras and bands to choose from, as well as part-time or free-lance jobs with off-campus groups. Organists can always find church work to do, and capable pianists are in tremendous demand as accompanists and banquet background suppliers.

5. ENTERTAINMENT

Musicians are by far the most common, most popular, and most successful student entertainers, but they still have to share the stage with a variety of other performers.

Student magicians command good fees at dozens of colleges, from the University of California at Berkeley to St. Mary's College in Winona, Minnesota. Magicians occasionally perform for college or adult groups, but their main audience is children. Most student magicians start off working small private parties, then graduate to carnivals and theater appearances. Puppeteers go the same route, but they rarely get as far; the demand is less, the pay is less, and the jobs are few and far between.

Comedians and masters-of-ceremony frequently earn up to $100 per appearance, but in the average college town there will be damn few appearances, however great your talent. Perhaps the best way to make money out of this sort of fast-talking talent is to work for a local radio station as a disc jockey. Most dee-jays earn about $4 an hour, and many students work up to 20 or 30 hours a week at it. Once you've learned the knack, you can get your studying done while the records are playing.

Other collegiate entertainers—jugglers, contortionists, and what-have-you—usually find themselves with a unique talent and nobody to buy it. If you're looking for an entertainment business that will pay for your books and your beer, you'd best stick to music or magic, and leave the sidelines for the unpaid fraternity clowns.

6. DRAMA AND DANCE

Student actors and dancers normally receive training and satisfaction for their on-campus work, but no remuneration. Even when a student play, show, or dance program earns a profit (which is not often, especially for dance programs), the money more usually winds up in the coffers of the college than in the pockets of the performers.

When student actors or dancers do manage to make a little

money, it is almost always off campus. The University of New Hampshire at Durham and Marywood College in Scranton, Pennsylvania, report profits for student actors, while dancers have been able to find outside jobs at Huston-Tillotson College in Austin, Texas, and Yankton College in Yankton, South Dakota.

The opportunities are severely limited, especially for dancers. Student actors may be able to find work with local radio or television stations, or with stock theatrical companies in town. Many small communities have their own semi-professional "drama societies," which split up whatever profits they make among themselves. College students are frequently able to work with these groups. A really good student dancer in a big city may be able to find part-time work with a ballet company or in a musical comedy. Less professional dancers have occasionally worked out their own routines and performed them for variety shows and similar events. And a few coeds have worked as go-go girls, much to the consternation of their parents.

In many parts of the country, the already serious job-hunting problems of the student dancer or actor have been increased by the growth of unions in these fields. If you do not plan a career as an actor or dancer and therefore do not want to join the union, you may find that amateur theatrics are the only opportunities open to you—and they rarely pay very well.

Students involved in theatrical production (stage hands, designers, grips, and so on) have it somewhat easier. Even campus drama clubs often pay for such work, and off-campus groups nearly always pay production people well in compensation for the glamor and public acclaim they are missing. Here, too, unions may present a problem, but a student stagehand can usually be dubbed an "apprentice" to avoid conflict with union regulations.

7. ARTS AND CRAFTS

Not every student can paint a portrait, knit a sweater, or make a bracelet. But for those who can, there are profits waiting.

Of all the forms of student handicraft, perhaps the most difficult to earn money from is painting. Artists are admired figures on most campuses, but the admiration rarely extends to purchasing their work. There used to be a time when student paintings sold easily to students and members of the community, to be hung and enjoyed. But today good prints of famous works are available at low cost almost everywhere, and the student artist is out of business.

There are two ways left to earn money from serious art work. One is to enter contests, and win. The other is to enter art exhibits, and have your work sold. Townies and even classmates who would never buy your paintings from *you* may visit an exhibition and decide to buy them there. Watercolors, drawings, pen-and-inks, and even block-prints can be sold through exhibitions. How much money you make will depend on how many exhibits you can find, how much you charge for your work, and how good you are. There is some disagreement concerning the relative importance of the third factor, but the first two are undeniably crucial. If you can keep your work constantly before the eyes of the local art-buying public, you may be able to sell four or five pieces a month at $15 or $20 each. That begins to add up to money—and you're building a reputation at the same time.

Student sculptors must play the same game, but both the number of sculpture exhibits and the number of sculpture buyers are comparatively small, so don't expect to support yourself on your sales.

The less "high-brow" your art gets, the more money you stand to make from it. Caricaturists can easily earn up to $10 an hour doing quick pastel impressions of classmates and townies. Any event which brings large numbers of people together is ideal for this sort of work; you should have no trouble making more than $100 in one day at a carnival. Between events, a simple tour from fraternity to fraternity will keep you in pocket money, at least until you run out of classmates.

Student cartoonists normally work for their school newspaper or humor magazine without pay, but the better ones have little difficulty getting their work accepted by local newspapers. Students occasionally place their best pieces in national magazines; if you can get into this racket, the pay can soar as high as $50 per cartoon.

Book and magazine illustrating is another possibility. This is a hard field to break into, but once you make it, you can have as much work as you like, and the pay is exorbitant. Your best bet is to start by getting your work published in college mags and local newspapers, then try to land a job illustrating a book by a local author. Talk to your university press, if you have one, and any small publishers located near your college. Once you have put together a fairly impressive portfolio, approach a few national magazines and major book publishers and see what you can work out.

One of the most profitable ways to make money from student art is to draw for advertisements. Bring a few samples of your work around to local merchants and businesses, and offer to design and draw illustrations for their ads. If you set your prices low enough, many small tradesmen should be enthusiastic about your offer, and you can make up in quantity what you lose through underpricing your talent. Several girls at Mary Baldwin College in Staunton, Virginia, earn good money by doing art work for local businesses. There is no reason why you shouldn't get in on the act.

Student artists who don't like any of these suggestions can refer back to Chapter Two, and go into business painting designs on sweatshirts. It doesn't look as snowy as the other ideas on your grad-school applications, but the money's good.

Midway between arts and crafts is decorating; many students have found it a more profitable business than either extreme. Hand-painted or hand-printed Christmas cards are a popular decorator item, followed closely by china, dishes, scarves, jewel boxes, coat hangers, shoe trees, and widgets. Decorating store windows is another possibility in this line. Large department stores hire professionals, but that leaves all the other merchants in town for you. As a sideline, you might try decorating for parties and fraternity dances.

The range of student handicrafts is fantastic. Student-made jewelry includes earrings, bracelets, pins, brooches, necklaces, and anklets—made out of wire, sea shells, beads, metal, or paper. Students manufacture novelty hats that sell for anything from $2 to $17.99. Hand-sewn products range from dresses and shifts to pillow covers, pajamas and pot-holders. Knitting, embroidering and crocheting yield bedspreads and handkerchiefs, sweaters and towels, doilies and antimacassars. Candies, cakes, jellies and pies stream out of countless sorority kitchens in a never-ending flow. Leather turns miraculously into moccasins and book bindings. Wood metamorphoses into cabinets, tables, and shelves. Clay transubstantiates into ceramic tiles and glazed pottery. Molten metals pour into molds and come out as toy soldiers, plaques, pitchers, and charms. In short, college students can make anything out of anything—and make money too in the process.

There are three basic ways to sell student handicraft. The first is to go directly to your customers, peddling your wares door-to-door. The second is to make your customers come to you, by starting a store of sorts in your room or elsewhere. The third is to meet your customers halfway, either by selling to established retailers or by setting up tables in convenient locations. Each system has its own advantages and disadvantages, and the choice depends primarily on the article to be sold. It is always possible, of course, to use a combination of methods.

Door-to-door sales are best adapted to seasonal goods and "impulse items"—the sort of gee-gaws that are charming when seen but don't turn up on very many shopping lists. Hand-painted Christmas cards are a good example. Few classmates and fewer townies are going to bother to visit you in your room to pick up a dozen cards. But when you or your salesman walks into *their* room or home and shows them a few samples, sales begin to skyrocket.

If you have something irresistible to sell, and can advertise it effectively through posters and newspaper ads, then you might consider making your customers come to you. Items which satisfy these criteria are comparatively unusual. But there is another situation in which it makes sense to operate your own store. This is when you have a large number of similar articles for sale. If you can get your classmates to the point where they visit you whenever they want "something artistic," then you can net big profits without ever leaving your room.

An example of a business of this sort is "The Gilded Gourd," a crafts concession operated by two freshman coeds at Ohio University in Athens, Ohio. Besides the title item, the girls sell hand-painted stationery, decorated boxes of all sorts, mobiles, icons, knickknacks and similar miscellany. An orange-crate showcase and a few signs on dormitory bulletin boards constitute their only advertising. The business operated for a month last year, before final exams forced it to shut down temporarily. It netted only $30 in that first month, but business was beginning to pick up toward the end. Meanwhile, the girls are "having a lot of fun and really learning something." As a direct result of The Gilded Gourd, one of them has decided to change her major to art.

Some 30 years ago, a group of artistic students at the University of Wisconsin banded together and formed the "Wisconsin Art Studio." The university lent them a room, which they redecorated and then filled with their work—paintings, etchings, Christmas cards, shades, screens, pewter, and so forth. They advertised in the university and Madison newspapers, and soon found themselves with a highly remunerative outlet for their talents. To the best of our knowledge, this approach has seldom been tried since. Fine arts students at Carnegie Tech in Pittsburgh run an annual sale of prints and paintings, but we know of no currently operating agency that carries a full line of student handicrafts. A student business on the Wisconsin studio model has a good chance of success, particularly at small-town schools where gift shopping is difficult.

The third approach we mentioned, meeting your customers halfway, is an excellent compromise between the inconvenience to you of door-to-door work and the inconvenience to your customers of a student store. On-campus business should flourish through the simple device of setting up a few tables outside the dining hall, in the dormitory lobbies, or in front of the library. Impulse items will sell as well as they're going to when displayed on these tables in conspicuous locations, and the work is far easier than door-to-door selling. To reach the off-campus market, try to get a few local stores to carry your goods. The best way to start is by offering the handicrafts on approval; the merchants receive a commission on each item they sell, and return the rest. Once you have proved the salability of your wares, local tradesmen will be more than happy to buy them outright for resale at a higher price.

However you sell them, student art and handicraft are excellent ways of turning talent into money. All you have to be is artistic, handy, and a little crafty.

8. FILM-MAKING

Every fairly large college has one or two students who dabble in the art of motion-picture-making. It is an expensive art to dabble in. Equipment and film cost money, developing and processing cost more, editing costs more still—and the final product is liable to get moldy in your attic before anyone pays you anything to see it.

Despite these hard facts of celluloid life, every fairly large college has one or two students who dabble in the art of motion-picture-making. And once in a while, somebody makes it big.

The biggest we've heard is a student at Carnegie Institute of Technology in Pittsburgh, Pennsylvania. This ambitious young man has produced a full-length feature film about the problems of three Center City youngsters. Both he and many of his actors have sunk considerable amounts of money into the film, but now it has been sold to a professional producer and will soon be shown in theaters across the country. He will be able to pay his actors and technicians, see his name in lights, and pocket a neat profit for himself.

We cannot in all conscience advise you to start right in on a feature film. If you insist on trying your hand at film-making, your best bet is to interest your college administration in hiring you to prepare a short movie on college life, to be shown to prospective applicants and alumni groups. If that succeeds, then you might try to talk some nearby industrial firms into a similar project for them. Only after you have three or four acceptable documentaries under your belt should you take a stab at anything with a story line.

Film-making is hardly a secure, routine student business. It is a magnificent, grand way to make money—or lose money.

9. PUBLICATIONS

One of the purposes of college, theoretically, is to teach you how to write better than the average man. If you possess this talent more than even the average college man, you should definitely consider a student business in the writing field. Many such enterprises are possible, ranging from ad writing to college journalism, from a weekly column in the town newspaper to a full-length book. In all cases, the essential requirement is the same: You have to be able to turn out clear, accurate, readable prose quickly and easily.

Most student writers work for their college newspaper, yearbook, literary magazine, or humor magazine—the choice depending on the sort of writing they do best. At nearly all schools these publications are supported (and controlled) by the college administration, or at best, the student government. This provides security should you fail to make as much money as you spend, but when you do manage to run in the black, the profit goes into the college bank account, not yours.

There are perhaps two dozen regular student publications in the country which can afford to stand alone, taking their own risks and pocketing their own profits. Most of them are daily newspapers. Many of the big state universities and nearly all the Ivy League colleges have papers which are independent of their administrations, and which split their annual profits among their members. In addition, a few college yearbooks and one or two humor magazines have made it on their own. We have never heard of a profit-making student literary magazine.

Profits from independent student publications can soar as high as $40,000 in a good year. Of course, that money gets split 30 or 40 ways, and each student editor's share inevitably comes out to less than $1.00 an hour—usually far less. Still, that's pretty good money for an enjoyable, instructive, and highly honored extracurricular activity.

Advertising and circulation provide much of the revenue for student publications, but the most successful ones supplement these sources with special projects of one sort or another. The Harvard *Crimson* recently published a highly successful guide to European travel; Princeton's *Daily Princetonian* put out *Where the Girls Are,* a humorous guide to women's colleges; the Yale *Daily News* has printed a series of special career guide issues which are distributed across the country.

If student newspapers can earn extra money from special publications, there is no reason why independent student writers couldn't do the same thing. As a matter of fact, many do. The list of books, pamphlets, magazines, newspapers and the like written and printed by unaffiliated student journalists at various colleges could run for pages. We will mention just a few. At Emerson College in Boston, Massachusetts, a student publishes a program guide for the college-operated FM radio station. Two "underground" magazines, one literary and one political, earn money for students at Utica College in Utica, New York. Four men at Carleton College in Northfield, Minnesota, produced a mimeographed *Dictionary of Carleton Slang,* and cleared a fast $200 profit on the deal. A student at Princeton University wrote and distributed a course guide booklet. And dozens of students at dozens of colleges have worked under contract to or in cooperation with their administrations to produce freshmen handbooks, college catalogs, and similar semi-official publications.

The procedures for putting out such works are essentially the same as those described in Chapter Two for blotters, programs and the like. The only important difference is that the projects listed here require not only the ability to sell advertising, but a great deal of writing skill as well. If you are a talented writer, the rest is easy; if you're not, the rest won't help much.

To get a better idea how these more ambitious student publications work, we will examine one in some detail. The *Unofficial Guide to Middlebury College* was first published in 1966, and has now weathered two successful editions. It was started by two freshmen at Middlebury College in Middlebury, Vermont. As the authors recall: "The idea was born of our frustration at knowing so little about the college and the town before we arrived on campus.... Our parents would have appreciated information on where they could stay and eat when they brought us in September. And then we could have used information on the stores and services Middlebury offered.... Also some information on air, bus, rail, and highway transportation leading to Middlebury would have been helpful. Not only did we know little or nothing about the town, we also had little idea of the new environment of college: what the dorms and dorm life were like;

the social life and where we could go on dates; what we should bring for our rooms, our studies, and the Middlebury climate; and then those many 'little things' that, had we known about them, would have helped us pass our first few weeks with less friction."

The *Unofficial Guide* was planned to fill in these information gaps for the coming crop of freshmen. After obtaining provisional approval from the college administration, our two authors set about their task—writing chapters, planning layout, pricing printers, selling ads. They had nearly finished when the administration decided that it would lend them the list of incoming freshmen only if it could exercise editorial control over the book's content. The ensuing dispute resulted in a compromise. Two chapters of the *Unofficial Guide*, "The Town" and "What to Bring and Buy," were made into a second book, entitled "Of Middlebury Town." New ads were hastily sold, and OMT was sent out free to the next year's freshmen, using the college list. The original *Unofficial Guide* was sold to freshmen for $1.50 when they arrived on campus.

The profits the first year were a disappointing $65. The editors attributed this to the surprise of suddenly having two books instead of one, and to the limited appeal of the *Unofficial Guide*. For the second edition, they re-edited both books to make them more attractive to a wider range of students and alumni. They doubled their sales, and nearly tripled their advertising revenue.

The second edition earned a profit of $1,385.

Middlebury has a student body of less than 2,000. An identical project on a larger campus would earn proportionately more.

Looking back on their first two years with the *Unofficial Guide*, the student editors view their work this way: "Whether we made a great deal of money or not, we have gained an inordinate amount of business experience. We have progressed from neophytes who didn't know a Bodoni Bold from a pica to editors who can put together a competent dummy. We shed our roles as 'just students' and took on a dubious and often hostile business world, selling a product uniquely our own. Finally, there is the great personal satisfaction of knowing we accomplished some-

thing in having recognized a need for our books and having acted
to meet it."

Perhaps the single most difficult sort of student publication to
make work is the competition newspaper. If you attend a large
college or university, and its student newspaper is poorly written
or not widely read (the two need not go together), you might be
tempted to start a competitive paper. Succumb to this temptation
only if you have a great deal of talent, time, money, and friends.
It can be done, no doubt, but it almost always fails. The latest
entry into this dangerous sweepstakes is *The Herald*, the brainchild of a University of Illinois sophomore. It seems to be giving
Illinois' *Daily Illini* a run for its money, but *our* money is on the
older paper. Your money is better off in your hip pocket than
invested in an operation of this kind.

A slightly more likely proposition is the multi-campus newspaper. Several years ago a group of students at Allegheny College,
Carnegie Institute of Technology, Chatham College, Duquesne
University and the University of Pittsburgh decided to publish a
joint newspaper. Since all these schools are in the Pittsburgh
area, the students figured that city merchants would prefer one
ad in their *Campus Dialog* to half a dozen in each of the individual college papers. They figured right, but the sheet folded
anyway, because it was taking its editors too much time and they
were in danger of flunking out.

There are so many possible one-shot student publications available, that it seems a shame to take the risk of a full-fledged newspaper. If you are a writer, the quick route to good money is
clear. Devise a booklet that would go over well at your school,
sell ads to local merchants, sell the book to classmates. You can
peddle your ads before you begin printing, so you needn't risk a
dime. If you hit on a good thing, profits of up to $5,000 should
provide sufficient reward for your caution and good sense.

10. WRITING

For students interested in writing but not in the other aspects
of publication work, there are still an ample number of money-
making possibilities to be found.

Perhaps the best of these is to land a job as a "stringer" for a large newspaper, magazine, or wire service. A stringer differs from a regular employee in that he is paid separately for each article he writes, and is free to work for more than one medium at the same time. The four largest networks of collegiate stringers are operated by *Time*, *Newsweek*, the Associated Press, and the United Press International. In addition, big-city newspapers often employ correspondents at colleges within their radius of distribution. Most college stringers cover events on their own campus; this may include anything from a football game to a student protest to a discovery in the biology department. They file their stories by press telegram, and receive an itemized check each month. Occasionally, a student stringer will be told to include his college community in his "beat." Very little of note happens at St. Peter's College in Jersey City, New Jersey, for example, but a great deal happens in the Jersey City area. Student stringers at St. Peter's are kept busy covering Jersey City for the New York City newspapers.

A campus stringer can earn anything from $10 to $200 a month, depending on the number of stories he writes. The news magazines pay the highest rates and also offer the most work; students are frequently asked to comment on some campus trend or interview faculty members about an international development. The two wire services pay the lowest wages, while newspapers usually fall somewhere in the middle.

Many colleges have organized "Press Clubs" composed of the student stringers for various media. At these schools, the only way to become a stringer is to be accepted by the press club. Elsewhere, the procedure is simpler. If there is no existing campus stringer for a given paper, wire service, or magazine, write a letter and offer your services. Be prepared to prove that your writing is up to professional standards; if it isn't, you won't last out the week.

A less journalistically inclined writer might consider hacking articles for magazines. Many of the teenage and campus-oriented monthlies are happy to accept contributions from college students. Subjects range from fashions to politics to dating behavior, and pay ranges from nothing-but-a-byline to $500 or more. Once you have sold a few articles, you will find that magazines will begin to commission you to write up a certain fad, activity, or whatever. When you reach that point, you are on your way to becoming a successful professional free-lance writer.

Do not neglect the media nearest your college. If your school puts out an alumni magazine, the odds are good that its editor is constantly in dire need of material. Offer to write a column in each issue about campus goings-on, and supplement this with occasional longer articles about student activities and opinions. Your local newspaper may be interested in running similar contributions. It is also possible to cover town events for a local newspaper, but in general your greatest asset is your knowledge of and involvement in student activities, and you should devote as much of your writing as possible to these matters.

Many college students earn good money by writing advertising and promotion for local stores and businesses. Visit a few town merchants and offer to put some extra oomph into their ads. If they accept, you've got yourself a business. Nearby corporations represent another potential source of income. Offer to write them a few recruitment ads on approval; if they like your work, they will pay you well for it. Success at these endeavors will soon lead to more lucrative opportunities, such as writing promotional booklets and the like. A Columbia University student currently writes advertising pamphlets for a correspondence school. His income from that one source alone is enough to pay all his college expenses.

If you are a good writer, you are one of a surprisingly small number of people. You should have absolutely no trouble finding a way to turn your valuable talent into cash.

11. PRINTING

In Chapter Three we described how a mimeograph machine can be made the basis of a thriving student agency. On large campuses, far greater profits can accrue to the student with a rudimentary knowledge of the art of printing.

The demand for printed advertisements, posters, letters, stationery, and so on is inexhaustible at any large college or university. If job printers in town are getting the lion's share of this business, it is only because no student at your college combines the necessary skills with the equally necessary ambition. If you have the skills, go find yourself some ambition. This business is too good to miss.

Of course the most profitable way to start a student printing agency is to purchase your own presses, type, and other equipment. A student at the University of Illinois has done just this, and his profits have justified his investment. But few undergraduates have the necessary capital to enter the printing business in this grand manner. Most student printing agencies use the facilities of the college press, the school newspaper, or a printer in town. It should not be difficult to find a printer who will let you borrow his shop and equipment in the evenings or on weekends. Whatever he charges you for the privilege, you can quickly earn back that much and more by taking orders from individual classmates, student organizations, your college administration, academic departments, and so on.

If you know something about printing, you owe it to yourself to investigate this business opportunity. Most student printing agencies net $3,000 or $4,000 a year, and some do better still. You needn't turn to counterfeiting to make money on a printing press.

12. PHOTOGRAPHY

Schools as far-flung as the University of Mississippi and the University of Delaware, Centre College in Danville, Kentucky, and Yankton College in Yankton, South Dakota, report the existence of one or more student photography agencies on their campus. They cite profits ranging from $20 to $400 a month.

The demand is obvious. Students need passport and application photos. Town newspapers and alumni magazines need pictures of campus events. News magazines and wire services need photographs of important goings-on, on campus and off. Colleges need portraits of faculty members and prize-winning students, and attractive photos of campus life. Fraternities, alumni groups, and student organizations need group photographs. Town residents (and lucky classmates) need wedding candids. And so on, *ad infinitum.*

The better your skill and equipment, the more business you will get. If you know something about cameras, lenses, strobes, etc., you will know what you need; if you don't, you're reading the wrong page. You will be able to provide much better, cheaper, and faster service if you do your own developing. The college newspaper or yearbook will probably let you use their darkroom for a small fee, or for nothing if you are a staff member. If not, see if the school itself has developing facilities that you can borrow.

Once you have taken care of the technicalities, all you have to do is advertise and wait for business. Pay a personal visit to each major potential customer. This includes your college office of public information, the alumni magazine, town newspapers, all stringers and other writers on campus, presidents of fraternities and student organizations, and the persons in charge of alumni reunions and homecomings. Newspaper ads and business cards should do for non-institutional customers; as word of your agency spreads you will begin to get your share of passport jobs, weddings, dances, and testimonials.

13. ATHLETICS

"Professionalism" is a "good word" in most college contexts, but when combined with "athletics" it becomes a very bad word indeed. Some college administrators might go so far as to call it a "nasty business."

Putting aside the issue of "athletic scholarships"—an athletic scholarship is the pay a professional athlete gets for playing college ball—putting that aside, there are still a number of likely ways of turning your athletic skills into pocket money. The best, of course, is to become an avowed and open professional athlete. Scores of students around the country spend part of their time at their studies, the rest of it at pro practices and games. Professional baseball, football, basketball, and hockey players have been known to attend school even while their sport was in season. Those few who made it to the major leagues in their particular sport were able to graduate with as much as $60,000 in the bank. That's a lot of pocket money.

Of course professional athletes are almost always prohibited from playing in collegiate contests, which might upset you a little and your school a great deal more. Still, some students have managed to avoid this dilemma by going professional in one sport and playing for Old Yahoo State in others. The most common examples are the student boxer, the student tennis pro, and the student golf pro. A boxer's earnings depend on his skill and his medical insurance, but the other two professions are well-paying and comparatively safe.

Other athletic opportunities are coaching for local teams, serving as an official at high school or other contests, instructing athletics for town organizations, or YMCAs, and helping out with the freshman team. If you are proficient at any sport, you should be able to think of a way to make your proficiency pay. Don't be scared off by that bugaboo of "professionalism."

14. COMPUTERS

A computer is a sinister machine invented by Rube Goldberg. *Nice* people refuse to have anything to do with computers.

As a result, nice people have to pay technically inclined college students a small fortune every year to do their computer work for them. If FORTRAN is your idea of racy language, you should be in the computer programming business.

Rutgers University in New Brunswick, New Jersey, and Massachusetts Institute of Technology in Cambridge, Massachusetts, both have active student computer programming services. M.I.T.'s is the bigger of the two, grossing nearly $25,000 a year. Its clients include faculty members, the college administration, and many private companies.

M.I.T. has another computer agency which programs "ideal dates" for customers throughout the East. It is one of several fairly successful imitations of a much larger Harvard-based enterprise called Operation Match. We will discuss this computer sideline in substantial detail in Chapter Six.

Independent one-man programming businesses are by far the

most common computer money-makers. They can be found on any campus with a computer or access to one. Their profits depend on the amount of business they get, but usually average out to $6 or $7 an hour. Computer time is prohibitively expensive, so you should think twice before going into the programming business unless you can get onto the "hardware" free of charge. Most universities allow student programmers this privilege on the grounds that they are training themselves while making money.

Typical of this new breed of technological student entrepreneurs is an undergraduate at Princeton University, who earns well over $1,000 a year at his labors. His employers have ranged from the Princeton admissions office to International Business Machines and from an undergraduate course guide to the American Association of University Professors. Not satisfied with pumping through the same programs again and again, this student specializes in designing new computer techniques for specific problems. Some of his original programs are now in use at research institutions from Washington to Alberta, Canada.

"It's fascinating as well as remunerative," he says about his work. "It's a whole lot better than waiting on tables."

"A Whole Lot Better than Waiting on Tables" could have been the title of this chapter. Turning an unusual talent into a profitable enterprise is undoubtedly one of the very best ways for a college student to make money. For one thing, such specialized businesses normally pay better than the average sales or service agency. More important, skilled work is more fun and more educational than a routine job or business. The suggestions contained in this chapter come closest to the ideal we have established for student money-making: an extra-curricular activity with pay.

CHAPTER 6

Moguls in
the Making

1. WARNING NUMBER ONE

This chapter is devoted to college businesses which earn five-digit profits. There are very few such businesses, so it will be a short chapter.

If you are planning to start a five-figure business, the next few pages are designed to disillusion and—we admit it—discourage you. Student businessmen who try to start big usually wind up losing big. But if you are just browsing, and are interested in reading about the five successful bigshots we have managed to unearth, please skip the warnings and start with Section Five of this chapter. Then, if the case studies tempt you to aim high, go back and read the first half of the chapter.

In a sense, there are many student businesses across the country which earn more than $10,000 a year. The catch is that nearly all of them are cooperative enterprises of one sort or another, and the ten grand has to be split into a number of smaller bundles. A student newspaper or a moving service or a grinder agency can easily take in this much cash, and still pay its top man only a couple of thousand.

It takes a very special kind of business to earn one man $10,000 or more. For one thing, it is not going to be a campus concession. It is a rare college that is large enough and wealthy enough to earn *anyone* that much dough. You have to figure that a business which nets $10,000 probably grosses at least $40,000. At a school with a student body of 4,000, that means $10 per student. If half your classmates buy whatever you're selling (which is a damn good average for any business), you must collect $20 from each customer to gross $40,000. And to make that $10,000 profit, you'll have to keep all your costs down to a total of $15 per sale. All in all, it's a good trick.

It might be easier on a giant campus with 30,000 or 40,000 students, but it usually isn't. If you have a good thing going, you can bet your life that a dozen competitors will spring up before the week is out, and your share of the market will quickly be pared down to the small-college level. The only way to avoid this is to wrangle an administration-enforced monopoly. This is usually impossible at a large school, and even where it is possible, the monopoly is invariably accompanied by price controls, salary minimums, and other restrictions designed to keep you from making more than your fair share. Your fair share will never amount to anything like $10,000.

We have searched a good deal, and we have not found a single campus business in existence today which nets one student $10,000 or more. You are highly unlikely to become the first exception to the rule.

2. WARNING NUMBER TWO

We do not mean to imply that there are no college students around with annual earnings of more than $10,000. If you inherit $170,000 and invest it safely at six percent, you can earn $10,000 a year just by clipping coupons—and there are college kids who do just that.

There are other ways. Be a professional athlete, or a professional singer. Write a best-selling novel. Invent a tarless cigarette, or a new psychedelic drug, or an automobile that runs without gasoline. Be a full-time corporation executive, and go to college at night. There are plenty of other ways.

Nearly all the college students who manage to earn five-figure profits earn them in a way that has nothing to do with their being college students. They make their wad out in the real world, by selling something that people want to buy. Their customers may not even know they are students; indeed, many of these young businessmen go to great pains to hide this shameful fact from those with whom they have dealings. They are creatures of two worlds. They have college classes and business appointments, school chums and working associates—and they keep their worlds as separate as they can.

In Chapter Four we discussed a student at Flint College who nets $9,000 a year from his sod-laying and landscaping company. His business is a perfect example of what we are talking about. Its owner-manager devotes a great deal of his time to laying sod; he spends the rest of it studying political science. His studies and his sod-laying are completely unconnected. He competes with other landscaping companies on an equal footing. He hires student labor only because it is the cheapest labor around. He is in every respect a successful young businessman who just happens, coincidentally, to be attending college as well. When he is finished at Flint he could very easily sell out to some other young businessman who doesn't happen to be attending college —and he might well do just that.

If you want a chance at earning $10,000 or more a year while you're in college, you will probably have to follow in the footsteps of our sod-layer. That is, find yourself a likely business in town and devote all your spare energies to it, forgetting about college and college life. Even this is no sure key to success. Lots of local business people earn ten thousand a year, but lots don't —especially in their first or second year. You will be additionally handicapped by two facts. First, you are a student, and will have to devote at least a minimum of time to your studies. Second, you are in all likelihood a transient. You probably plan to go on to graduate school, or to military service, or to a career in another line and another state. You have only a couple of years to build your business to the $10,000 milepost.

Still, in the sweepstakes that is American business life, $10,000 is not such an unusual prize. You have almost as much chance of success as a non-student would if he entered the same business. Of course you also face the possibility of losing money. But if

"Ten Thousand or Bust" is your motto, you'd better hang your shingle off campus. You won't find that kind of money anywhere else.

3. WARNING NUMBER THREE

The college student who decides to run an off-campus business loses a great deal. Not only does he pass up the pleasures and satisfactions of college life and college friends, he also throws away the chance to make money from the thing he knows best: the wants and needs of the college student. We have already explained why it is almost impossible to earn a five-digit profit on a college campus. But there is another alternative, one which enables a student businessman to work with other students, yet does not restrict him to the limited market of a single school. This is the multi-campus business.

People whose job it is to know about such things are agreed that the "youth market" is gigantic, growing ever larger, and still more or less "underdeveloped." In other words, college students have a lot of money to spend, and there are a large number of items on which they would be willing to spend it—if the items were made readily available to them. The typical student agency takes advantage of this underdeveloped market at one college. The multi-campus business does the same thing at many colleges at once.

Multi-campus businesses can fail, and when they do, they fail resoundingly. Two years ago, a sophomore at Princeton Univeristy decided to organize a traveling fashion show. Working with his brother, also at Princeton, a friend from Yale, and a girl from Vassar, he founded Beau-Duane Fashion Enterprises, and set to work.

For an entire year, the group struggled to get the show going. A price of $500 was established for each outfit; for that sum, a manufacturer was guaranteed that his garments would be modeled in at least twenty fashion shows on twenty different college campuses. A full-length program, with photographs of each outfit, was designed and prepared. Girls were contacted at colleges throughout the East, and were told to get ready for the show. Dates were set, models were found at each college, advertising was printed, problems of all sorts were met and mastered.

But not mastered well enough. The original goal of 75 outfits had to be revised to 60. Many manufacturers expressed interest in the plan, but wanted to wait a year to see how the first series of shows went. To get sponsors for that first series, the managers were forced to offer fantastic bargains; one manufacturer exhibited six costumes for a mere $400 total.

It was thought that local stores would be an important source of profit, with tradesmen paying as much as $50 each to have their names listed in the program as places where students could buy the garments exhibited. Nearly $1,000 was spent to find the names and locations of the popular clothing shops, and to prepare rate sheets and other material for prospective advertisers. But the group found itself without enough capital to hire salesmen on the various campuses, and so this whole aspect of the business was dropped.

Great plans were also made for the show program, which was to be ornate, complete, and attractive. Manufacturers of accessories and cosmetics were invited to advertise in the program, but they were invited too late. Most had already committed their advertising budgets, and asked Beau-Duane to come back next year. Finally, after $2,000 had been spent to prepare the program, this too was scuttled—because there was not enough money left to print it. When the program dropped out, so did some of the sponsors—decreasing even further the group's working capital. .

A $5,000 bank loan was arranged, and the money was quickly spent. The Princeton founder tossed in $8,000 of his own money. That too was soon gone.

The fashion show was a smashing success. It toured 28 colleges, played to full houses at nearly all of them, and was immensely popular wherever it went. But when the books were balanced, Beau-Duane Fashion Enterprises was $1,000 in the red. The Princeton originator, now a senior, accepted his loss gracefully, and remarked that he was glad to get out with only $1,000 and two years of work down the drain.

The story has a happy ending. An executive with one of the clothing firms which participated in the show thought the idea was sound, and decided to buy out the business. He felt that the failure of the first series was due to undercapitalization—the group had been constantly short of money, and had therefore been unable to do things properly. He offered 50 percent of the profits from the second tour, plus 10 percent of all tour profits from then on. The deal was made. The second tour netted $20,000, half of which was duly turned over to the originators of Beau-Duane Fashion Enterprises. The third tour is now in preparation, and promises to be still bigger and more successful.

The happy ending should not diminish the importance of this object lesson, for it was a totally unexpected fluke. The important point of the story is that multi-campus businesses can fail, and when they do, they involve a far greater loss of time, energy and capital than an unsuccessful single-campus venture. Our Princeton entrepreneur considered himself very lucky when he thought he was losing just a thousand bucks and two years of work. He could have lost his shirt—literally.

4. WARNING NUMBER FOUR

It is clear from what we have already said that the college student who is resolved to earn $10,000 or more in a single year has two options. He can forget about being a college student and start a local business, or he can expand beyond his own school to form a multi-campus business.

Nine out of ten cocoon tycoons choose the former approach. The chances of success are greater, the need for originality is smaller, and the risk of capital is less. All you have to do is think of a business that you are capable of running, and that is needed in your community—and then go ahead. Your business can be anything from a restaurant to an advertising agency, from a catering service to (our old friend) a sod-laying company. You start small, investing as little capital as you can. If the need for your business is less than you estimated, you'll stay small, and your loss will be small. If the need is great, you'll grow quickly, and soon reach the $10,000 mark. Chances are you'll stay small, but you have as much likelihood of making it big as the next man.

A few adventurous souls try the other route. Here it is crucial to find a product or service that just isn't available so far to students in your area. The more creative and original you are, the more likely you are to think of an idea that will succeed. Plan it out carefully, to make sure it can be done, and done profitably. Conduct a "pilot project" on your own campus, and see how your business is received there. If all goes well, you are ready to take the big plunge. Find competent campus representatives at other colleges, offer them a liberal commission, furnish them with whatever they'll need in the way of promotional materials, samples, and such, and then hope. As things get going, plough back all your profits into the business, expanding to new campuses as soon as the old ones are secure. By these methods, you will soon soar past the $10,000 figure—or lose everything.

Whichever option you choose, remember that any business which nets its owner $10,000 is a big business. It will take all of your ability and most of your time. To succeed, you will need not only a good instinct for business, but also a lot of quickly acquired knowledge. Chapter Eight of this book will help orient you in the legal and financial thickets of big business. For the rest, you will have to delve into the mammoth literature on business techniques and related matters.

Because it has nothing to do with college students *per se*, the off-campus big business is of little interest to us here. We have already given one example (the sod-laying company), and will give only one other. The remainder of the chapter will be devoted to a discussion of four successful multi-campus businesses. We would include more, but we have been able to find only four which earned their managers five-digit profits.

5. BUSINESS FORMS

Four years ago, a freshman at Amherst College in Amherst, Massachusetts, decided to go into business selling forms of various sorts to other businesses. He organized Titan Business Systems in his home town of Philadelphia. The enterprise has been going, and growing, ever since. It earns its manager, now an Amherst graduate, well over $10,000 a year.

It is hard to imagine a student business which would have less to do with college. Roughly once a month during the school year, Titan's manager flies down to Philly for the weekend, to make sure that his employees have everything under control. Other than that, he handles the business by mail from Amherst, running a Massachusetts "branch office" in his college room. There he designs, promotes, and sells a variety of business forms, from sales books and ledgers to invoices and computer cards. He works about 20 hours a week while at school, full-time during vacations.

Titan Business Systems is currently undergoing extensive corporate reorganization, branching out into management consulting and similar fields. Its originator envisions the development of a sort of "business supermarket," capable of providing a wide range of services to businessmen. To this end, he is pumping nearly all his profits back into the business, building up both his list of services and his list of clients.

Aside from the money, Titan's manager says he derives great satisfaction from his business. "It's a teriffic feeling to be able to accomplish something people twice my age can't accomplish," he admits. "I get particular pleasure out of implementing new ideas and talking old-fashioned businessmen into trying my systems." He speaks with something like joy about a streamlined check-writing procedure he has devised, which employs shingles of patterned carbon to enable businessmen to write a check, a check stub, and a tax journal entry at the same time, without having to write any word more than once. "It's hard work convincing people that the extra convenience is worth the extra cost," he says. "But once the system begins to catch on, the satisfaction is tremendous."

Any disadvantages of the business? "Well," he says, "it doesn't have much to do with college." To make up for this deficiency, he worked for a semester as business manager of the Amherst student newspaper, and in that short time managed to wipe out an $8,000 debt and put the paper in the black. "That was fun too," he says, "and gave me a different kind of satisfaction." But there was no money in it, and so Titan Business Systems remains his first love.

6. CHARTER FLIGHTS

In Chapter Three we discussed the possibility of making money from a campus charter flight. Four years ago, a student at the University of Texas at Austin tried it, and was successful. He decided to expand his program, incorporated it as Student Travel, Inc., and set to work. Now a senior at the University of Texas law school, he handles charter flights for all 63 Texas colleges and universities. His gross revenue comes to $350,000 a year, and his net profit, while undisclosed, is well beyond the $10,000 mark.

The process of expansion was easily accomplished. After incorporating, he established a liaison with the Texas Intercollegiate Student Association, which helped him to find campus representatives at various schools. His size enabled him to charter planes at a discount rate, and he passed the savings on to his customers. Smaller campus charter flight groups were unable to compete, and he soon found himself with a virtual Texas-wide monopoly on college charters.

From the very beginning, this entrepreneur decided to depend less on campus reps and more on his own advertising and his comparatively low prices. Besides placing ads in all the campus newspapers, he designs and prints a special brochure each year. He estimates that he makes one sale for every hundred brochures distributed. Last year he sent more than 1,000 people overseas—the fruit of 100,000 brochures and a lot of work.

The work is lightened by half a dozen employees, in addition to campus representatives. Student Travel's manager is currently expanding his business to include non-collegiate charter flights, and will no doubt have to hire more full-time help. It will be worth it. He's got a good thing going, and he knows it. After law school is finished, he plans to stay in the charter flight business —at least for a while.

7. BIG-TIME BOOKING

We talked about campus entertainment booking agencies in Chapter Three. At Brigham Young University in Provo, Utah, there is a student booker who is earning more than $2,000 a month. Needless to say, he doesn't make it all, or even very much of it, on the BYU campus.

In fact, wherever you are in Utah, Idaho, Colorado, Montana, or Wyoming, if you want to hire a band, put on a variety show, sponsor a speech, or take 100 of your friends out canoeing, you will probably be advised to get in touch with SAK United Entertainment. You will then become a part of that $2,000-a-month profit.

The guts of SAK's business comes from supplying student bands to student organizations. BYU has 30 or 40 bands and combos, and nearly every one is on the SAK payroll. Most of their performances are not at Brigham Young, however. The entrepreneurial genius behind SAK has learned that, as he puts it, "college talent which is of no great interest on its home campus can be a real marquee-value attraction 100 miles away." SAK transports its bands the 100 miles, or more—and has them playing at colleges, high schools, churches, cotillions, and private parties throughout the Southwest. Once outside their hometown area, some of his student groups command as much as $500 a night— and are considered a bargain at the price.

Big-name entertainment is another major source of SAK's income. Suppose a local high school calls and says it wants, say, the Beach Boys for its senior prom. SAK gets in touch with the national agency that handles this popular group, and finds out whether they are available. If they are, it buys a week of the Beach Boys' time from the agency. The high school that made the original request pays most of the expense of bringing the Beach Boys out to the Southwest. SAK then arranges five other engagements for the group in the same week, and makes a tidy profit on each one.

SAK does not limit itself to musical entertainment. Among its other attractions is a completely packaged variety show, which varies in length and make-up depending on the desires of the customer. Composed almost entirely of Brigham Young students, the show usually includes a comedian or two, a master of ceremonies, singers and instrumentalists of various sorts, and a few miscellaneous acts. The complete package sells for between $500 and $1,000 a performance. To give his entertainers the training they needed, SAK's manager took the show on a three-month tour of South America—and thereby earned himself some additional profit as well.

SAK will cater a dinner dance, hire a lecturer, arrange a hayride, organize a barn dance, guide a camping trip—or set up and carry out any other kind of entertainment you can think of. The company manages seven or eight recreational facilities in the Provo area—including a dance hall and several boating lakes. It does public relations work for the Miss Utah contest, and has even supplied attractive coed enthusiasts for political rallies —for a price. The SAK letterhead lists "entertainment, conventions, pageants, assemblies, concerts, public relations" as its chief services. It couldn't possibly give a complete list without filling the page and leaving no room for the letter.

And letters are very important to SAK's success. They are sent out in droves to potential customers all over the Southwest. Together with brochures and word-of-mouth, they constitute the company's only method of attracting new clients. A typical letter reads:

> SAK United Entertainment represents a very unique position in the college, high school and special entertainment field.
> Since our beginning we have represented the entertainment market on the "buying side" as well as the "artist side" of the picture. Our experience has given us a thorough grasp of all aspects of the artists and their agencies. The colleges and high schools no longer have to worry about unsigned contracts, routing, confusing contract riders, etc. Our entertainment areas include. . . .
> SAK United Entertainment offers . . . .
> Free publicity materials. We absolutely supply everything at no charge. Including: posters, flyers, pictures, records, newspaper

mats, radio and television tapes, television slides, news releases, etc.

Professionally produced shows. Our trained staff works with you in the selection of an artist who will "complement" your particular need. . . .

Personal representative. To each and every show, we send a personal representative to help you in any manner possible. He will help make adjustments with sound, lights—or even the artist!

We are very much interested in helping you plan your next attraction—regardless of budget and the entertainment that you have in mind. We can help. Please feel free to call at any time—about anything.

Once contact has been established with a customer and the first booking has been successfuly completed, everything is easy from then on. "Satisfied customers keep coming back," explains SAK's founder and manager. "They give us a phone call whenever they need some entertainment help. We meet their needs within their budget, and then bill them. It's as simple as that."

Simple or not, it certainly is profitable. SAK United Entertainment was started in August of 1966. By the following April it was in full swing. In April and May, 1967, the company earned a total income of $5,500, gave part-time employment to more than 50 college students, worked on behalf of 18 different schools and 25 different civic and private organizations, arranged more than 50 concerts and dances in five states, and took over the management of four recreational sites in Utah. A senior in political science, SAK's manager plans to set up "branch" offices in New York and Los Angeles as soon as he graduates. Eventually, he will probably sell out the buisness at a nice profit and go on to something new.

Meanwhile, SAK United Entertainment has its non-financial advantages too. SAK's manager had to drop his course load to 12 hours a week to make the time to run his business, but he says it was worth it. "This is perfect training for a dozen careers," he exults. "You learn how to handle money, and how to deal with individuals and groups of all sorts. You meet men in all kinds of positions and learn what their problems are and how they go about solving them. No business could be better for any student going into business, counseling, politics, psychology, group relations, or any profession involving the solution of group or organizational problems." That covers a lot of ground.

8. DISCOUNT SALES

Three years ago, a student at Trinity College in Hartford, Connecticut, founded Varsity International Sales Association. The idea of the business was to sell special VISA cards to college and high school students in the Hartford area. These cards would entitle their owners to a substantial student discount at any store which was a participating VISA "sponsor." Sponsors would be charged to have their names listed in the VISA directory, which was to be handed out free to every purchaser of a VISA card.

VISA was launched in four cities simultaneously. Our Trinity student handled Hartford himself, and interested three friends in following the same procedure in Philadelphia, Boston, and Washington. The idea was a good one. In three short years, VISA has grown to the point where it now publishes 11 directories in 11 different states, sells more than 100,000 VISA cards a year, and grosses well over half a million dollars. New branches are about to open in Denver, Chicago, Pittsburgh, and Los Angeles, and within the next decade the company expects to expand to every state in the union.

Now a national organization with headquarters on Madison Avenue in New York City, VISA purposely retains its decentralized structure. Each regional manager is free to set his own prices and advertising rates, hire his own employees, design his own distribution system, and so forth. When a student from a college which is not yet covered applies to VISA for permission to set up a new region, the group conducts market research on the area, and personal research on the applicant. If both are deemed to be good risks, a VISA "trouble-shooter" is sent out to help start the new region. The regional manager-to-be is trained in the VISA system and the VISA philosophy—and then left to work out his own procedures. Only national advertising in the

VISA books and the appearance of the VISA decal and card
are controlled from above.

VISA makes its highest profits in big cities, but it is more
than willing to open up branches in small college towns as well.
The smallest VISA operation so far is at Williams College in
Williamstown, Massachusetts, which earns its regional manager
a steady if unimposing profit. As the original founder of VISA
(now regional manager for Connecticut) sees it: "Even in the
smallest college town, our operation can work. There may not
be enough merchants to justify publication of a new VISA guide
for the area, but card sales can always succeed. After all, a student
who goes to school in Williamstown might live in New York
City. He can get his money's worth out of his VISA card when
he goes home on vacation."

VISA makes money from three principal sources. The first is
the sale of VISA cards. High school and college students seldom
need more than a glance through the local VISA guide to realize
that the card is a bargain at almost any price. To get maximum
distribution, most regional managers price the cards as low as
they dare. We say "dare" because VISA has found that if the
card is priced too low, students will not bother to use it, and
sponsors will therefore become dissatisfied with the program. In
Hartford, for example, $3 was tried and found to be too high;
students weren't buying the cards. The price was reduced to $1.00
the next year, but this was too low; students weren't using the
cards. Now the price is established at $1.50, which seems to be,
as Goldilocks would say, just right.

The second source of revenue is the local sponsors. Tradesmen
pay an average $25 a year to be included in their local VISA
guide. For that sum, they get their name, address, and phone
number listed, plus a short description of the goods they carry
and the particular discount they are offering. Nearly all the discounts last the entire year, and students with VISA cards may
return to the same store many times to take advantage of their
savings. Merchants who don't want to offer a permanent bargain
may place discount coupons—good for one time only—in the
back of the VISA guide. The $25 fee also entitles the sponsor
to post a distinctive (if ugly) purple VISA decal in his window.

Walk through the streets of Philadelphia, Boston, or Hartford these days and you'll be able to count hundreds of these decals, adorning the displays of restaurants, movie theaters, and stores of all kinds.

The third source of VISA's profit is advertising in the VISA guides. Some sponsors take out ads to increase the appeal of their stores, but most of the advertising comes from manufacturers. Corporations interested in recruiting college students are another major category of advertisers; though these companies have nothing to do with VISA's discount program, they realize that the VISA guide is an ideal spot for advertising aimed specifically at college students.

VISA charges $2,500 for a full-page national ad. Local ad prices vary with the size of the regional program. A full page costs $500 in Washington or Boston, only $250 in Philadelphia or Hartford. The minimum advertisement size for non-sponsors is one-third of a page.

A regional manager's net profit will depend on the size of his operation, but it is not going to be astronomical for the first couple of years. This is because VISA is still growing, expanding, and developing, and is committed to what it calls an "account-development approach." In other words, nearly all the profits are put back into the business. In his first year at Trinity, our correspondent netted $400. He doubled that figure in his second year. Last year he pocketed a $4,000 profit on a gross revenue of roughly $30,000. "I could have netted more than $10,000 without much trouble," he says, "but that would have nearly wrecked the project for the future."

The regional managers are normally planning to stay with VISA for a number of years, so they can afford to wait around for their efforts to bear fruit. Meanwhile, temporary VISA employees are certainly not complaining about their earnings. The average commission for salesmen is 25 percent on each advertisement sold, 33 percent on each VISA card sold, and 40 percent on each sponsorship sold. Most salesmen average at least $150 a week for part-time work. One crackerjack employee in Connecticut set to work selling VISA cards to high school student governments. In one week he sold 2,400 cards, earning himself a very impressive $1,200.

Regional managers frequently hire employees on a commission basis to cover outlying areas of their states. In Connecticut, for example, the regional manager in Hartford pays a Yale student to sell cards, ads, and sponsorships in New Haven. This procedure helps expand the business for those who plan to stay with it, while at the same time earning good money for students who are just "passing through."

Varsity International Sales Association has gone a long way since the first mimeographed VISA guide was printed in Hartford three years ago. The company recently incorporated as the sole subsidiary of "Shield, International," and is planning to branch out into real estate, national marketing, and many other areas. VISA's unique discount program will continue to expand, as a service to students, an advertising medium for national corporations, and a marketing gimmick for local tradesmen. If VISA has not yet come to your college town, you may rest assured it will.

9. COMPUTER DATING

Ask any student at any college to name the biggest student business of them all, and the odds are he'll answer "Operation Match." He'll be right. You probably know already, but just for the record Operation Match is the nation's first and largest computerized dating service. The story of its growth from a kooky idea in the minds of a couple of Harvard roommates to a far-flung business empire is destined to become the rags-to-riches fable of our generation.

It all started in the winter of 1965. Two Harvard juniors were sitting in their room, discussing dating in general and blind dates in particular. Recalls one of them: "It seemed to us that a very extensive but unsophisticated method of 'fixing up' one's friends with each other had become an accepted way of meeting people on campuses everywhere. The results were often painful for everyone concerned. . . . The essential idea behind Operation Match is the pooling of resources into the biggest little black book ever, and using a computer as a clearinghouse for the information. At the time the idea seemed like a natural for college students who have learned to avoid the cattle shows known as 'mixers.' We really didn't know then how right we were."

To test their idea, the two students designed a questionnaire that would give the vital statistics of both the customer and his "ideal date." An IBM 1401 computer was programmed to match up the questionnaires and send each applicant the names of all other applicants who were ideal for him (or her), and for whom he (or she) was ideal. Operating on a shoestring budget of $1,250, they printed up 10,000 questionnaires and had them distributed on college campuses in the Boston area. Each applicant had to send $3 with his completed questionnaire to receive his ideal matches.

Within three months, 7,800 students from 100 New England colleges had paid the $3 fee, and had their qualifications punched onto computer cards and scanned by Operation Match's rented computer. By mid-April the results were out: 7,800 lists of names and addresses arrived in 7,800 college mailboxes on the same morning. A Cornell University medical student received 154 matches, over 125 of them from Wellesley College. Top among the girls was a blond, blue-eyed Vassar College sophomore, who got 112 names in the mail. Most applicants got five or six, and were more than satisfied.

It was clear to the two Harvard founders that they were not the only lonely collegians in New England. Students were not only willing to pay the $3 fee and answer the 135 questions about their interests, background, sexual attitudes, personal appearance, and personality—they also added enthusiastic comments and instructions to the questionnaire answer sheet. Examples: *Dartmouth*—"No dogs please! Have mercy!" *Harvard*—"Have you any buxom blondes who like poetry?" *Mount Holyoke*—"None of those dancing bears from Amherst." *Williams*—"This is the greatest excuse for calling up a strange girl that I've ever heard." *Sarah Lawrence*—"Help!" *Columbia*—"Just hurry!" News of the new service spread faster than questionnaire forms could be printed, and the Match headquarters in Cambridge was deluged with requests for applications.

By the summer of 1965, Operation Match had incorporated as Compatibility Research, Inc., a full-time staff of a dozen had been employed, and an established New York City firm had been pulled in to provide working capital and technical assistance.

Figuring that what was good for New England should be good for the world, the fledgling company spent the summer setting up shop in eight other college-heavy cities—San Francisco, Los Angles, Chicago, Bloomington, Ann Arbor, Lansing, Detroit, and New York. Campus representatives were hired at hundreds of schools to distribute questionnaires, answer questions, and arrange for advertising. By fall, Operation Match was on 500 campuses in large cities across the country. By spring, it had spread to 2,000 campuses throughout the United States and Canada. The price went up to $4, the questionnaire got longer and more complicated, and applications continued to pour in by the thousands. In 1966, more than 100,000 students were matched.

The service was constantly expanded and improved. An IBM 7094 was substituted for the old 1401 model. An office in an old warehouse was acquired, outgrown, and replaced with one in a posh hotel. Continuous processing was introduced, to give customers more matches for their money, as new questionnaires were paired off with old answers stored in the computer's memory banks. Zip codes were used to assure that all matches were in the same geographical area. Operation Match had gone professional.

It was to get more professional still. A Washington columnist suggested an Operation Match for "the not so dewy-eyed and callow"—meaning Washington high society. A man in Maplewood, New Jersey, hired Match to re-pair 76 married couples for a party. The only complaints came from the two couples who were paired with their own spouses: "Why did this have to happen to us?" they moaned. Match saw the light, and started thinking about the adult lonely-heart business.

Potential sidelines in the student market were not ignored. Plans are now afoot for an Operation Match Privilege Card, which will offer Match subscribers a significant discount on national products. A Match Magazine, to be devoted to Match and its participants, is also planned, with an initial circulation of 100,000. Advertising in this magazine will move Match into the marketing business, and plans are already being formulated to market-test new products aimed at college students.

Back on the dating frontier, the next step will be a coin-operated date machine. As envisioned by Match directors, the machine will consist of a keyboard, located perhaps in the student union, with a direct connection to the Match computer. Anyone desiring a date for the evening will type in the answers to a few questions, wait about ten seconds, and then read out the name of a suitable date —nearby, free for the evening, and ideally matched.

Operation Match has little choice but to innovate or atrophy, for already it has plenty of competition in the computerized dating field. Nearby Massachusetts Institute of Technology was the first school to invade the Match domain, with a reasonably successful and very similar venture called Contact. Dozens of smaller versions are now flourishing around the country. Operation Match has refused to reveal its volume of business in the fall of 1966 and the spring of 1967, on the grounds that the company is now involved in litigation concerning its ownership. But we suspect that its total business was less than the year before—and so new areas seem to offer the best chance for new profits.

Whatever its future, Operation Match has contributed more than its share to American college life. Punch cards are now preferred over punch bowls as the "in" way to meet dates. In its three years of existence, Operation Match has earned itself a permanent place in the annals of student business—not to mention a whopping profit.

10. WARNING NUMBER FIVE

The handful of student big businesses we have described in this chapter are the *only* student big businesses we have heard of. The vast majority of student money-makers start small and end small. A tiny percentage start small and end big. Those that start big inevitably end—completely. They leave the overambitious entrepreneur who masterminded them with nothing but debts and wasted effort. Remember that.

CHAPTER 7

In Loco Parentis

1. THE NEGATIVE APPROACH

In talking about the role of college administrations in student money-making, you have to start with the same premise that the administrations do: Making money is not the purpose of college. Hundreds of administrators from all over the country have written to tell us that, as one Midwestern dean phrased it, "the proper business of students is study." Everything else is secondary at best.

If you button-hole an administrator and press him hard enough, you can usually get him to admit the possibility of a student business or job with an educational value of its own. But you will have to press very hard indeed, for the admission goes against the academic grain. The popular administrative attitude toward student money-making is that it is a more or less necessary evil. In formulating college policy on the subject, the administrator therefore asks himself two questions: How necessary? How evil?

The usual answer to the first question is very necessary. There are colleges in existence with sufficent scholarship and loan money to go around, but they are rare. There are schools where the student body is wealthy enough to pay its own way without working, but they too are uncommon. Nearly every college in the country is faced with a substantial number of students who *have* to earn money, and a still larger group who *want* to earn money.

The second question therefore becomes the deciding one. College administrations give their reluctant approval to those forms of student money-making which they consider least evil—that is, least inconsistent with the ideals and demands of the academic life.

2. THE STUDENT EMPLOYMENT OFFICE

At most colleges, the least evil form of student money-making is evidently off-campus employment. It is hard to tell why this is the case. Perhaps administrators feel that students who work off campus will keep their studies and their employment well separated, and therefore give due attention to both. Perhaps they feel that off-campus student jobs are good for town-gown relations. Perhaps they're just glad to have someone else foot the bill and handle the problem. Whatever the reasons, the frenetic activity that goes on in nearly every college employment office attests to the administrator's preference for this kind of student work.

You just can't complain about the student employment office. If there is a regular part-time job available in the community, you can count on them to know about it. When the job openings run out, you can count on them to talk some friendly local businessman into inventing a few. Some schools go so far as to enlist the aid of nearby alumni in their unending search for student employment opportunities. A few even train students for their off-campus jobs; you can learn computer programming or short-order cooking at Harvard, bookkeeping or bartending at Columbia. Most student employment offices fall down a bit when it comes to one-time-only jobs (baby-sitting, car washing, and the like), but you can't really blame them for that. Their goal is to get every student who wants to earn some money into a regular, well-paid, part-time job off campus. Usually it is an impossible goal, but they come as close to it as is humanly possible.

3. ON-CAMPUS EMPLOYMENT

We've said it before and we'll say it again: On-campus jobs do not pay well. At most schools, they pay miserably, and you're lucky if you can get anything over $1.00 an hour. Nevertheless, on-campus jobs are second only to off-campus jobs on the adminis- trator's list of lesser evils.

The range of student jobs on campus is tremendous in one sense, tiny in another. Which is to say, there are a lot of different jobs, but somehow they all sound the same. If you don't believe us, consider this typical list, from Louisiana State University in Baton Rouge, Louisiana:

Category I (paid between 65 cents and 90 cents per hour)—bus boy, counter girl, dormitory office assistant, factory worker (un- skilled), farm laborer (unskilled), file clerk, gardener, grade re- corder, information clerk, laboratory assistant (unskilled), library assistant I, library page I, lifeguard, messenger, monitor, office assistant (unskilled), office machine operator (simple operations), receptionist, shop assistant (unskilled), sorter.

Category II (paid between 75 cents and $1.20 per hour)—book processor, building service worker, cartographic assistant, cashier, checker (meal tickets), checker (swimming pool), draftsman (semiskilled), factory worker (semiskilled), farm laborer (semi- skilled), file clerk (reference assistant), food service worker, laboratory assistant (semiskilled), library assistant II, library page II, microfilm camera operator, museum assistant, office assistant (semiskilled), office machine operator (semiskilled), paper grader (checker), proofreader, registration assistant, reporter, beginner, research assistant (semiskilled), seamstress, shop assistant (semi- skilled), statistical clerk (semiskilled), stock clerk, student driver, telephone operator, traffic assistant, typist, waiter.

Category III (paid between 85 cents and $1.30 per hour)— accompanist, accountant, artist, book repairer, coder, draftsman, editorial assistant, electronics technician, factory worker (skilled), farm laborer (skilled), head lifeguard, illustrator trainee, labora- tory assistant (skilled), language lab attendant (skilled), law library desk attendant, letterer, library assistant III, library page III, loan desk attendant, mail clerk, multilith machine operator, museum assistant (skilled), nurse, office assistant (skilled), office machine operator (complex), orchestra librarian, paper grader (evaluation), photostat operator, reader, receiving clerk, reference assistant, reporter (advanced), research assistant (technical skill), revisor, searcher, shop assistant (skilled), stage technician, statistical clerk (complex operations), stenographer, student supervisor, translator, visual aids assistant.

See what we mean?

We should add that the list is four years old, though we doubt it's grown much. At most schools the selection would be smaller and a good deal *less* varied. Few colleges have factories, farms, or the like in which to employ students. The most common jobs, available on nearly every campus, are food service worker, clerk-typist, secretary-stenographer, library assistant, paper grader, janitor, and research assistant.

The last job mentioned is the only one worth having. By the time you're an upperclassman, you are presumably "semiskilled" in one academic discipline. Also, you are presumably reasonably interested in that discipline. If you must accept a campus job, try to get one in your field of concentration. The pay will be a little better, and at least you'll learn something.

There is one other on-campus job which is interesting—not because it is of any particular significance to students, but because it shows the cleverness of at least one administration in creating new campus job openings. In 1960, Northland College in Ashland, Wisconsin, inaugurated a plan whereby each faculty member was given a drawing account of $100 every fall. The money could be used to hire students for a variety of chores throughout the year. Rates were predetermined, with payment handled by the college business office. A monthly statement was sent to each faculty member telling him his operating balance. Among the services performed by students under the plan were baby-sitting, typing, proofreading, yardwork, car washing, driving lessons, music lessons, and painting. As an enticing fringe benefit for faculty members and an added employment opportunity for students, the Northland program shows unusual resourcefulness.

Of course if you don't happen to go to Northland (and only 400 students do), your choice of on-campus jobs will be limited to the more routine ones listed above. And if you go to a small-town college that doesn't believe in student business, your choice of money-makers will be pretty much limited to on-campus jobs.

As a matter of fact, this may be true whatever the size of your college community. Vassar College in Poughkeepsie, New York, places 460 girls a year in campus jobs; this is a little less than one-third of its student body, about average for a small women's college. Princeton University finds on-campus jobs for 1,600 undergraduates a year, roughly half the student body and the normal ratio for a large college or a small university. The University of Illinois has 8,000 students on its payroll, representing a little over a third of its enrollment, about par for a large state university.

Overall, approximately twice as many college students hold on-campus jobs as off-campus jobs. The two together account for about 99 percent of all working students. One student out of a hundred operates his own business, on or off campus.

4. COOPERATIVE EDUCATION

College administrators give tacit recognition to the educational potential of student money-making by supporting programs in cooperative education. Commonly known as "work-study" or "five-year" plans, these programs involve alternating periods of study and employment. They offer the student a chance to gain valuable on-the-job training while paying his way through college.

The cooperative education movement began in 1906 with 27 engineering students at the University of Cincinnati. Today, cooperative education enrolls some 40,000 students at more than 70 different colleges and universities. The National Commission for Cooperative Education, established in 1962, hopes to see at least 75,000 cooperative students a year by 1972.

The first "co-ops" (as cooperative students are usually called on campus) alternated a week of work with a week of classes throughout the school year. Today, most cooperative programs alternate terms instead. This permits use of the campus the year round, and allows a college to admit a greater number of students each year. By putting two students on each job, the program guarantees full-time help for every employer.

College administrators tend to stress the educational advantages of cooperative education. They talk about things like "integration of theory and practice," "increase in student motivation," "development of maturity and a sense of responsibility," "orientation to the world of work," and so on. They seem to soft-pedal the major non-educational asset of the program, which is money. Over a five-year period of alternating work and study, the average engineering student earns $7,000. Business administration students average $5,600, while students in the liberal arts earn around $3,700. Nearly all cooperative students use their earnings to defray college costs and living expenses. The economic value of a cooperative program to a college administration can be seen from a single example: The 1,000 co-ops at Georgia Institute of Technology earn $3,000,000 a year; it would take an endowment of $75,000,000 to provide enough scholarship money to replace these annual earnings.

Employers of cooperative students include many of the country's largest manufacturers, research laboratories, airlines, banks, professional groups, hospitals, newspapers, department stores, school systems, and child-care centers. The University of Cincinnati cooperates with 500 companies in 30 states, Drexel Institute of Technology with 600 companies in 16 states, and Northeastern University with 900 companies in ten states. In addition, the federal government employs several thousand students a year on a work-study basis.

Cooperative education started in an engineering college, and the program still has its greatest popularity in technical schools. The next most popular subjects are science and business administration. Education and the liberal arts trail behind, but are beginning to catch up. At some schools, including Antioch College in Yellow Springs, Ohio, and Fenn College in Cleveland, Ohio (both pioneers in cooperative education in the liberal arts), all students, regardless of their major, participate in the cooperative program. Other colleges require all students in certain areas to be co-ops. Still others offer the cooperative plan on an optional basis, often as an honors program.

All cooperative programs afford the student an opportunity for earning while learning. This is the basis for their great appeal to students and administrators alike.

5. VARIATIONS ON THE THEME

Most work-study programs alternate terms on a staggered basis, so that the college and the job are both kept filled at all times. A few schools, notably Bennington College in Bennington, Vermont, run on a different schedule. The school term at Bennington is organized in such a way that students have several months free during the winter. During this "work period" every student is expected (and helped) to find a job which is relevant to her studies and her career goals. A girl planning to go into teaching will work as a practice teacher, while a dance major will find a job dancing.

Several colleges offer work-study programs of their own—without the cooperation of private industry. Berea College in Berea, Kentucky, is the best-known example of this procedure. Berea students pay no tuition, but every student is required to work during the academic year to help meet expenses—his own and those of the school. To provide the necessary employment, Berea operates a bakery, a candy kitchen, a ceramics factory, a print shop, a needlecraft workroom, a bookcraft factory, woodcraft and weaving shops, a creamery, a dairy farm, and a hotel. Every student must work at least ten hours a week, and the school guarantees a minimum of 24 hours a week of gainful employment to those students who want it. The program is designed in such a way that no student who is willing to work is *ever* required to drop out for lack of money.

Blackburn College in Carlinville, Illinois, operates a similar program. All 500 men and women at Blackburn are required to work 15 hours a week at chores which range from building the new library to cooking the college meals. No payment is made for this work, but tuition and fees have been whittled down to a little over $1,000, roughly half the cost at comparable private liberal arts colleges without work programs.

There is another kind of work-study plan which should really be called study-work, for it involves full-time employment and part-time study. Many large corporations and industrial firms, for example, operate training progams in which students are encouraged to study part-time at nearby colleges and universities, with tuition and fees paid by the company. The Chase Manhattan Bank in New York City refunds as much as $200,000 a year to employees who have completed approved college courses related to banking. International Business Machines matches the tuition payments of employees who go to school part-time. The Insurance Company of North America does the same. So do many other firms.

A few companies even operate their own college. The General Motors Corporation, for instance, runs the General Motors Institute in Flint, Michigan, a five-year cooperative engineering college. Students at the Institute alternate periods of classroom study with periods of work at G.M. plants. They earn enough to pay almost all their educational expenses. And when they graduate, they are offered permanent G.M. jobs with their diplomas.

Work-study, whether through a cooperative plan or financed entirely by a college or an industry, provides an excellent solution to the college cost problem—even if that is not its *raison d'être*. A work-study program will guarantee you a far greater income than you would be likely to earn from a regular part-time job, on campus or off. At schools where student businesses are frowned on and scholarship money is scarce, work-study may be your only means to a college education.

6. BACK TO NEGATIVISM

The typical college administrator is enthusiastic about cooperative education, and reluctantly tolerant of off-campus and on-campus employment. That is as far as he'll go. At most colleges, the independent student business is looked on as something suspect at best, outright dishonorable at worst. More than 80 percent of the administrators contacted in connection with this book expressed the view that students should be discouraged from starting business enterprises of their own.

It is easier to document this attitude than to explain it. Undoubtedly a good deal of it is caused by genuine administrative concern for student welfare; a job is secure, while a business can lose money, or fail to earn as much as expected. But this hardly accounts for the whole phenomenon. For one thing, it fails to explain why students who can afford their tuition and simply want to try to earn some extra spending money are prohibited or discouraged from doing so. Nor can the argument be used to support the curtailing of already successful student business activities.

A second line of reasoning involves concern for the welfare of the campus as a whole. Again and again we have heard administrators express their fear that if student business were allowed to run rampant, the college atmosphere would come to resemble a carnival more than an institution of learning. This fear may be real, but its object is illusory. There is nothing carnival-like about the activities of a student laundry agency or a charter flight. Nor have schools like Princeton or Harvard (which encourage student business) found themselves burdened with an over-frivolous student body. Strangely enough, the very colleges which are most critical of student business on these grounds are the ones which permit the most frenetic, rambunctious fraternity and sorority goings-on. For carnival spirit, student businesses can't begin to equal these hallowed institutions.

Lying behind the arguments of most administrators is the view that, somehow, student business just isn't consistent with the ideals and goals of academia. The student employee will keep his working hours separate from his study hours, and will rarely be tempted to work overtime. The student entrepreneur, on the other hand, is in danger of discovering that his business is more meaningful to him than his classes. He may neglect his work for his money-making, and before the very eyes of his deans and professors, may turn into what one administrator frankly termed "a decadent bourgeois capitalist."

It is this anti-capitalist prejudice, combined with a strong academic inferiority complex, that seems to be the basis for most administrative opposition to independent student business. We would like to argue against this prejudice—and in a sense this whole book constitutes such an argument—but at the moment we are concerned with what is, not what should be. Accordingly, we will forego theoretical discussion and go on to talk about the nature of college regulations governing student business activities.

7. REGS AND MORE REGS

The most stringent possible college policy concerning on-campus business is complete prohibition. It is by no means rare. The regulations of Georgia College at Milledgeville, for example, explicitly state that "no individual or organization may sponsor a money-making or fund-raising plan on campus." Other schools which expressly forbid all student on-campus business include: Cedar Crest College, Allentown, Pennsylvania; University of California at Riverside; Georgia Southern College, Statesboro, Georgia; Newark State College, Union, New Jersey; North Georgia College, Dahlonega, Georgia; Ohio State University, Columbus, Ohio; University of Texas at Austin; Ursinus College, Collegeville, Pennsylvania; Valdosta State College, Valdosta, Georgia; and Wheeling College, Wheeling, West Virginia.

Ursinus College is a particularly interesting case, since student business flourished at that school until recently. In 1965, profits from student concessions on the Ursinus campus totaled more than $2,500. But in September, 1966, the business manager of the college issued a directive ordering the abolition of all student businesses on campus as of the following January.

Many colleges which do not specifically outlaw all student businesses pass regulations which have very nearly that effect. For example, the University of California at Santa Barbara has a rule that "University facilities shall not be used for any commercial purpose except in accordance with the written approval of the Chancellor." Now if a drama society or a debating club wants to sell doughnuts in the dorms to earn money for its activities, written permission from the Chancellor is soon forthcoming. But if some impoverished sophomore wants to do the same thing, permission is denied. With a few rare exceptions, individual students with money-making ideas do not get the go-ahead from the Santa Barbara administration.

Or consider a still more obvious example. The University of Massachusetts in Amherst, Massachusetts, has no rule forbidding student businesses on campus. But it does hold that "students are not allowed to sell or solicit on campus." If you can think of an on-campus business that does not require selling or soliciting, you're doing better than us—and better than the U Mass students, who have come up with no on-campus businesses to date.

Nearly one-third of the colleges surveyed for this book have regulations which either explicitly or indirectly prohibit all on-campus student businesses.

An additional quarter of our administrative respondents have stated that they do not forbid on-campus businesses, but rather "discourage" them. "Discourage" in this context can mean many things. On some campuses it seems to mean that students are heartily advised to look for a job instead. At other schools, it means that regulations which hinder but do not exclude on-campus businesses are in force. At still others, it means only that no assistance or cooperation is given the prospective campus entrepreneur. But at a few schools at least, we know that "discourage" has a very special meaning—namely that, while there is no college regulation against student businesses on campus, every student who approaches the administration and requests permission to start a business is turned down. Several administrators have admitted to us that this is their current policy. We have no way of knowing how many other schools follow the same procedure, and refer to it as "discouragement" of student businesses.

Of those colleges which do not in one way or another completely prevent the development of on-campus student businesses, most have regulations which at least hinder this development.

The most common is the rule prohibiting business use of the dormitories or other college facilities. Roughly three-fifths of the schools surveyed forbid solicitation in the dorms, usually on the grounds that students should not have their privacy invaded—especially when they're studying. A glance at Chapters Two and Three of this book will demonstrate the effectiveness of this prohibition; nearly every student business in the two chapters depends upon door-to-door solicitation of some kind.

Almost as effective is the very frequent regulation prohibiting the use of dormitory rooms as salesrooms, storerooms, or money-making workrooms. Dartmouth College in Hanover, New Hampshire, justifies this ruling on the grounds that "to operate a profit-making enterprise in a dormitory would possibly endanger the college's exemption from property and other taxes." But most schools offer no such rationale. At least in some cases, we suspect that the purpose of the rule is simply to deter students from trying to start on-campus businesses.

Another very popular regulation forbids students from starting businesses which would compete with a college-sponsored service or agency. This is reasonable enough, but it can often be extremely limiting. If the college co-op carries book covers, say, most students would be content not to peddle book covers in the dormitories. But if the co-op also stocks new books, does this mean that students should not be permitted to start a used book agency? At many schools, this is how the regulation has been interpreted. When a rule of this sort turns up at a large university with an extensive on-campus employment set-up, it can come very close to preventing the development of any student businesses at all. If the school operates its own laundry, general store, restaurant, linen service, tutoring agency, typing agency, etc., etc., etc., there is very little left for the independent entrepreneur to do.

A similar prohibition against competition with established *student* agencies is considerably more justified, since it prevents would-be capitalists from destroying each other. About half the colleges that permit on-campus student businesses at all say that they protect their agencies against encroachment by other students.

Nearly all colleges require students to consult with some administrative official before starting an on-campus business. At that point, if the proposed enterprise is "against the best interests of the college," they forbid it. Interpretations vary as to what constitutes the best interests of the college. Dartmouth College turns down any plan which is not "an essential student service." For reasons of sanitation and health, Baldwin-Wallace College in Berea, Ohio, Bridgewater College in Bridgewater, Virginia, and Luther College in Decorah, Iowa, all forbid the selling of student-prepared food. Bridgewater even prevents soft drinks from being peddled in the dorms on these grounds. West Virginia University in Morgantown, West Virginia, will not allow a student humor magazine to get started. Rocky Mountain College in Billings, Montana, has a rule against raffles. Bethel College in St. Paul, Minnesota, prohibits student entertainment groups "of the sort commonly found in nightclubs," and also all enterprises that "conflict with the moral and ethical values held by the school." Findlay College in Findlay, Ohio, won't let coeds work in local taverns, or in any job or business that might require them to stay out beyond dormitory curfews. And of course every college has rules against illegal businesses.

Supplementary regulations vary tremendously from college to college. Many schools insist on determining prices and salaries for all campus agencies. Some require that permits of various sorts be applied for whenever on-campus solicitation is planned. Most have special locations where posters may be placed, tables may be set up, and so on. A few colleges forbid money-making organizations from locating in the student activities building, but allow them to develop elsewhere on campus. Others have special regulations governing the use of the college seal for advertising purposes. Wherever you go to school, there are bound to be special regulations not mentioned here. Find out what they are, and obey them.

8. THE BRIGHTER SIDE

We do not want to make the student business outlook seem blacker than it actually is. A little over one-third of the colleges surveyed for this book have essentially no policy concerning student business. They maintain instead a passive attitude, permitting on-campus entrepreneurs to exist, but in no way encouraging them. Such schools usually have less than their share of money-making enterprises. Therefore, they may actually yield higher profits than would be forthcoming at a more commercially active college. They lie dormant, waiting for the arrival of a student entrepreneur with the initiative, ambition and push to "develop" them properly.

Even where on-campus business is discouraged, it is rarely impossible. At least half of the administrators who took stands in opposition to student business activity also expressed an open-minded interest in reading the results of our survey. Many told us frankly that they were "open to argument." A good number commented that their obstructionist policy had not been revised primarily because there had been little demand on their campuses for such revision. There is a good chance at almost any college that if you approach the administration with a plan that would benefit your classmates as well as yourself, it will be accepted. Offer students a chance to buy something they need cheaper than they could get it in town, and you are likely to get a provisional go-ahead from even the most recalcitrant dean—particularly if your proposed business would also open up new on-campus job opportunities.

Furthermore, it should be noted that a large percentage of the colleges which are opposed to on-campus business activities have good reason for their opposition; specifically, their schools are too small to support such activities in any case. No one on a campus with 300 students is going to make much money peddling hamburgers in the dorm(s). At a college of this size, a prohibition against on-campus money-making may make good business sense. If it doesn't, you may be able to reverse the ruling simply by demonstrating to the administration that a campus business could be profitable and useful.

Commuter schools are in the same boat. A college where 95 percent of the student body lives at home may permit no campus business simply because it has no campus. You lose nothing by obeying the regulation.

Many of the colleges and universities which restrict on-campus money-making are endeavoring to protect their scholarly surroundings more than their student body. They have no objection to students starting businesses with other students as customers, so long as the atmosphere of the college is not "defiled" by such activities. They therefore permit solicitation by mail or telephone, but only deliveries in person. Dartmouth College, for example, despite its strict limitations on door-to-door selling, permits and even encourages a wide range of unobtrusive student agencies.

Even where the prohibition of on-campus business is total, it is often possible to start a student agency—by moving off campus. If the majority of students at your college live outside the campus, in fraternities, sororities, or rooming houses, you should have no trouble operating an agency of any sort, regardless of the policy of your school administration. This situation is particularly common at the large state universities, many of which are required by law to forbid all on-campus student money-making. The administrations of these schools sometimes go so far as to help students set up businesses which cater to their fellow students—as long as the businesses are off-campus.

Finally, whatever the administration policy and practical situation at your school, the odds are that an off-campus business aimed at the surrounding community will be acceptable. Bryn Mawr College in Bryn Mawr, Pennsylvania, is the only school we have heard from that has regulations governing off-campus businesses. At Bryn Mawr, students are not allowed to canvass the immediate neighborhood of the college or to solicit parents of other students. Elsewhere in the country, the attitude of the University of Texas at Austin is typical: "On-campus business enterprises are not permitted. Off-campus student-run businesses are left to the ingenuity of students."

We are now in a position to list the characteristics of a college where student business is impossible. The school must be: (1) in a town so small that an off-campus business would be impracticable; (2) organized with all or nearly all students living on-campus, making an off-campus student agency unfeasible; (3) opposed to all forms of on-campus student business, no matter how valuable to students or how unobtrusive; and (4) possessed of an administration that is wholly unmovable and will not listen to reason.

Schools which meet all four of these criteria are rare. Anywhere else, you will have a fighting chance of earning money as an independent student entrepreneur.

9. THE STUDENT AGENCY SYSTEM

The individual would-be student businessman may have a fighting chance at nearly every college, but some schools will make him fight less than others. There are about two dozen colleges and universities in the United States which actually go out of their way to encourage student entrepreneurial activity, by providing assistance, advice, capital, facilities, and so forth. As any student lucky enough to attend one of these schools can tell you, it makes a difference.

Colleges that wish to encourage campus businessmen normally

set up some sort of student agencies system. Before discussing some actual examples, we would like to present a hypothetical case of a student agencies program, just to show how such a system may develop.

Phumph College is a fairly small, coeducational, liberal arts college in a suburban town. The school has 3,000 students and about 250 faculty members. It also has more job requests than openings.

Roughly half of the Phumph student body must work part-time in order to stay in school. An additional 500 students a year express a desire to work in order to earn extra money, bringing the total number of job requests to 2,000 a year. For decades, Phumph has had a student employment office which handles these requests. The office currently places 800 students a year in on-campus jobs, and locates employment in town for another 600. The remaining 600 must shift for themselves, making do with whatever they can find in the way of baby-sitting, typing, tutoring, and odd jobs.

In recent years, the Phumph administration has become somewhat concerned about this situation. Besides the 600 jobless students to worry about, there have also been complaints from a number for whom jobs have been found. Too many students seem to feel that their work is valueless and dull, and many resent the low wages paid by both college and town employers. Students have occasionally requested permission to organize independent businesses, but the administration fears that such enterprises might endanger the scholarly atmosphere of the school and the scholarly achievements of the would-be entrepreneurs. Among themselves, however, top administrators admit that there is a need both for more jobs and for more student services.

Out of these circumstances a new program is born—Phumph Student Agenies (PSA). A member of the Phumph administration is given charge of the program, and is instructed to work out a structure which will provide students with more jobs, a chance for business and leadership experience, and valuable new services—all at the same time.

PSA resolves to move slowly and simply, growing in accordance with the needs of the campus. For its first student agency, it decides on a souvenir concession for home athletic contests. This activity has traditionally been handled by the athletic department, which hired one or two students a year to do the selling. One of last year's salesmen is called into the new PSA office and asked what could be done to expand the concession. He suggests that more salesmen be hired, and a wider range of souvenirs offered. He thinks he knows where the hawkers should locate themselves for maximal sales, and says he'd like to try his hand at managing the concession.

By the end of the year, the Phumph Souvenir Agency has netted a $4,000 profit, more than twice the figure for previous years. Most of the money is split among the ten salesmen who worked the games, but the manager keeps $1,000 for his own efforts. The result of this trial effort: 11 students working instead of two, better wages for the salesmen, a good profit for the manager, and a more enthusiastic grandstand filled with souvenir-clutching students and alumni. PSA decides to expand.

Inside of five years, PSA has 15 different student agencies. The most profitable is undoubtedly the student linen service, which earns its manager, two assistant managers and 20 salesmen a total of $12,000 a year. The magazine subscription agency is also doing well, the Christmas gift salesmen are earning good holiday profits, and even the tiny button agency is running in the black. In all, the 15 agencies are netting just under $30,000 a year for their 200 managers and employees. New ideas are springing up nearly every week. Plans for a catering service and an odd-job agency in town are progressing nicely, and the new student tutoring agency looks like it should be out of the red by next year.

As business increases, the Phumph Student Agencies office grows too. A full-time accountant (a student of course) is hired to keep the books straight. Negotiations are begun to grant a $3,000 interest-free loan to a sophomore who wants to start a student laundry. A food permit is applied for to enable students to peddle sandwiches in the fraternities. And next year PSA plans to incorporate as part of the college, to gain certain tax advantages and liability protections for its various agencies. PSA's director prophesies that within ten years every Phumph student who is looking for work will be able to find it under the aegis of Phumph Student Agencies—whether he wants to hold down a part-time job or start his own business.

The development of Phumph Student Agencies closely parallels that of Harvard Student Agencies, Inc. (Harvard University, Cambridge, Massachusetts), Rutgers Student Agencies (Rutgers University, New Brunswick, New Jersey), the Associated Student Agencies of Yale (Yale University, New Haven, Connecticut), Columbia Student Agencies (Columbia University, New York, New York), Technology Student Enterprises, Inc. (Massachusetts Institute of Technology, Cambridge, Massachusetts), and the Princeton Bureau of Student Aid (Princeton University, Princeton, New Jersey).

The student agency organization at all these schools is very nearly the same. Each agency is actually a small business, operated and directed entirely by students. Freshmen and sophomores are hired as employees, and normally are paid either a straight salary or a commission on sales. Juniors are frequently promoted to assistant managerial positions, and may receive a percentage of the agency's profits. The senior manager is usually elected by his employees, with the approval of the student agencies director. He is responsible for running his business, and his pay depends on his running it well. If he does a good job, his share of the profits should be more than ample reward; if he does a poor job, he may earn less than his most junior employee.

The role of the central office is to provide guidance and assistance. Students with ideas for new agencies are given the advice and aid they need to develop their plans. Seed money is often supplied for new ventures, and capital may be advanced to on-going businesses as well, if they need it to expand, purchase stock, or whatever. The legal and technical aspects of each agency (permits, insurancè, taxes, bookkeeping) are usually handled centrally.

The student agencies director screens each proposed business before he accepts it. The agency must have a good chance of earning a reasonable profit, and must offer a product or service of genuine value to the student body or the surrounding community. Student agencies are normally not permitted to compete with each other, unless there is a large enough market to make both businesses pay off.

In return for its services to the individual agency, the central office rakes off a small percentage of the profits for itself. This tithe—usually less than 10 percent of the annual net profit—enables the system to be self-supporting. It also permits the establishment and maintenance of a "sinking fund," to be used to buoy up any agency that fails to show a profit in a given year.

In order to ensure that each agency continues to operate in the best interests of the college, most student agencies offices retain control over the operations of their member agencies. Student managers are usually permitted to establish their own prices, but an administrative veto power assures that the rates will be reasonable. Similarly, wages and commissions may be set by each individual manager, but they are subject to revision if they fail to provide student employees with a "living wage." At a few schools these goals are achieved by putting a ceiling on the profits of the manager. A manager who knows he will not be permitted to walk away with more than $2,500 for his year's labor will tend to reduce prices and increase wages if his expected profits are greater than that amount.

Policies vary on the question of student employment within the agency system. At some schools, managers are permitted to choose their own employees as they wish. Most colleges allow managers to pick their employees, but stipulate that all scholarship students who want jobs must be employed before non-scholarship students can be accepted. One or two schools arbitrarily assign students to the various agencies.

The value of the student agencies system has been proved on every campus where the program has been tried. Columbia University now has 16 agencies, in which 200 undergraduates earn more than $75,000 a year. Massachusetts Institute of Technology has 11 agencies, earning a total of $35,000 annually. Harvard University has nearly 40 agencies, netting well over $100,000 a year. Other colleges and universities show similar profit figures.

Besides providing business experience for managers and employment for hundreds of students, these businesses also offer valuable services to the student body and the outside community. Says former Harvard dean John U. Monro: "Students here are pretty bright, with lots of energy and initiative. They ought to be able to earn money faster than by digging ditches or stacking books in the library." Through the student agencies system, they do just that.

A number of colleges have programs which are somewhat less elaborate than the student agencies system, but which still provide assistance and encouragement to campus entrepreneurs. In this context we particularly want to mention Carnegie Institute of Technology in Pittsburgh, Pennsylvania, Middlebury College in Middlebury, Vermont, the University of Pennsylvania in Philadelphia, and Swarthmore College in Swarthmore, Pennsylvania. Vassar College in Poughkeepsie, New York, is a fifth school which deserves credit for encouraging student business, though Vassar's program is very different from the others. In order to ensure its girls an adequate return for their work, Vassar turns nearly every student business into a student job, paying managers and employees appropriate salaries regardless of whether the business succeeds or fails. An entrepreneur at Vassar can't make much of a killing, but she can do pretty nicely for herself—and she's safe.

The student agencies system has been so successful at the colleges where it is used that administrators across the country are beginning to show an interest. The system is currently being considered at the University of New Hampshire, Rensselaer Polytechnic Institute, and Syracuse University. It has been a topic of discussion at several meetings of financial aid directors from various schools. The student agencies system has by no means fully exploded the traditional administration prejudice against on-campus student business, but it has made a few dents and cracks —and may yet break through.

10. THE MONEY-MAKING ATMOSPHERE

The student agencies system has a way of growing on itself. A few successful ventures are launched, and students begin to see the profit potential of the agency set-up. So they generate a number of new ideas, which turn into "second-generation" agencies. Once these start running in the black, the temptation to add a few more businesses is irresistible. The cycle continues to operate, and before very long as much as half the student body may be working with one agency or another.

Princeton University is an excellent example of this process in action. Dating back only as far as the Depression, Princeton's agency system now includes more than 50 student businesses. Some barely manage to make a profit for one student manager and his sole employee, while others hire hundreds of students every year and gross as much as $80,000 annually. The total annual gross sales of all the agencies together comes to more than a quarter of a million dollars. Net profits each year total almost $100,000.

In alphabetical order, the list of currently active student businesses at Princeton reads as follows: air travel service, art agency, baby-sitting, beer mug, bicycle, birthday cake, calendar, canoe, cashier, catering, chapel watchmen, Christmas card, Christmas tree, Christmas wreath, club tie and belt, Collegiate Enterprises (booking agency), directory (telephone numbers), doughnut, Esquire Sales (gifts), Europe by Car, Express-Reunion (furniture and moving), firewood, flower, Freshman Herald (frosh directory), Fuller Brush (gifts), gatemen (for sports events), hi-fi, laundry, linen, magazine, newspaper, nightie, odd job, parking squad, perfume, photography, pipe, pizza, record, refreshment, refrigerator, ring, room (for dates), room decoration, reunion buttons, rubber apron and goggles, scarf, rug, shirt, soft drink, souvenir, stationery, survival kit, sweater, sweatshirt, T-shirt, thesis binding, tie, typing, and wall banner.

The existence of such a large number of profit-making agencies on campus attunes students to the profit potential of non-agency enterprises as well. Every major airline has a student representative at Princeton. Individual campus tutors, barbers, jewelry-makers and the like abound. The campus newspaper, humor magazine, and yearbook are all organized as profit-making organizations. Dozens of students each year start small off-campus businesses, earn money writing for newspapers or magazines, and so on.

The Princeton administration has also got into the spirit of the thing, and has organized many on-campus jobs on the agency model. The University Food Services set-up is a good example. This department operates all on-campus faculty and student dining rooms and provides food for reunions, receptions, banquets and other functions. It also handles food peddling at athletic games, and in the dormitories each evening. Like most colleges, Princeton hires students for food service work. But unlike most colleges, Princeton has a complex student managerial system for its food service employees. Some professional workers are of course needed, but every student employee is under student supervision. Each division of food services has its own senior director, headwaiters, senior and junior managers, supervisors, payroll clerks and, finally, run-of-the-mill employees. Food services now provides Princeton students with more than 700 jobs a year; its annual undergraduate payroll is over $250,000.

The athletic department and the library, the next largest employers of student labor, are also organized on a student managerial system. The result in all three cases is better wages for students, greater incentive to work, more rewarding jobs, and happier student employees.

Princeton now possesses what we have termed "the money-making atmosphere." Nearly two-thirds of all Princeton students earn money during the school year. A good percentage of these are their own bosses. Nearly all the rest have a fellow student for a boss—and the knowledge that if they do well they might be boss next year.

But if the Princeton experience is any guide, a money-making atmosphere is not (as many administrators at other schools fear) a carnival atmosphere. There is no evidence that Princeton students study less than those at other colleges, or are less interested in their academic work. There is no evidence that they become money-grubbing capitalists with no other goal than to make their million in the business world and then retire to the country club.

In fact, the trend seems to be in the opposite direction. A survey conducted at Princeton in the late 1950's found that a disproportionate majority of flunk-outs had engaged in no extra-curricular or money-making activities at all while at school. Less than 8 percent of students in academic trouble showed any adverse effects from too much non-academic work. Comments W. Bradford Craig, director of Princeton's Bureau of Student Aid: "A strong challenge and a full daily schedule will normally act as a stimulus which will bring the student to do his best in course work, extracurricular activities, and term-time employment." The consensus among Princeton deans and faculty members is that working students are *more* likely than non-workers to have top grades, participate in "unprofitable" extra-curricular activities, and go on to graduate school and a profession.

The three words most often used to describe student business at Princeton are "profitable," "unobtrusive," and "worthwhile." We challenge any administrator anywhere to find something objectionable in these three adjectives.

11. DEALING WITH THE DEAN

Whatever the policies of your college with respect to student businesses, if you plan on starting one you will have to have a talk with the appropriate member of your administration. When you see him and what you say, however, should depend greatly on what you expect his attitude to be.

If you are fortunate enough to go to a school where student businesses are encouraged, it would be a good idea to see the dean early in the planning stages of your proposed agency. Simply tell him what you have in mind, and ask for his opinion. If your idea is a bad one, he will be able to explain why, and thereby save you hours of senseless labor. If your plans are good, he will help you to develop them and get your business off the ground. Either way, you cannot lose by seeking his advice and assistance as soon as you have a fairly clear proposal in mind.

But if you expect a hostile response to your idea, you should plan your tactics differently. Work out the business to a fare-thee-well. Investigate your expenses and your market; calculate your prices and your profits. Make out a list of the advantages of your business to the college—the service it will render to undergraduates, the money it will save them by underselling existing establishments, the number of employees it will provide work for. Anticipate any objections that might be raised, and be ready to respond to them. Design a sales and solicitation procedure that will not cheapen the college atmosphere. Work out advertising and distribution systems that are low-key and dignified. Think about the non-financial advantages of your plan to yourself and your employees—specialized training, business experience, contact with fellow students, and so on. Only when your case is as airtight as it could ever be should you phone for an appointment.

If you can sell your dean on your idea, you should have little trouble selling your customers.

CHAPTER 8

Shalts and
Shalt Nots

1. LEGALISM AND REALISM

This chapter will be devoted to the legal and quasi-legal requirements that pertain to the operation of a small business, particularly a student business.

Bugs Baer once wrote that "if you laid all our laws end to end, there would be no end." His maxim is even truer today than it was when he wrote it. Law is a messy business at best, and business law is messier than most law. In one short chapter we cannot possibly hope to explore this tangled network fully. We won't even be able to get completely through all the relevant laws of one state or one municipality—and there are 50 states and thousands of municipalities in the country, each with its own unique set of laws.

But though we cannot guide you through the legal thicket, we can at least sketch in a rough map of it for you, pointing out where the most dangerous patches are, and where the best guides are to be found.

Of necessity this is going to be a legalistic chapter. By that we mean not only that it will be a bit complicated, but also that it will be rather cautious. We are in no position to tell you which laws are safe to ignore, because theoretically *no* laws are safe to ignore. Yet we feel it is only fair to give you this piece of factual information at the outset: Most student businesses ignore many laws, and get away with it. Silly Sally, who sells sea shells by the seashore, probably doesn't bother with the excise tax. If the people at the seashore are her friends, and she sells three shells a season, she's almost surely safe and not so silly after all. But as soon as she starts a sea shell store, she should seek out a lawyer and see what he says.

2. TAXES

All citizens and residents of the United States with a gross income of $600 or more, including minors and foreigners, must file a federal income tax return. Full-time students who make less than $900 a year may include their earnings as part of their parents' incomes on their parents' returns, but the tax is almost always less if you pay it yourself. In any case, even a full-time student must file his own federal return if his gross earnings are more than $900 in a given year. His parents may still include him as an exemption if they pay for more than half of his support.

State income taxes vary. Some states have none at all. Others have minimum taxable earnings ranging from $600 up. The local office of your state tax commission will tell you what your income must be before you have to file a state return. If you ask nicely, they may also tell you what special tax benefits exist for students. In some states these are considerable, so you should ask nicely.

If your legal residence is in one state, but your college (and hence your part-time business) is in another, head for the nearest law library. Some states tax the earnings of all residents, regardless of where they earn their money. Some states tax all money earned within the state, regardless of the legal residence of the earner. Some states have one policy for some kinds of businesses, another for different kinds. The only thing you can do is inquire at the tax commission office in both states and see who you owe money to. Don't be surprised to find that both states claim your taxes. Even then, it is sometimes possible to deduct the taxes paid to one state from what you must pay the other. State taxes are always much lower than federal taxes anyway, so don't worry too much about it—but make sure you pay somebody.

Business income taxes are still more complicated. If you are in business for yourself, but are not incorporated, then you have no federal business income tax to pay. Your gross business earnings must be reported on your personal tax return, and your business expenses may be included as deductions. A formal partnership also pays no federal income tax, but must file an "information return" with the federal government, the figures in which are then used to calculate the personal income tax of each of the partners. A corporation must pay a federal corporate income tax on its net earnings. Then each individual must pay a second tax on his share of the profits.

State business income taxes usually follow the same procedure, but not always. Some states have "unincorporated business taxes," which are levied against partnerships and sometimes individually owned businesses as well. In such cases, you must pay the business tax on your net earnings, then pay a personal tax on the same net earnings.

In general, the rule is this: If you have no business tax to pay, then the *gross* earnings of your business must be listed on your personal income tax, and business expenses deducted. If there is a business tax which applies to you, business expenses are deducted there. Your personal income tax is then based on the *net* profits of your business, plus income from various other sources.

It should be pointed out that small corporations are frequently able to avoid the payment of business taxes simply by disbursing their total profits in the form of salaries. Suppose, for example, that the three owners of an incorporated student travel agency earn a profit of $6,000 in a given year. They could vote themselves a salary of $2,000 apiece for the year, leaving the company itself with no taxable profits. A partnership or individually owned business which is subject to state taxes can do the same thing. Of course, the money must still be included on the personal tax return of each owner-employee, but the additional business tax can usually be avoided in this manner.

The federal government and many state governments require that withholding taxes be deducted from the wages of all employees, to be applied against their personal income taxes. If your business is incorporated, then you yourself are technically an employee, and must deduct your own withholding taxes as well. The federal withholding tax rate is usually 20 percent after all exemptions have been deducted. State rates vary. Contact the nearest office of the Internal Revenue Service for information about the federal withholding tax, and see your state tax commission to find out about state withholding taxes.

State unemployment insurance taxes vary from state to state. In general they come to a little under 3 percent of wages, and must be paid by the *employer* to the state government. Most states exempt businesses which employ fewer than four persons. The federal unemployment insurance tax is less than one percent of wages; businesses with fewer than eight employees are exempt.

Federal social security taxes must be paid for all employees, even if there is only one. Currently, the employer must contribute 4.4 percent of the wages of each employee until total wages pass $6,600. The employee contributes an equal amount, which must be deducted for him by the employer and sent to the federal government once a month. Self-employed persons may pay a similar percentage of their earnings in social security, but their participation in the program is optional. State social security and old-age taxes vary greatly, and the only thing to do is to check.

State and municipal sales taxes normally depend upon the item sold and the manner in which it is sold; door-to-door sales, for example, are often treated differently from store sales. In all cases, the tax is paid by the purchaser, but must be collected and recorded by the seller, who eventually turns it over to the appropriate government. The same is true for federal and state excise taxes, which must be added to the price of luxury items such as jewelry and cosmetics.

Miscellaneous state and local taxes are many and varied. Corporations must often pay special state franchise taxes on their earnings. Local communities usually assess a property tax or an occupancy tax on premises occupied for business purposes. Other states and local taxes on business must be investigated individually in each state and each municipality. You may be sure there will be some.

If you are employed, the only tax you'll have to worry about will be your personal income tax, federal and state (if any). Your unemployment and social security taxes will be deducted from your wages by your employer. He will also do your withholding for you, and will send you a "W-2 form" each year telling you how much money has been withheld. This sum is deducted from your personal income tax. If your tax comes to less than what has been withheld—which it should if your tax bracket is less than 20 percent—then you may apply for a refund.

The most crucial tax question for student businesses is the role of the college or university. Non-profit corporations are exempt from most taxes, and get special breaks on others. Since just about every college is incorporated as a non-profit organization, it may be possible to gain certain substantial tax benefits by organizing your business as a subsidiary of the school. This is a complicated matter, since the laws governing profit-making activities of non-profit corporations are complex and in many cases ambiguous. Still, the possibility is worth looking into, especially if your school has a student agencies system in operation. We will discuss this further when we talk about non-profit corporations.

Employees of colleges may also take advantage of special tax benefits under certain circumstances. As a paid employee of a non-profit corporation, you will still be obliged to file a regular personal income tax return. But some states allow a student employed by a college to reduce his tax by the amount he pays back to his "employer" in the form of tuition and fees. Furthermore, the fact that you receive money from the college only to pay it back to the college should alert you—and your school—to the possibility of eliminating the transaction altogether. If instead of paying you $1,000 a year for your work, the administration is willing to reduce your tuition by $1,000, you will have no "earnings" on which to pay taxes. Similarly, the school may stipulate that your employment is a part of its regular educational program, and save you some tax money that way. It may go against the administrative grain to admit that student employment can be educational, but a number of colleges have swallowed their prejudices and made the admission, thereby saving their students thousands of dollars every year.

Whatever sorts of taxes you wind up having to pay, you will save time, energy, and money by keeping good books. All businesses are required by law to make their books available to the proper authorities if requested—and Lord help you then if your records are incomplete.

The paperwork necessary for tax records and payments is considerable for a large business, but may be less onerous than you imagine for a small, part-time, student-run enterprise. You may find yourself exempt from many tax requirements because of the size of your operation, your status as a student, or your association with a college or university.

Taxes are something you shouldn't play around with. Get what information you can from your school's financial aid office, then ask your remaining questions at the municipal, state, and federal tax offices. If things get really complicated, see a specialist. The college lawyer or accountant may be able to help you without charge.

3. EMPLOYEES

Aside from withholding, social security, and unemployment taxes, the employer's responsibility to his employees is governed primarily by two laws—the minimum wage and workman's compensation.

The Federal Fair Labor Standards Act, which sets minimum wages, overtime rates, and so on, applies only to industries which are directly or indirectly involved in interstate commerce. Retail and service establishments are specifically exempted, as are executive, administrative, and sales personnel of all businesses. It is very unlikely, then, that a student business would be covered by this statute.

Comparable state laws are another matter entirely. Most apply to a far wider range of businesses than the federal statute, and the likelihood of their including your business is fairly great. In New Jersey, for example, employees beyond the age of 18 in nearly all businesses must earn at least $1.40 an hour. Those who work more than 40 hours a week must receive time and a half for each additional hour. Tips may be included in the $1.40, but at least 66 cents of the amount must be paid by the employer himself. Various states may make exceptions for businesses with very few employees, for part-time jobs, or for college students, but the state minimum wage requirements are definitely something to check out.

Workman's compensation laws also vary from state to state. There is always a minimum number of employees before you must be covered, but that figure ranges from two in some states up to fifteen in others. Part-time employment is covered by workman's compensation in ten states, exempted in the remainder. But the definition of "part-time" is different in each state anyway, so all you can do is write your state's department of labor and see what's what.

In most states, employees of non-profit corporations need not be covered by workman's compensation. This will include nearly all employees of colleges, and many employees of student businesses which are associated with colleges. Your school administration can tell you the law on this point. Many colleges accept workman's compensation coverage even though they are not legally compelled to do so. If your school is one of these, it is likely that the college coverage extends to your business. Similarly, most employees of colleges are not eligible for minimum wage guarantees, either because the college is a non-profit corporation, or because student jobs are considered educational rather than financial, or because student employees work only part-time. This exemption may extend to your business as well—or it may not. The controller, business manager, or financial aid director of the college should be able to give you an answer. If not, ask the state labor department.

Every state has a large collection of laws designed to protect workers from exploitation at the hands of evil capitalists. As an evil-capitalist-in-the-making, you must inform yourself about these statutes. Most of them specifically exempt small businesses, but not all of them do, and they set up a variety of criteria as to what constitutes a small business. If you operate a "place of business"— that is, a store or office—you will find regulations on the books concerning proper lighting, ventilation, lunch breaks, bathroom size, and heaven knows what else. If your employees work on their own, life will be somewhat easier, but you should still look out for laws governing working hours, vacations, and the like. And if you plan on hiring anyone under the age of 18, be sure to check the law concerning employment of minors.

It almost pays to run your business yourself and hire nobody.

4. ACCOUNTING

Except for tax records on behalf of yourself and your employees, your bookkeeping is your own problem, and there are very few laws which specify uniform accounting systems. Nevertheless, if you don't keep accurate and complete books, you are bound to run afoul of some law before very long.

Business record forms are available in most large stationery stores. So are handbooks on how to keep business records. Buy the handbook first, then come back for the forms you need.

Two annual statements are customary, and will be essential if you have business taxes to pay. The first is an "annual balance sheet," which lists the assets and liabilities of the business, and thereby calculates its net worth. The second is a "profit and loss statement." This lists the income and expenses of the business, and thereby calculates its net profit or loss. The difference between the two must be clear: The balance sheet reflects the financial condition of the enterprise as of a given date, while the statement of profit and loss shows the results of business operations over a given period. Standardized forms and instructions for both statements are available.

In addition, every business should keep a general ledger of assets and liabilities; that is, accounts receivable and merchandise inventory balanced with accounts payable. A cash book for cash receipts and disbursements is essential for tax purposes, as is a sales and purchases book. A variety of other forms are useful for one sort of business or another. Your handbook and a year's experience will make it clear which ones you need.

An accountant is a handy man to have around, but it is a rare small business that can afford one. It is fairly likely, however, that your college administration will loan you the use of one of theirs on occasion, and you should take advantage of this opportunity to receive a little free professional advice and assistance.

5. INFANCY

Without knowing it, you may be an infant. In fact, the odds are that you still have a few good years of infancy left.

The law holds that everybody is an infant until he or she becomes an adult. In most states this is at the age of 21, but the following exceptions should be noted: In Florida, Iowa, and Utah you attain your majority on marriage or at age 21, whichever comes first; in Kansas and Louisiana you become an adult when you marry if you are over age 18; Arizona males are adults at 19; in Hawaii males are adults at 20, Nebraska females are adults as soon as they marry; in California and Alabama married females are adults if they're over 18; all females are adults in Alaska when they pass 19, in Hawaii when they pass 20; and everybody over 18 is an adult in Arkansas, Idaho, Illinois, Montana, North Dakota, Oklahoma, and South Dakota.

Just how much of a difference all this will make depends less upon you than upon the people with whom you do business. Most states hold that a contract between an infant (a minor) and an adult may be voided at will by the infant or his legal guardian (usually his father). There are six states in which the infant is required to compensate the other party to the contract if he rescinds an agreement which has already been acted upon, but throughout the rest of the country a legal infant can get away with legal murder if he has a mind to.

As a result, you may find your business associates justifiably reluctant to sign any long-term agreements with you. This can be most inconvenient if you want to rent an office, negotiate a loan, or take merchandise on consignment.

A few solutions to the problem are possible. One is to incorporate your business; so long as he can perform the duties required of him, a minor is qualified to enter into binding contracts on behalf of his employer. In some states a formal partnership will achieve the same goal. The usual solution for a student business, however, is to arrange for a member of the college administration to countersign all contracts and long-term agreements. If your business has some sort of semi-official connection with the college, your administration will probably insist on this procedure anyway, since it might get stuck for the tab should you fail to fulfill a contract. If you're organized independently of the college administration, your best bet is to find some friendly adult who trusts you—either that, or talk your business associates into trusting you.

6. INSURANCE

As we have already mentioned, your business may be legally required to carry workman's compensation insurance. Non-profit corporations normally have a "charitable immunity" from workman's compensation liability, but most colleges carry the insurance anyway for ethical reasons. Your school's coverage may include your business. If you are not required to carry workman's compensation, fine, but make sure you have immunity as well. The one bind you want to avoid is liability for on-the-job injury to your employees without insurance to cover it.

Aside from workman's compensation, the only other form of insurance you will have no choice about is automobile liability insurance. If your business owns a car, the law will force you to carry a minimum amount of accident liability coverage.

Everything else is up to you. Fire insurance is good to have if you stock a great deal of merchandise. So is theft insurance. Public liability insurance will protect you from lawsuits arising out of injuries to the person or property of others resulting from the operation of your business. Misplaced confidence insurance (also known as "bonding") covers you for dishonesties of most sorts on the part of your employees. Casualty insurance is an all-purpose form of coverage which includes public liability, accident and health liability, auto collision, theft, and four or five other things. Hundreds of other sorts of insurance are available. Your needs depend on the size and nature of your business. A student who peddles home-made jewelry in the dorms doesn't need much insurance; one who operates a restaurant or rents motorcycles does.

Before running to a broker to find out what *he* thinks you could use, have a talk with the appropriate dean at your college. The school undoubtedly carries a greater number of insurance policies than you have customers, and a few of them may extend their coverage to your business. This is especially true if your business operates entirely on campus, or if you are part of a student agencies set-up. In any case, do some thinking and talking before you do any buying. Insurance costs a lot of money. You want to be covered for everything you should be covered for—but not a thing more.

7. LICENSES AND PERMITS

A license is a permission granted by a governmental agency to carry on a business or occupation which would be illegal without such license. Technically, a permit is the same thing as a licence, but in practice permits are usually local affairs, while licenses are granted by the state government.

The assortment of businesses and activities that are licensed or permitted is fantastic, and growing every year. In most states, you need a license to operate an auto driving school, a bank, a salvage business, a storage business, an insurance agency, a liquor store, a collection agency, a drugstore, a theater ticket agency, and so on; the list runs into the hundreds. Permits are even more plentiful. If you own a store, an office, or a warehouse you need a building permit; if you sell food you need a food permit if you use gas in the operation of your business you need a gas permit; if you sell door-to-door you need a peddling permit.

Some licenses and permits are hard to get; others come easy. A fee is usually required, which may run you anywhere from $2 to $200. In some cases (such as insurance licenses), an examination is involved; in others (such as liquor licenses) a public hearing must be arranged. Often there is a minimum age to cope with. Application forms in triplicate and fingerprint records in duplicate are all part of the necessary bother in some cases.

Just to make life a bit more difficult, any business that is directly involved in interstate commerce may need a license from the federal government. If you think you might qualify, contact the Interstate Commerce Commission and find out.

Again, the wise procedure is to talk to the college authorities before visiting the legal authorities. If your business is operated entirely on the campus of a privately owned college, you may find that many license and permit requirements don't apply to you. The school may also have a few licenses, permits, and special dispensations of its own that might cover your business. At the very least, your administration can sound out local officials on your behalf to find out what you need and how hard it will be to get it.

The applicability of many licenses and permits to very small businesses has never been determined, simply because small businessmen have tended to assume that they did not apply, and nobody bothered to try to prove otherwise. This is a convenient—but dangerous—bandwagon to jump onto. In the long run, it pays to make sure that what you are doing is within the law. Still, a little discreet inquiry through a friendly college administrator makes a lot more sense than striding into the nearest town clerk's office and asking for trouble.

8. COPYRIGHTS

Many student authors think of a copyright as a terribly technical legal document which isn't worth the effort unless you plan on printing at least 100,000 copies. Most therefore neglect to copyright their writing. A good number regret the omission within a few years.

Nothing could be easier than copyrighting a book or article. All you have to do is publish the work with a correct notice of copyright in it. Thereafter, if you ever want to go into court to protect your copyright, it is necessary to register your work with the Copyright Office in Washington. The Copyright Office will mail you the appropriate form, which you return with a $6 fee to complete your registration. But your work is fully copyrighted as soon as it has been published with the proper warning; in most cases, registration will never even be necessary. Once you publish your book or article without the warning, however, it cannot be copyrighted at a later date, no matter how many forms you are willing to fill out.

The copyright notice must include either the word "Copyright," or the abbreviation "Copr.," or the symbol "©." For maximum protection, include both the word and the symbol; this will give you a legal copyright in most foreign countries as well as the U.S. The notice should also state the name of the proprietor of the copyright, the date of first publication, and the date of the current publication, if it is not the first. The proprietor of a copyright is usually the author, the publisher, or both.

In a book, the copyright notice should appear on either the title page or the page immediately following. Copyright notices for periodicals may be placed on the title page, on the first page of text, or under the title heading of the periodical. Articles in a periodical should be copyrighted on the title page or first page of text of the contribution.

Unpublished manuscripts may be covered by "common law copyright" if an appropriate warning is printed or typed on the title page. A common law copyright notice should indicate that the manuscript is for restricted distribution only and is not for publication. A typical notice might read: "For confidential use only. Not for circulation, distribution, or publication. All rights to this work are the property of————."

In addition to literary works of various sorts, song lyrics, all forms of music, television and motion pictures, and some kinds of art can be copyrighted. In all cases the copyright lasts for 28 years and may be renewed on request for another 28; thereafter, the work is in the public domain.

Copyrights may be "assigned" by their proprietor through contractual agreement. An assignment is a transfer to another individual of all or a stated portion of the rights guaranteed under the copyright. A transfer of partial rights is also termed a "license." Assignments and licenses need not be registered with the Copyright Office to be binding, but the assignee must record the transfer with that office within three months of execution to protect his rights.

A copyright guarantees the proprietor a complete monopoly over the copyrighted work. It gives him sole control of all reprintings and reproductions, adaptations, and sales. A work is considered to infringe on another work's copyright if it substantially duplicates its predecessor in language, development, treatment, arrangement, or sequence of ideas and facts. The ideas and facts themselves are not covered.

More than one student author has had the experience of turning out a "minor" piece of writing, publishing it in a campus newspaper or magazine, and forgetting it—only to find several months later that it is beginning to get some unexpected attention. Somebody wants to reprint it in a national-circulation magazine; someone else thinks it could be turned into a series of syndicated columns; someone else would like to buy the movie rights to the title and format. If the article has not been copyrighted, anyone can do what he wants with it without paying a dime. The moral of the story is: Copyright everything. Nine times out of ten it will do you no good, but the tenth time it could save you a fortune—and all it takes is two extra minutes at the typewriter.

9. PATENTS

Patents are to inventions what copyrights are to books and articles. According to the U.S. Department of Commerce, "a patent may be obtained by any person who has invented any new and useful art, machine, manufacture or composition of matter, or any new and useful improvement thereof." Only the inventor himself can apply for a patent, but he may assign his rights to another party if he wishes.

A patent grant gives the inventor the exclusive right to make, use, or sell his invention for a period of 17 years. Anyone may apply, even a minor, but the procedure is complicated and more or less necessitates the aid of a patent lawyer. Patent application forms may be obtained from the Commissioner of Patents in Washington. If your brainchild meets the Patent Office criteria for novelty, utility, and invention, a patent will be issued. The patent application must be accompanied by a $30 filing fee and a sworn oath as to your status as inventor. If the patent is granted, another $30 fee is required to register it.

College students seldom have occasion to apply for a patent. But it can happen. Ideas and concepts are not patentable, but in some cases procedures are, and processes, recipes, and mechanical devices almost always are. If in the course of your business operations you come up with something that you think might be patentable, you should think about seeing a patent lawyer. If your invention could be of value to others, you should definitely pay him a call—and as soon as possible. Pre-patent sale, manufacture or use of an item can sometimes endanger its patentability, which could cost you a mint of money if your invention is a good one.

To find out more about patents, write the U.S. Government Printing Office in Washington, D.C., and ask for their pamphlet entitled "General Information Concerning Patents."

10. TRADEMARKS AND TRADE NAMES

A trademark is a word, letter, device, sound, or symbol used in connection with an article of merchandise or a service. A trade name is an invented or arbitrarily adopted name given to an article, service, or business establishment. Both trademarks and trade names are intended to help identify the product, service, or company. They may therefore be protected from infringement through registration with the U.S. Patent Office.

Trademarks will be accepted for registration only if they do not contain immoral or scandalous matter, do not consist primarily of a geographic name or a surname, and are not merely descriptive (or mis-descriptive) of the product or service. Examples of trademarks that could not be registered are "Eat It Raw Peanut Butter," "Oklahoma Peanut Butter," "Jones Peanut Butter," and "Good Peanut Butter." Registration of national insignia, such as the Red Cross emblem, is not permitted. The name or portrait of a living individual can be registered as a trademark or part of a trademark only with his written consent. Merchandise trademarks must be included on the article or its container to be registerable; use of the trademark on advertising is not sufficient. Finally, the trademark cannot resemble an existing registered trademark closely enough to be confusing. You may call your new haircream "Greasy Kid Stuff," but you may not name it "Bitalis," or "Better than Vitalis."

Normally, your own name may be used for the name of your business without registration. If you use some form of assumed or trade name, however, a certificate must usually be filed with the county clerk setting forth the pertinent information as to the ownership of the company. This is to enable anyone doing business with your firm to identify its owner or owners. No assumed name which is likely to confuse your product or service with another may be adopted. If your name is John Klean you *might* be permitted to call your home detergent "Mr. Klean," but if your name is John Jones you *certainly* would not be allowed to do so.

The fee for registering trademarks and trade names in Washington is $35. Generally, national registration will be refused unless the trademark or trade name is "in commerce"—that is, involved in sales beyond the immediate neighborhood. State registration procedures may protect smaller businesses.

A college student operating a part-time business that is not expected to continue beyond his graduation has little need to register his trademarks and trade names. Unfortunately, an unregistered trademark or trade name might be an actionable infringement on a previously registered one, and the only sure way to find out is to seek registration yourself. A very small local business can probably afford to forget about it, since no infringement on its part is going to do very much damage to the "wronged" company anyway. But if you're growing and plan to stay around awhile, you'd best write away to Washington.

11. FINANCES

Underestimation of capital requirements has often been termed the single most important source of business failures. Money makes money, as they say; it is equally true that no money makes no money. Throughout this book we have repeatedly warned student businessmen to start small—but even starting small means starting, which means working capital. Getting bigger means still more working capital.

If you have $10,000 in the bank, and are willing to risk it, capital presents no major problem for you. If you don't or aren't, the odds are good that at one point or another you are going to have to borrow money.

The usual source of capital for small businessmen is short-term credit. Credit may be obtained in three ways. The easiest to arrange is trade credit from your suppliers. If the prospects for your business look good, most suppliers will agree to wait one, two, or even three months for payment. The disadvantage of this arrangement is that the supplier will probably jack up his price in return for waiting, and will cut off your supply if you fail to pay within the stated period. This can very often drive a small businessman to bankruptcy just when everything is beginning to click. Short-term bank loans, usually from two to six months, are a second source of credit, but they are hard to get, especially for students. The third and often the best solution is a six-to-twelve month loan against collateral. These loans are available from banks and from commercial credit firms. Your inventory or accounts receivable should be sufficient collateral to make the loan easy to negotiate.

It is an axiom of banking and business that the more money a company has, the easier time it has borrowing more. A.T. & T. can negotiate a loan wherever and whenever it wants, but *you* are bound to have trouble, especially at the beginning. Try to start small enough so that you won't have to borrow money until you are well established and want to expand. By that time it will be easier.

A sympathetic college administration can make a world of difference when it comes to borrowing money. No bank is going to refuse a loan if the college is willing to stand behind it. Better still, some administrations will lend money to student businesses themselves if they think the business is good for the school and likely to do well. If you can borrow seed money or expansion capital from your school administration, you will save yourself not only a lot of argument, but also a lot of interest.

12. FORMS OF BUSINESS ORGANIZATION

The three possible forms of business organization are individual ownership, partnership, and corporation. We will take each in turn and discuss its advantages and disadvantages.

Individual ownership is by far the most common organization for a small business. Its advantages are: (1) lower taxes than either of the other two forms; (2) least difficulty and cost in starting; (3) least government interference and paperwork required for operation; and (4) greatest flexibility in management, organization, structure, and activity. The individually owned company has no legal existence at all. Its owner assumes all responsibility for its actions, reports its income on his personal income tax return, and signs all contracts and holds all business assets in his own name.

The major disadvantages of individual ownership stem from the same source as its advantages. Since the business is not a legal entity, it may have difficulty negotiating loans and contracts. If its owner gets ill or dies, the business is very likely to fall apart. Most important, the owner has total personal liability for business losses and debts. His private property can be confiscated as the result of a lawsuit against his business.

A partnership is a formal association of two or more persons on mutually agreeable terms. In most states, a partnership agreement must be in writing, and must include a great deal of specific information about the structure and plans of the business. Forming a partnership is a fairly complex process, and usually requires the services of a lawyer. Specific requirements, forms, and procedures vary from state to state, and must be checked.

The main advantage of a partnership over individual ownership is simply that it allows several persons to combine their resources and abilities to conduct a business. In most other ways the two forms of organization are treated alike. That is to say, a partnership (1) pays no federal income taxes; (2) pays no state franchise taxes; (3) is comparatively free from government interference, regulation, and paperwork; (4) is comparatively free to change the nature of the business; and (5) may operate in any state without first obtaining permission from any government. Partnerships also share the principal disadvantage of individual ownership; each partner is liable to the full extent of his personal assets for business debts contracted by himself or by any other partner.

In addition, partnerships have a few disadvantages of their own. Though they pay no federal income tax, partnerships must file a tax return with the federal government. Some states have special unincorporated business taxes for partnerships. Finally, state laws regulating the activities of formal partnerships, while not nearly so stringent as those governing corporate behavior, are substantially more restrictive than laws covering individually-owned businesses.

A corporation is a statutory form of organization, a legal entity which may exercise the powers conferred upon it by its charter, and no others. Legally, a corporation is an individual.

The procedures for incorporating are far too complex to justify discussion here. If you're considering the possibility, see a lawyer; you'll need one anyway.

The major advantage of a corporation is the limited liability of its shareholders. On receiving its charter, every corporation is required to sell stock. Very large corporations may decide to put their stock on the public market, but the usual procedure for small corporations is to hold a private sale, open only to directors of the company, important employees, and perhaps a few interested investors. Thereafter, shareholders are financially responsible for the corporation only to the extent of the value of their stock. This means that if three college students incorporate their business and distribute all the stock among themselves, their personal assets are safe should the business fail. They can lose the business itself, and all of *its* assets, but that is the full extent of their risk.

In addition to limited liability, a second advantage of the corporate structure is its existence as a legal entity. The corporation may sign contracts in its own name. It may bring a lawsuit against an individual or another corporation. It may own property. It may change ownership through the sale of stock, or change management through election of a new board of directors.

In return for these benefits, state law puts a large number of limitations on the activities of corporations. A corporation may sell stock only in the state from which it receives its charter. Unless it obtains permission from the government of another state (which usually entails a fairly large fee), it may not do business in any state except the one in which it is chartered. It must pay a number of special taxes, including an annual federal corporate income tax, an annual state franchise or income tax, a state organization tax (on receiving its charter), and special income taxes in other states in which it does business. It must submit burdensome annual reports to the federal and state governments. It may not alter its business structure or activities beyond what is stated or implied in its charter without receiving special permission from the state government. Its initial charter must conform with all state laws, and must be approved by the state government.

The specific advantages and disadvantages of individual ownership, partnership, and incorporation must be weighed separately in each individual case before a decision is reached. In general, the smaller and less permanent a business, the more sense it makes to organize on an individual-ownership basis. A small business is not likely to lose very much money, so the protection of limited liability is not too essential. On the other hand, a small business is not likely to make very much money either, so the minimization of taxes, government interference, and paperwork is very essential. An informal partnership can be drawn up among several students who want to go into business together; no lawyer will be necessary, and no special restrictions will result.

But if your business extends beyond the confines of your college town, or if it nets an annual profit of more than $5,000 or $6,000, or if it will be continued after your graduation by you or someone else—then you should consider a formal partnership or a corporation. Talk to the college lawyer first, and see what he advises. If he thinks some sort of formal organization might be a good idea, hire your own lawyer and get down to brass tacks.

There is one other situation in which it is advisable to incorporate, regardless of the size or expected duration of your business. This is when your college administration has done the work for you. We have already mentioned that nearly all colleges and universities are themselves incorporated. Depending on the terms of the charter of your college, you may be able to "join" its corporate structure simply by asking the administration to include you in. This is especially likely at schools which operate on the student agencies system. Many student agencies offices are incorporated, either as part of the college or separately from it. Every new agency becomes a part of the corporation, and the paperwork is handled by the central office.

Joining a college corporation may be particularly advantageous because of the special nature of colleges. Most private schools are chartered as non-profit corporations, while most state-owned colleges and universities have special agreements with their state governments which amount to the same thing. If you can make your business a part of a non-profit corporation, you stand to save a great deal of money. This will be the subject of the next section.

13. NON-PROFIT CORPORATIONS

The main legal differences between a non-profit corporation and a regular corporation are as follows: (1) non-profit corporations have greater freedom in establishing and altering their internal organization; (2) non-profit corporations normally receive partial or total exemption from state franchise and corporate income taxes; (3) non-profit corporations are usually exempt from the federal corporate income tax; (4) non-profit organizations must file special annual financial reports with both the state and federal tax authorities; and (5) non-profit corporations are generally exempted from workman's compensation requirements, and sometimes from minimum wage and unemployment insurance legislation as well.

The catch, of course, is that a non-profit corporation isn't supposed to earn a profit. The paradigm case of a non-profit organization is a charity or a social club that exists for service alone and does not make any money. However, the definition has been extended to include a variety of other institutions. A cooperative store may be a non-profit corporation if all its profits are returned to members in the form of rebates. A church may be a non-profit corporation despite the fact that it owns stores, hotels, and real estate companies. And of course the charity, social club, cooperative, and church may all hire paid employees.

The rules for determining what's non-profit and what isn't are extremely complex, and different in each state. In general, two criteria are used. The "functional" criterion concerns the activities in which the organization is engaged, while the "economic" criterion has to do with the financial relationship between the organization and its members or stockholders. Either or both of the two parameters may be applied by statutes or court decisions in various states. The articles of incorporation, constitution and by-laws of an organization are important in determining its status—but so are its actions. Government regulation of non-profit corporations is on the increase, and a number of "loopholes" have already been blocked off. For example, the federal government and some state governments now tax the "unrelated business income" of otherwise non-profit corporations. As a rule, non-profit tax exemptions are strictly construed, and any ambiguities in construction are generally resolved against the taxpayer. The burden of proof is on the organization that wishes to be included under the exemption.

It is a rare student business that applies for and receives its own charter as a non-profit corporation—but it has happened. College newspapers are particularly likely to achieve this goal, by virtue of the fact that they are "educational organizations" which teach the fundamentals of journalism to students. The profits of such papers are distributed to reporters and editors in the form of salaries. We would hardly advise the average student businessman to apply for his own non-profit charter. Not only are the odds against him, but it is also likely that he will have long since graduated by the time the papers come through.

Achieving non-profit status on the coat-tails of your college administration is far more practical. Non-profit corporations are permitted to have affiliated or subordinate units, which then have the choice of filing their own tax returns or being included in the parent corporation's return. Whether or not a student business may be included in this category is a fine legal question. Its answer depends on the state, the articles of incorporation of the college, and the relationship between the college and the student business. Another determining factor will be the nature of the student business itself—specifically, does it serve any educational function for its members or customers?

It can be done. At several schools which operate on a student agencies system, it has been done—usually after a great deal of discussion with a good tax lawyer, a representative of the Internal Revenue Service, and a man from the state capital. If you can interest your administration in opening negotiations, you might be able to save yourself and other student businesses on campus thousands of dollars a year.

14. REALISM AGAIN

If you're willing to generalize a bit, it is possible to group all student businesses into three categories. The first consists of large, independent student entrepreneurial endeavors. The category is nearly empty; it contains only the half dozen enterprises we discussed in Chapter Six, plus one or two more we might have missed. These businesses need to know a great deal more about business law than what is said in this chapter. Since they have grown nicely and are prospering well, they undoubtedly know it already.

The second category includes all those student businesses, large and small, that are associated in one way or another with their college administrations. It should be clear by now that the legal obligations of these enterprises depend almost entirely on the nature of that association. The more closely tied you are to the college, the better your legal position. However close your association is or is not, it is probable that the administration will want to look after your legal problems itself, or at least give you the necessary guidance to help you do what you must.

The third category is composed of those student businesses which are small and more or less independent of their college administrations. This is by far the largest grouping. The legal problems of a small independent business are in one sense mammoth, because there is no one to give you a hand. But in another sense they are miniscule, because there is no one to give a damn what you do or don't do. Silly Sally is still securely selling her sea shells, and nobody has knocked on her door yet to ask about that excise tax. They might catch up with her tomorrow, but as of today she's doing fine.

Silly Sally, though she doesn't know it, is living dangerously. We can't advise you to follow her example. For one thing, she has an ethical advantage over you in that *she* never heard of an excise tax; if you've read this far, you have been amply forewarned. And illegality is a shaky foundation for any business that hopes to grow beyond the Silly Sally stage.

Nevertheless, we do not advise you to go overboard in your search for technicalities to worry about. Perhaps the best solution is to talk to some people in similar businesses, either on campus on in town. What they do, you should do; what they don't do, you may be safe not doing.

You should also contact the Small Business Division of the U.S. Department of Commerce. This government agency publishes a long series of pamphlets about the legal, financial, and technical problems of small businessmen. Pick up copies of them, and read them carefully. What the pamphlets don't bother about, you needn't bother about.

Probably.

CHAPTER 9

Concluding Remarks

1. REMARKABLE CONCLUSIONS

(1) Three-quarters of all college students earn money during the school year. Roughly two-thirds of these hold on-campus jobs, while the other third take jobs off campus. Only about one percent of all students go into business for themselves. The small percentage of student entrepreneurs is partially a result of the increasing availability of skilled part-time jobs. Another contributory cause is the greater academic pressure at most colleges, which forces students to seek out the security and limited responsibility of employment.

(2) The major reason for the small number of student businessmen, however, is the opposition of most college administrations to this sort of student activity. This opposition, in turn, is partly the result of genuine concern for the well-being of the would-be entrepreneur and the atmosphere of the campus. But its most important source seems to be a school-teacherish distaste for business, born of a virulent academic inferiority complex. Administrative opposition may take the form of total prohibition of all student businesses, but it more often expresses itself as an informal policy of discouragement, aided by a network of regulations which hamper the would-be campus businessman.

(3) Despite opposition, student business continues to do nicely. It flourishes best, of course, on those few campuses where it is encouraged through a student agencies system—but it is kept alive by a few ambitious students at almost every college in the country. And wherever they are, student businessmen seem to

be considerably more satisfied with their work than student employees. In particular, they cite business experience and the sensation of independence as the special advantages of their choice. In addition, the financial return to the student businessman is usually much greater than the salary of the student employee. This is equally true of both total earnings and remuneration per working hour.

(4) The most profitable student businesses are those which extend across many campuses. These are extremely difficult to set up, however, and only a very few have been successfully organized. The next best alternative is the community business. Here the problem is that such a business separates a student entrepreneur from what he knows best: his classmates. Any very highly profitable business is by definition large, and any large business is by definition dangerous. In general, students are well advised not to aim for top profits when they begin, but rather to start small and grow large only if the demand for what they offer is clearly sufficient.

(5) The small student business may choose between three fields —selling goods to fellow students, selling services to fellow students, and selling goods or services to the surrounding community. Except for individual door-to-door peddling, the third alternative is the least popular. It requires entrance into the real world beyond the campus, where things and people are a bit tougher than one expects. Venturing off campus is usually desirable only if you are shooting for top profits (which isn't a good idea) or if you have an extremely recalcitrant college administration which must be by-passed. Once the decision to sell to students is made, the choice between selling goods and selling services is not crucial. In general, however, service agencies earn the largest and the smallest profits, depending on whether the particular service is actually needed or not. Merchandise sales usually fall somewhere in the middle.

(6) Profits are by no means the only factor which should be considered in choosing and organizing a business. Among the others which are frequently mentioned by student businessmen are the development of special skills; enjoyment and satisfaction; contact with fellow students and with non-students; independence; business training; minimum investment of time and capital; secur-

ity. The most important factor is feasibility. This means choosing a business that *you* can do, and that *your customers* want done.

(7) Whatever business is finally chosen, *learning* will be an essential part of its operation. You will have to learn about selling and buying, advertising and soliciting, billing and bookkeeping, law and finance. Regardless of his particular product or service, a small businessman must be something of a jack-of-all-trades. That is the danger of a small business, and that is a large part of its appeal.

2. WAYS AND MEANS

(1) FIRST STEPS: The first step in organizing a student business is thinking—thinking about what needs to be done, what you can do, what you would enjoy doing. The second step is planning—investigating prices and markets and expenses, turning a good idea into a concrete outline. The third step is visiting—visiting your college administration for permission, advice, and perhaps even help, visiting the legal authorities for guidance and information. The fourth step—which should never begin until the first three are finished—is starting.

(2) BUYING: If you plan on selling something, you'll have to buy it first. Even if you sell a service or manufacture your own product, you will have to buy equipment and materials. The most important thing to remember about buying is to take your time looking around. Comparison-shop, and let your potential suppliers know that you are comparison-shopping. Whenever possible, buy wholesale. Buy in as great quantity as you can, or place a standing order for so many widgets per week or month. Buy as many of the items you need as possible from the same supplier; this will not only gain you a quantity discount, it will also make life a good deal easier. Where you can, buy on approval or consignment, so that you can return whatever you can't sell. If possible, offer to pick up what you order yourself, and offer to pay cash. These last two will go a long way toward assuaging your suppliers' reluctance to do business with students.

(3) SELLING: Sales are the lifeblood of every business. How you decide to sell will of course depend upon what you decide to sell. In general, setting up your own store is a dangerous

proposition. A store in town is a full-time responsibility, which is pretty pointless when you're running a part-time business. A store in your dormitory room is likely to incur the wrath of your college administration, and is not likely to incur the interest of your classmates—not to mention townies. Door-to-door sales, on campus or off, are an excellent way to sell anything, and the only way to sell impulse items such as Christmas cards or late-night snacks. But door-to-door selling is hard work, requiring a great expenditure of time and a small army of salesmen. A variety of compromises are possible, among them telephone solicitation, mail solicitation, use of sales tables in strategic locations on campus, and placement of hand-made items in established stores off campus.

Salesmanship, we are told, is an art, not a skill. It is supposed to be an art which college students possess in greater measure than any other part of the population. If selling does not come naturally to you, there are dozens of books written on the subject which might help—but your best bet is to hire salesmen who already know how.

(4) ADVERTISING: Successful advertising and promotion are crucial to the success of any student business, especially when it is just beginning. Be sure to take advantage of all free advertising possibilities. These include news articles in the campus newspaper and perhaps town papers, posters, placards and notices on campus and off, and word-of-mouth. Paid advertising campaigns make sense for most student businesses, especially since campus ad rates are usually very low. Handouts and flyers can also be cheaply prepared and distributed. In all that you do, do not shy away from "college-boy humor." Anything that attracts attention is good, and anything funny will attract attention. Kooky advertisements, outrageous names, and slightly off-color sales pitches are all part of the game, and all employed by nearly every successful business.

(5) PROFITING: We hate to tell you how many student businesses have sold well and lost money. The art of turning a profit is the art of figuring things out in advance, and figuring them out right. It is the art of keeping good books, and staying within the law; of paying your employees well enough that they'll work, but not so well that they'll earn more money than you;

of pricing your goods and services as high as the market will take, but not a penny higher; of purchasing everything you need, but nothing you don't need; of knowing when to borrow money for expansion, and when not to; of publicizing your product fully and interestingly, but not lavishly—in short, it is the art of running a business.

For the student businessman, the most important component of this art is the realization that your profit is not the difference between what you pay for an item and what you sell it for. Separating the two are salaries, overhead, publicity expenses, equipment purchases, taxes, and a hundred other little details, not the least of which is working time. The student entrepreneur who graduates with money in the bank is the one who calculates these operating expenses before he starts. He is certain before he spends a penny that if his product or service sells, his business will earn him money—and enough money to be worth his trouble. The vagaries of customers you can do little about, except to pray. But every other business variable can be estimated in advance. The great majority of student business failures fail not because their product or service doesn't sell, but because their expenses are greater than their income. Terrific sales will do you absolutely no good if you're selling at a loss.

3. ENVOI

The research conducted in the preparation of this book has conclusively demonstrated that the entrepreneurial spirit is still alive on the American college campus today. We consider this a wholly good thing. We believe that an independent business enterprise is usually the most profitable, the most rewarding, and the most practical way for a college student to earn money. We have found plentiful support for this belief in the comments and experiences of student businessmen across the country.

This book is a guidebook to student business. Like all guidebooks, it only hits the high spots—and not all the high spots at that. We have offered some clues, some hints, some suggestions. The rest is up to you.

If you come up with something good, send us a postcard.

The Colleges

LISTED BELOW ARE all the colleges and universities consulted in the preparation of this book. An asterisk (*) is used to denote schools whose administrations replied to our questionnaires. The remaining schools fall into one or both of two categories: Some are discussed in published articles on the subject of student business activities; others are schools whose student businessmen responded to our questionnaires, though their administrations did not. The fact that a given school is not mentioned in our discussion of a given business should not be construed to mean that that business does not exist at that school.

Agnes Scott College, Decatur, Georgia
**Albright College, Reading, Pennsylvania*
**Alfred Agricultural and Technical College, Alfred, New York*
**Allegheny College, Meadville, Pennsylvania*
Amherst College, Amherst, Massachusetts
Antioch College, Yellow Springs, Ohio
**Appalachian State Teachers College, Boone, North Carolina*
Arizona State College, Tempe, Arizona
**Avila College, Kansas City, Missouri*
**Baldwin-Wallace College, Berea, Ohio*
**Ball State University, Muncie, Indiana*
**Bany College, Miami, Florida*
**Barat College, Lake Forest, Illinois*
Barnard College, New York, New York
**Belmont Abbey College, Belmont, North Carolina*
Bennington College, Bennington, Vermont
Berea College, Berea, Kentucky
**Bethany College, Lindsborg, Kansas*
**Bethel College, North Newton, Kansas*

*Bethel College, St. Paul, Minnesota
*Blackburn College, Carlinville, Illinois
*Bloomfield College, Bloomfield, New Jersey
*Bowdoin College, Brunswick, Maine
*Bridgewater College, Bridgewater, Virginia   •
Brigham Young University, Provo, Utah
*Brown University, Providence, Rhode Island
*Bryn Mawr College, Bryn Mawr, Pennsylvania
*Buena Vista College, Storm Lake, Iowa
*University of California, Berkeley, California
University of California, Los Angeles, California
University of California, Pasadena, California
*University of California, Riverside, California
*University of California, Santa Barbara, California
*Capital University, Columbus, Ohio
Carleton College, Northfield, Minnesota
*Carnegie Institute of Technology, Pittsburgh, Pennsylvania
*Cazenovia College, Cazenovia, New York
*Cedar Crest College, Allentown, Pennsylvania
*Centre College of Kentucky, Danville, Kentucky
*Chaminade College, Honolulu, Hawaii
*Chatham College, Pittsburgh, Pennsylvania
University of Chicago, Chicago, Illinois
University of Cincinnati, Cincinnati, Ohio
*The Citadel, Charleston, South Carolina
City College of New York, New York, New York
*Claremont Men's College, Claremont, California
*Clarke College, Dubuque, Iowa
*Clark University, Worcester, Massachusetts
*Clemson University, Clemson, South Carolina
Colby College, Waterville, Maine
*Colby Junior College, New London, New Hampshire
Colgate University, Hamilton, New York
*Columbia University, New York, New York
*Concordia College, Moorhead, Minnesota
*University of Connecticut, Storrs, Connecticut
*Cooper Union, New York, New York
*Dartmouth College, Hanover, New Hampshire
*Dean Junior College, Franklin, Massachusetts
University of Delaware, Newark, Delaware
*Denison University, Granville, Ohio
*University of Detroit, Detroit, Michigan

Dickinson College, Carlisle, Pennsylvania
*Dominican College, San Rafael, California
*Drew University, Madison, New Jersey
Drexel Institute of Technology, Philadelphia, Pennsylvania
Duke University, Durham, North Carolina
Duquesne University, Pittsburgh, Pennsylvania
*D'Youville College, Buffalo, New York
*Elizabethtown College, Elizabethtown, Pennsylvania
*Emerson College, Boston, Massachusetts
*Emory University, Atlanta, Georgia
*Eureka College, Eureka, Illinois
*Fairleigh Dickinson University, Madison, New Jersey
Fairleigh Dickinson University, Rutherford, New Jersey
Fenn College, Cleveland, Ohio
*Ferris State College, Big Rapids, Michigan
*Findlay College, Findlay, Ohio
*University of Florida, Gainesville, Florida
*Flint College of the University of Michigan, Flint, Michigan
*Fordham University, New York, New York
George Washington University, Washington, D.C.
*Georgia College, Milledgeville, Georgia
*Georgia Institute of Technology, Atlanta, Georgia
*Georgian Court College, Lakewood, New Jersey
*Georgia Southern College, Statesboro, Georgia
*Gordon College, Wenham, Massachusetts
Grinnell College, Grinnell, Iowa
*Hamilton College, Clinton, New York
Harvard University, Cambridge, Massachusetts
*Harvey Mudd College, Claremont, California
*College of the Holy Names, Oakland, California
*Hood College, Frederick, Maryland
*University of Houston, Houston, Texas
Hunter College, New York, New York
*Huston-Tillotson College, Austin, Texas
*College of Idaho, Caldwell, Idaho
Illinois Institute of Technology, Chicago, Illinois
*University of Illinois, Urbana, Illinois
Indiana University, Bloomington, Indiana
*Indiana University, Indiana, Pennsylvania
*Kalamazoo College, Kalamazoo, Michigan
*Kent State University, Kent, Ohio
*Keystone Junior College, La Plume, Pennsylvania

*King College, Bristol, Tennessee
Knox College, Galesburg, Illinois
*La Grange College, La Grange, Georgia
*Lake Erie College, Painesville, Ohio
*Lakeland College, Sheboygan, Wisconsin
*Lamar State College, Beaumont, Texas
*La Sierra College, Riverside, California
Louisiana State University, Baton Rouge, Louisiana
*Loyola University, New Orleans, Louisiana
*Luther College, Decorah, Iowa
*MacMurray College, Jacksonville, Illinois
*Manchester College, North Manchester, Indiana
*Mary Baldwin College, Staunton, Virginia
*Maryhill College, Austin, Texas
*Marymount Manhattan College, New York, New York
*Marywood College, Scranton, Pennsylvania
*Massachusetts Institute of Technology, Cambridge, Massachusetts
*University of Massachusetts, Amherst, Massachusetts
*Medical College of Virginia, Richmond, Virginia
*Mercer University, Macon, Georgia
Michigan State University, East Lansing, Michigan
University of Michigan, Ann Arbor, Michigan
*Middlebury College, Middlebury, Vermont
University of Minnesota, Minneapolis, Minnesota
University of Mississippi, University, Mississippi
University of Missouri, Columbia, Missouri
*Mitchell College, New London, Connecticut
Montana State University, Missoula, Montana
Mount Holyoke College, South Hadley, Massachusetts
*Mount Mercy College, Cedar Rapids, Iowa
*Mount Mercy College, Pittsburgh, Pennsylvania
*Mount Saint Agnes College, Baltimore, Maryland
*Mount St. Mary's College, Los Angeles, California
*Mount St. Scholastica College, Atchison, Kansas
Muhlenberg College, Allentown, Pennsylvania
*Muskingum College, New Concord, Ohio
*Nazareth College, Nazareth, Kentucky
*Newark State College, Union, New Jersey
*New England Conservatory, Boston, Massachusetts
*University of New Hampshire, Durham, New Hampshire
New York University, New York, New York
*Northeastern University, Boston, Massachusetts

Northeast State College, Monroe, Louisiana
*North Georgia College, Dahlonega, Georgia
Northland College, Ashland, Wisconsin
Northwestern University, Evanston, Illinois
*Northwest Nazarene College, Nempa, Idaho
*Ohio State University, Columbus, Ohio
*Ohio University, Athens, Ohio
University of Oregon, Eugene, Oregon
*Oswego College of the State University, Oswego, New York
*Otterbein College, Westerville, Ohio
*Pembroke College, Providence, Rhode Island
*University of Pennsylvania, Philadelphia, Pennsylvania
University of Pittsburgh, Pittsburgh, Pennsylvania
*Princeton University, Princeton, New Jersey
*Radcliffe College, Cambridge, Massachusetts
*Randolph-Macon Woman's College, Lynchburg, Virginia
Reed College, Portland, Oregon
*Reinhardt College, Waleska, Georgia
Rensselaer Polytechnic Institute, Troy, New York
*Rhode Island School of Design, Providence, Rhode Island
*Ripon College, Ripon, Wisconsin
*Rochester Institute of Technology, Rochester, New York
*Rocky Mountain College, Billings, Montana
*Rollins College, Winter Park, Florida
*Rose Polytechnic Institute, Terre Haute, Indiana
*Rutgers University, New Brunswick, New Jersey
*St. Andrews Presbyterian College, Laurinburg, North Carolina
*St. Benedict's College, Atchison, Kansas
*College of St. Catherine, St. Paul, Minnesota
*St. Edward's University, Austin, Texas
*St. John College, Cleveland, Ohio
*St. John's University, Collegeville, Minnesota
*St. Louis University, St. Louis, Missouri
*St. Mary's College, Winona, Minnesota
*St. Mary's University, San Antonio, Texas
*St. Peter's College, Jersey City, New Jersey
*St. Procopios College, Lisle, Illinois
San Fernando Valley State College, Northridge, California
Sarah Lawrence College, Bronxville, New York
*Seattle Pacific College, Seattle, Washington
*Simmons College, Boston, Massachusetts
University of Southern California, Los Angeles, California

Southern Methodist University, Dallas, Texas
Stanford University, Stanford, California
*Swarthmore College, Swarthmore, Pennsylvania
Syracuse University, Syracuse, New York
*Temple Buell College, Denver, Colorado
*University of Texas, Austin, Texas
*Transylvania College, Lexington, Kentucky
Trinity College, Hartford, Connecticut
*Upsala College, East Orange, New Jersey
*Ursinus College, Collegeville, Pennsylvania
*Utica College of Syracuse University, Utica, New York
*Valdosta State College, Valdosta, Georgia
*Vassar College, Poughkeepsie, New York
*Waldorf College, Forest City, Iowa
*Wagner College, New York, New York
*Washington and Jefferson College, Washington, Pennsylvania
*Washington and Lee University, Lexington, Virginia
University of Washington, Seattle, Washington
*Wayne State University, Detroit, Michigan
*Wellesley College, Wellesley, Massachusetts
*Wesleyan University, Wesleyan, Connecticut
*Western Reserve University, Cleveland, Ohio
*West Virginia University, Morgantown, West Virginia
*Wheeling College, Wheeling, West Virginia
Whitman College, Walla Walla, Washington
*William Jewell College, Liberty, Missouri
*Williams College, Williamstown, Massachusetts
University of Wisconsin, Madison, Wisconsin
*University of Wisconsin, Milwaukee, Wisconsin
*Wittenberg University, Springfield, Ohio
*Wofford College, Spartanburg, South Carolina
*Yale University, New Haven, Connecticut
*Yankton College, Yankton, South Dakota

An Index
to Jobs and Colleges

378.365
S21   80446

AUTHOR
Sandman, Peter M.

TITLE
How to succeed in Business before

DE 16 68				